# ArtScroll® Series

Rabbi Nosson Scherman / Rabbi Gedaliah Zlotowitz
*General Editors*
Rabbi Meir Zlotowitz ז״ל, *Founder*

# A Tap on the

Published by

## ARTSCROLL
Mesorah Publications, ltd

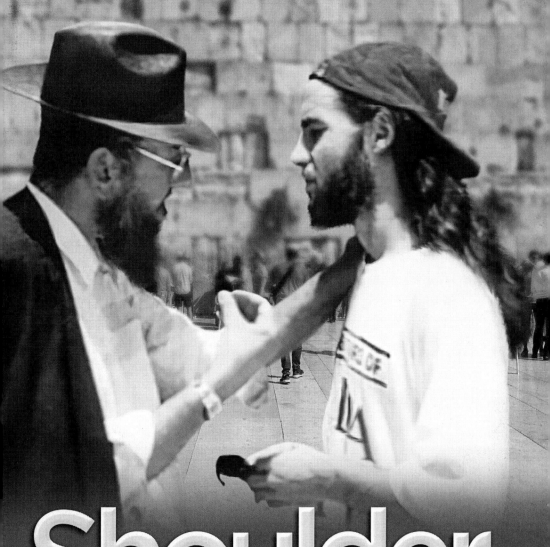

# Shoulder

## RABBI MEIR SCHUSTER
### and a magical era of teshuvah

#### YONOSON ROSENBLUM

FIRST EDITION
*First Impression … June 2021*

Published and Distributed by
**MESORAH PUBLICATIONS, LTD.**
313 Regina Avenue / Rahway, N.J. 07065

*Distributed in Europe by*
**LEHMANNS**
Unit E, Viking Business Park
Rolling Mill Road
Jarrow, Tyne & Wear NE32 3DP
England

*Distributed in Australia & New Zealand by*
**GOLDS WORLD OF JUDAICA**
3-13 William Street
Balaclava, Melbourne 3183
Victoria Australia

*Distributed in Israel by*
**SIFRIATI / A. GITLER — BOOKS**
POB 2351
Bnei Brak 51122

*Distributed in South Africa by*
**KOLLEL BOOKSHOP**
Northfield centre, 17 Northfield Avenue
Glenhazel 2192, Johannesburg, South Africa

---

ARTSCROLL® SERIES
A TAP ON THE SHOULDER
© *Copyright 2020, by* MESORAH PUBLICATIONS, Ltd.
*313 Regina Avenue / Rahway, N.J. 07065 / (718) 921-9000 / www.artscroll.com*

---

ITEM CODE: TAPH
ISBN 10: 1-4226-2842-6
ISBN 13: 978-1-4226-2842-3

Typography by CompuScribe at ArtScroll Studios, Ltd.

Printed in the United States of America.
Bound by Sefercraft, Quality Bookbinders, Ltd., Rahway NJ

$\mathcal{M}$rs. Esther Schuster and the Schuster family
wish to express their gratitude
to all those who have made possible
the perpetuation of the legacy of

**Rabbi Meir Tzvi Schuster** *zt"l.*

$\mathcal{F}$irst and foremost, to **Mr. Sam Friedland**,
who spearheaded the project.
And to all those who donated generously:

**Mr. Sam Friedland**

**Mr. Yaakov (Tom) Steinberg**

**Mr. Dov Friedberg**

**Mr. Michael Kaufman**

**Mr. Amir Jaffa**

**Mr. Reuven Dessler**

**Mr. Jake Koval**

**Mr. Gary Torgow**

**Mr. Joseph Nussbaum**

**Mr. Jerry Hoffnung**

**Mr. Eli Rubin**

**Mr. Mark Geller**

# TABLE OF CONTENTS

## ৵§ Part I: Laying the Foundation

## ৵§ Part II: Soul-Searcher

# AUTHOR'S PREFACE

I WAS AT THE BAR MITZVAH RECEPTION FOR THE SON OF A CLOSE friend when in walked another old friend who sat next to me in kollel approximately thirty years earlier. I was puzzled because I could not figure out how the *baal simchah* and my friend from kollel could have known each other. They had, I was pretty sure, never lived in the same neighborhood. In addition, the *baal simchah* is a baal teshuvah, which my old friend from kollel is not, and I could not imagine they had ever learned in the same yeshivah or kollel together.

Finally, my curiosity got the better of me, and I asked my kollel friend how he knew the host. "We were the family Meir Schuster brought him to for his first Shabbos," he replied. At that time, I was already working on a biography of Rabbi Schuster, and it suddenly struck me that most of the baalei teshuvah of a certain period — from the mid-'70s to the turn of the millennia — came to yeshivah or seminary via Rabbi Schuster.

When I was writing a biography of Rabbi Noach Weinberg, *zt"l*, one of the founders of Shema Yisrael (which became Ohr Somayach) and later of Aish HaTorah, for instance, I soon discovered that most of the former Aish students whom I interviewed were brought to Aish HaTorah directly from the Kotel by Rabbi Schuster. Yet unless I asked, they often did not even mention that fact or skipped over it perfunctorily, as if it were unnecessary to mention, sort of like starting a fairy tale, "Once upon a time."

My wife and I are baalei teshuvah from that period. We came to Israel on our honeymoon in June 1979, and have remained in Jerusalem since. Though we are among the minority who did not come to Ohr Somayach, in my case, or Ohr Somayach's women's school, in my wife's, through Rabbi Schuster, he nevertheless played a role in our lives as well, and even more directly in the lives of several family members.

To this day, many, if not most, of our closest friends are drawn from those who went through the process of turning their lives upside down along with us. So in writing the story of Rabbi Schuster, I feel that I am at the same time writing the story of a generation of which my wife and I are very much a part, the story of a magical era in Jewish history, lasting a little over a quarter-century, in which baalei teshuvah proliferated. Rabbi Meir Schuster was at the very center of that magical era.

As a talmid in Ohr Somayach for two and a half years, I would see Rabbi Schuster on an almost daily basis. At some point in the day — and often more than once — he would turn up with a group of bewildered-looking, usually hirsute, young men trailing in his wake. I don't remember who it was — it might have been me, or it could have been a friend — who once looked out the window and commented, "The Pied Piper is back," upon spotting Rav Schuster pulling up to the front entrance of Ohr Somayach.

From the looks on their faces, it was evident that the young men with him had no clue as to how they got there or even what a yeshivah is. Most did not stay for very long, but enough did so that the rooms in Ohr Somayach were always packed. And today, when we entertain young men and women at our Shabbos table from mainstream yeshivos and seminaries, it no longer surprises us when they mention that one or both of their parents are baalei teshuvah, and that Rav Schuster first brought them to yeshivah.

In our early years living next door to Ohr Somayach, we did have a good deal of personal contact with Rabbi Schuster. Within two or three months of our arriving in Jerusalem, he was already sending us Leil Shabbos guests on a regular basis. Often one of Rabbi Schuster's assistants brought our guests to the door, but he personally made the call to determine whether we could take guests.

On Thursday night the phone would ring, and I would answer. I would venture a "Hello," but at the other end there was only silence. At that point, I quickly learned to say, "Is that you, Rabbi Schuster?" My "guess" always seemed to catch him by surprise, and he would stumble briefly before asking, "Can you take guests tomorrow night? How many?" There were never any pleasantries or small talk, and as soon as his mission was accomplished, there would be a click at the other end, as Rabbi Schuster hurried to make his next call.

At the end of each such call, I would always wonder to myself, "How can a person so shy that he cannot initiate a phone conversation with someone he knows somehow force himself to start conversations with dozens of complete strangers every day?"

This volume seeks to answer that question.

# INTRODUCTION

With *Siyata d'Shmaya*

"**H**E WAS, IN MY OPINION, THE MOST SUCCESSFUL PERSON who ever lived," Rabbi Dovid Refson, the founder of Neve Yerushalayim women's seminary, says of Rabbi Meir Schuster — i.e., he did more with the particular *kochos hanefesh* (personal strengths) with which he was blessed than anyone else.

The achievement of Rabbi Meir Schuster defies naturalistic explanation. Let us first define that achievement. From the early 1970s until the outbreak of the second intifada just before Rosh Hashanah of 5761 (2000), Rabbi Schuster brought thousands, if not tens of thousands, of young Jewish men and women to the major baalei teshuvah yeshivos and seminaries in Jerusalem — chief among them Ohr Somayach, Aish HaTorah, Dvar Yerushalayim, Diaspora Yeshiva, and Neve Yerushalayim. Those institutions would never have flourished as they did in the last quarter of the twentieth century but for Rabbi Schuster. Their existence depended on the ability of Rabbi Schuster to bring them a steady stream of potential students.

But how did he do it? How did he convince young men and women, who were often rebelling against their upbringing and all the "uptight" rules of the society in which they had grown up, to experience a yeshivah — something of which they had in many cases never heard — and simultaneously open themselves up to a discipline and set of rules more intense and more comprehensive than those against which they were rebelling?

One thing we know for sure: It was neither his charismatic personality nor his eloquence that proved decisive. It is by now a commonplace that Rabbi Schuster would have been voted the person least likely to spend virtually his entire adult life trying to convince complete strangers from weak or nonexistent Torah backgrounds to learn more about their Jewish heritage. He was almost pathologically shy and tongue-tied. He used to joke that were someone to give him a watch he would have no way to start a conversation. "Do you have the time?" was one of his traditional icebreakers.

Rav Elazar Menachem Mann Shach once said of Rav Yechezkel Levenstein, the great Mashgiach of both Mir and Ponevezh, "In the previous generation, Rav Yechezkel Levenstein was the exemplar of overcoming one's natural *middos* to serve Hashem." In our generation, Rabbi Meir Schuster was such an exemplar.

So, how did he do it? No answer suggests itself other than with incredible *siyata d'Shmaya* (Divine assistance). That *siyata d'Shmaya* can be inferred from decades of success in a mission for which he would at first glance have seemed so thoroughly ill-suited. But it was also manifest in the countless stories of how he always seemed to turn up at precisely the moment when someone whom he had previously brought to a yeshivah or to a meeting with a "wise man" was going through a crisis, and had decided to return home to his previous life. Or in the many stories in which he assured someone with an expiring airline ticket that he had connections with the airlines and would take care of it, and then had to somehow come up with the money on the spur of the moment to pay for a new ticket.

What does it take to be the beneficiary of *siyata d'Shmaya?* Rabbi Meir Schuster's life serves as the answer. One must first believe in *siyata d'Shmaya*. Rabbi Schuster did.[1] He possessed a crystal-clear understanding that success or failure comes only from Hashem. "My husband believed that one must do whatever is humanly possible to merit the Divine assistance. But in the end, the result will be determined only by Hashem," says his wife, Mrs. Esther Schuster.

From the time he was a young boy, Rabbi Schuster was engaged in an intense, ongoing dialogue with the Ribbono shel Olam (Master of the

---

1. Mrs. Esther Schuster, as told to Bracha Goetz.

Universe). His *bensching* (Grace After Meals) alone was a life-changing event for the children growing up in the homes in which he stayed, and for many of their parents as well. "It was impossible to listen to him lead the davening at the Kotel," remarked one frequent companion, "without turning around immediately afterward expecting to see Mashiach arriving on a white donkey."

One of the few people with whom Rabbi Schuster spent much time in private conversation was Rabbi Noach Weinberg, the legendary founder of Shema Yisrael (later Ohr Somayach) and Aish HaTorah. Rabbi Weinberg spoke constantly of the power of one person to change the world, and of how few ever achieve large goals because they fail to appreciate the source of that power.

The power of one which Reb Noach spoke about was actually the power of the One Above. If a Jew attaches himself full-heartedly to advancing Hashem's goals in the world, there is nothing he cannot achieve because Hashem is the Al-mighty, capable of doing anything. For Reb Noach, Rabbi Schuster was the proof of his teaching, the personification of the power of one.

He exemplified that attachment to Hashem's goals of which Reb Noach spoke. His own ego played no role in his chosen mission — only what Hashem needed. And because he had so little ego of his own, Hashem's *Hashgachah* (Providence) shone through him.[2]

If most of us were paid a king's ransom to try to initiate conversation with dozens of strangers every day, we would still not last a week in the job. While no one can know for sure the ratio of those who accepted Rabbi Schuster's invitation to "speak to a wise man," "learn something about your heritage," "visit a yeshivah," to those who ignored him, or expressed no interest in what he was offering, or simply told him to "get lost," the rejections almost certainly vastly outnumbered the acceptances.

Yet the constant rejections, and what would have been seen by anyone else as the concomitant humiliation, did not deter him one bit or call into question his mission. For more than three decades, he approached long-haired young backpackers at the Kotel (the Western Wall), Jerusalem's Central Bus Station, and anywhere else where young Jewish travelers were likely to congregate. Had he not been willing to accept upon himself the humiliation of those rejections, the modern baal

---

2. I am indebted to Rabbi Jeremy Kagan for this insight.

teshuvah movement would never have flourished as it did.

The most famous story about Rabbi Schuster demonstrates best his almost superhuman devotion to his mission — a devotion that calls to mind Avraham Avinu at *Akeidas Yitzchak*. On Isru Chag Pesach 5735 (1975), the Schusters' 6-year-old daughter Yocheved Faige Dina ("Shatzi") was hit and killed by a truck driven by an Arab as she went to the local grocery store to buy herself a post-Pesach treat. During the week of *shivah*, Rabbi Schuster grew increasingly agitated by the thought of all the young Jews at the Kotel who might miss the only opportunity that they would ever have to experience a full Shabbos with a religious family because he was not there to make the necessary arrangements.

Finally, he could bear it no more. He had decided that his presence at the Kotel fell into the category of *pikuach nefesh* (saving a life), and posed the question of whether he could go to the Kotel during *shivah* to Rav Aharon Feldman, today Rosh Yeshivah of Ner Israel Rabbinical College in Baltimore, Maryland. Rav Feldman pronounced the question as beyond his level, and asked Rabbi Yehudah Samet of Ohr Somayach to present it to the *posek hador*, Rav Yosef Shalom Elyashiv.

Rav Elyashiv did not dismiss the query out of hand. Indeed he said that Rabbi Schuster's calculation of what was at stake was correct. Since so few of us live at the level to make that calculation, however, his leaving the *shivah* house would be misunderstood, and he should therefore remain at home.

But as soon as he heard the question. Rabbi Elyashiv declared that if there was a Jew in the world who could ask such a question, he must make a *shivah* call to him. The next day Rav Elyashiv came to the Schuster home, where Rabbi Schuster and his wife were sitting *shivah*, even though he almost never left the Meah Shearim neighborhood where he lived and learned.

Perhaps Mrs. Esther Schuster described most succinctly the interplay between her husband's intense love of Hashem — which led him to devote himself to helping every single Jew experience that same closeness to Hashem that he felt — and the young Jews he approached. "He saw through them and they saw through him," she said. Where others might have seen only the long hair, scraggly beard, and bedraggled clothes of young adults exploring their identity, Rabbi Schuster saw nothing besides Hashem's beloved child, the pure, unsullied *pintele Yid* standing before him. Everything else was extraneous and did not exist.

And where an outside observer might have seen a gangly, decidedly uncool, inarticulate figure, thousands of young Jews saw someone who cared about them more than anyone had ever cared about them before, and who wanted what was best for them more than they did for themselves. His sense of urgency when he asked them whether they were interested in knowing more about their Judaism did not escape them. Nor did his pain if they responded in the negative. Young Jews trusted and followed the awkward stranger to a degree they had never trusted anyone before.

"It just seemed the most natural thing in the world to follow him to yeshivah," said one young man, who not only went to yeshivah, but today teaches at Aish HaTorah.

Rabbi Eli Glaser, who managed the Heritage House men's hostel for two years, wrote of Rabbi Schuster after his passing, "He had been bestowed with the blessing and burden of totally and completely feeling the pain of another Jew. So much so that it was his pain. He embraced it. He nurtured it. He lived it." Rabbi Yisroel Rakofsky, who knew Rabbi Schuster from his very early days at the Kotel, explained his success: "*Ess iz eim ungegangen in leben* — it bothered him so much because he cared so much."

Ultimately, the biography of Rabbi Meir Schuster challenges us in ways that those of great Torah scholars often do not. With respect to the latter, we are quick to attribute their greatness to preternatural intellectual gifts and often to having been born into a family of distinguished Torah lineage. And in that fashion, we convince ourselves that their biography has nothing to say to us: How can the life of someone possessing natural gifts with which we were not blessed, or born into a house steeped in Torah learning, obligate or even prod us to push ourselves a little bit harder?

But what can we say about Rabbi Meir Schuster and the source of his epoch-changing achievements? That he loved Hashem more than we do? That he took more seriously than we do that Hashem is the Al-mighty, capable of doing anything? Will we try to convince ourselves that the thirst for *deveikus* (cleaving to Hashem) is also an inborn trait, and so we cannot be blamed for not being more like Rabbi Schuster?

Yet he had no obvious advantage over any of us in this respect. He did not imbibe *yiras Hashem* and *ahavas Hashem* with his mother's milk. He too, like many of those whom he picked up at the Kotel, was a spiritual seeker, albeit at a much earlier age, and without anyone like Rabbi Meir Schuster to take him by the hand and show him the way.

It is the way of the world that we will eventually find ways to distinguish Rabbi Meir Schuster from ourselves in order to explain why he accomplished so much more and did so much more to bring the light of Torah to this world than we have. But it will not be easy. And the question will continue to niggle at us. And that is why the biography of Rabbi Meir Schuster is so important. It forces us to confront how much more each of us can do.

# ACKNOWLEDGMENTS

ONE OF THE GREAT JOYS OF COMPLETING A BIOGRAPHY SUCH as this one is the opportunity to publicly thank those without whom it could not have seen the light of day.

Sam Friedland solicited the lion's share of the money for the project. Over the nearly seven years from the inception of the project, he and his wife Laurie have become not only partners, but among my closest friends. His gentle prodding, growing ever so slightly more insistent with the passage of time, was a key ingredient in the successful completion of the biography of Rabbi Meir Schuster, *zt"l.*

The Friedlands hosted Rabbi Schuster for a week or more each year for nearly two decades and loved him dearly. That love is reflected in all the many contributions Sam made to the biography, including reading each chapter multiple times.

Yaakov (Tom) Steinberg has been a friend for nearly forty years, and was close to Rabbi Schuster for even longer than that. He provided the first contribution needed to get the project started, and his story forms one of the pillars of Chapter Five.

Rabbi Avraham Edelstein worked in tandem with Rabbi Schuster for a quarter-century. Over that period, no one was closer to Rabbi Schuster. Despite his own busy schedule as Educational Director of Neve Yerushalayim Seminary, he invariably answered every question I posed quickly, in addition to submitting to multiple interviews.

Michael Kaufman was a lay partner and *chavrusa* of Rabbi Schuster over many years, and an invaluable source of information for this biography. I have quoted liberally from his autobiographical work *In One Era and Out the Other* (and not just because the title is so good).

Rabbi Yirmiyahu Abramov was Rabbi Schuster's daily *chavrusa* for decades and his closest partner in Shorashim, his final major undertaking. Moishe Mendlowitz served as the director of the men's Heritage House hostel in its final stages prior to closure, and was probably the person with the greatest day-to-day contact with Rabbi Schuster over his final decade of good health, as well as the person in whom Rabbi Schuster confided the most. Both have made considerable effort to ensure the accuracy of the portrait of Rabbi Schuster in every way possible.

Dena Estrin's *It Happened at Heritage House* provided many of the best stories from the first decade of the Heritage House women's hostel, and is a highly enjoyable read to boot. Mrs. Chaya Weisberg, the codirector, with her husband, Rabbi Matan Mordechai Weisberg, of the women's hostel since 2004, sent me many moving stories from the ongoing activities of the women's hostel, after I thought I had completed the manuscript. They serve as a source of many valuable lessons about the teshuvah process, and insights into why the environment of the women's hostel bore so much precious fruit.

I personally interviewed over seventy people for the biography, many of them multiple times, and their contributions have been duly noted in the text and footnotes. Still, much of the richness of the material would have been lost without access to the website created by Joe Reback, whom my wife and I first welcomed for a Seder nearly forty years ago, and with whom I became reacquainted in the course of this project. I have drawn heavily on the capsule biographies of those first brought to yeshivah or seminary by Rabbi Schuster found at www.rebmeirschuster.org.

I am deeply grateful to Project Inspire for its powerful and moving documentary on Rabbi Schuster, "The Man at the Wall," and for having allowed us to incorporate a great deal of visual material from that documentary, as well as to quote freely from the interviewees. Project Inspire has kindly made access to its inspiring documentary on Rabbi Schuster's life and legacy available at http://projectinspire.com/man-at-the-wall. It provides a wonderful supplement to this volume.

And finally, I would like to pay tribute to the remarkable woman with whom Rabbi Schuster shared his life and built his family, Mrs. Esther Schuster. In addition to providing a mini-library of articles written on Rabbi Schuster and a large collection of photographs, she was always available to discuss any issues that arose and to provide clarification. Her ready wit furnished a frequent boost along the way.

In an entirely different realm, there are those whose support extends far beyond this biography to my entire life. My mother, Mrs. Miriam Rosenblum, may she live and be well, continues to supply all the maternal encouragement any son could ever ask for, even at the outset of her tenth decade. Fortunately, she remains as sharp as ever and fully able to take pleasure in the achievements and *smachos* of her plentiful offspring, of whom I am the first.

My wife Judith, my life partner in everything, remains a continuing proof that one good decision made early in the journey will continue to bear fruit forevermore. Truly, all that is mine is hers. In addition, she remains my best editor.

This is my first book in almost a quarter-century that did not benefit from the rigorous critique of my dear and very much missed brother, Rabbi Matisyahu Rosenblum, *zt"l*. Even in his final months, he continued to push me to complete this volume, and it is a source of deep pain to me that he never had a chance to see the work complete. The only consolation for my failure in that regard is that I did not distract him, as his strength and energy ebbed, from the completion of his own collection of Torah essays, *Rays of Torah Wisdom: Thoughts That Light Up Our Understanding of the World.*

On behalf of Mrs. Esther Schuster and her family and myself, I would like to express our gratitude to ArtScroll/Mesorah Publications for their enthusiasm for this biography of Rabbi Meir Schuster and for their dedication to bringing it to fruition in the most attractive fashion possible. Though this is my tenth book to be published by ArtScroll, it is the first in over ten years. A lot has changed in the book publishing business and at ArtScroll in the interim, including, of course, the passing of my dear friend and mentor Rabbi Meir Zlotowitz, zt"l. And I was working, in the main, with a brand new team.

Mendy Herzberg, who managed the production from start to finish, has a remarkable ability to keep a handle on a myriad of details and different production streams, while always retaining his cool. I am grateful to Mrs. Judi Dick and Mrs. Tova Finkelman for their meticulous proofreading. Each possesses an uncanny ability to seemingly hold the entire manuscript in front of them at all times in order to prevent any inconsistencies. Every author hopes for a cover that will draw readers to his work, and Eli Kroen has certainly provided that with his beautiful cover design. Thanks to Shmuel Blitz, director of ArtScroll's Israel operations, for getting all the photos to the U.S. during the coronavirus — not an easy task — and to my friend and neighbor Mrs. Miriam Zakon, ArtScroll's acquisitions editor, for providing the title: A Tap on the Shoulder. Mrs. Estie Dicker undertook the arduous task of placing many photos in the manuscript and carried it off with aplomb. I am indebted to Chanie Ziegler for her superb work on the photographs and to Mrs. Felice Eisner for undertaking the laborious task of producing a name index. Just knowing that my friend of three decades Rabbi Nosson Scherman, with whom I have worked closely on so many books, was available for consultation of matters of style was a comfort. Finally, it was a pleasure to work for the first time with Rabbi Gedaliah Zlotowitz, and to experience the same commitment to excellence that was his late father's hallmark.

And finally, I am truly blessed by HaKadosh Baruch Hu to have spent my life immersed in the lives of those, like Rabbi Schuster, whose example can only uplift us and make us better Jews, in pursuit of our own individual missions in life.

# Part I

# LAYING
# THE FOUNDATION

# Part I

# LAYING
# THE FOUNDATION

## Chapter One
# MILWAUKEE

**L**ITTLE IS KNOWN OF RABBI MEIR TZVI (STANLEY MARTIN) Schuster's early life. He rarely spoke about himself.

What is known? He was born in Manitowoc, Wisconsin, a city of less than 75,000, on Lake Michigan, about ninety minutes' drive north of Milwaukee, on Tu BiShevat 5703 (January 22, 1943). How the Schuster family arrived in Manitowoc, and why and when they left for Milwaukee, is unknown, like most aspects of Rabbi Meir Schuster's childhood.

His parents, Morris (Moshe Chaim) and Mary (Myrke) Schuster, were both Polish-born, and Morris earned his livelihood as a carpenter. The Schuster family was not religiously observant, though like many Milwaukee Jews of that period, they may have observed some level of kashrut at home and been members of Orthodox congregations. A religious grandmother, Gittel, after whom Rabbi Schuster would one day name a daughter, oversaw his religious education and was heartened when he began to show interest in learning Torah. The most Reb Meir ever ventured about his parents in later years was: "They were good people."

Stanley had two siblings, an older sister, Rosalie, and a younger brother, Michael.

TO SAY THAT MILWAUKEE'S RELIGIOUS LIFE IN THOSE DAYS WAS NOT vibrant is an understatement. The initial Jewish settlers in Milwaukee in

## Milwaukee's Jewish Community in the '40s and '50s

the 1840s were from Germany, and brought with them religion affiliated with classical German Reform. Only later did Jews begin to arrive from Eastern Europe. By the time Stanley came of age, most of the religious Jews were older and European-born. Rabbi Avraham Yehoshua (Shea) Twerski MD (b. 1930) had only one religious contemporary in his youth, other than his brothers. And apart from Rebbetzin Twerski, his mother, only two women in Milwaukee covered their hair, both of them wives of shoemakers.

One poignant story told by Reb Shea captures the difficulty the older generation had in passing the torch of Yiddishkeit to their children. One of the aforementioned shoemakers was fasting on Tzom Gedaliah. He did not feel well, and called his son, an accountant, to come to his home. The father wanted to show his son the deed to his burial plot in the cemetery of the Poilishe shul. The son, irritated at having been interrupted in the middle of the work day, asked his father, "For this you interrupted me at work?" The next day the father passed away.

Here and there, one could still find examples of the *"pashute* Jews" so beloved by the Baal Shem Tov. Herschel Katz, a peddler, would use a horse and buggy to transport freshly cut *schach* for his succah. When he was in the hospital during his final illness, he instructed his son to open up a sack with instructions left in a drawer. The sack turned out to be filled with silver dollars.

"I've tried to be honest in business my whole life," he told his son. "But who can be sure that one has not transgressed? The money in the sack is money I received as a Kohen for *pidyon haben.* It is absolutely kosher *gelt* (money). And I want you to use it to pay my burial expenses."

Little in the way of Jewish education was available in Milwaukee in the 1940s and early '50s. Not until the mid-'50s would there be enough students to establish a religious elementary school, Hillel Academy, long after most cities of a comparable size had Jewish day schools. Such Jewish education as the younger generation picked up was in after-school Talmud Torahs associated with the various shuls, where the youngsters learned to read Hebrew and perhaps the cantillation prior to bar mitzvah.

IN 1939, REBBE YAAKOV YISRAEL TWERSKI PURCHASED A BUILDING FOR his Congregation Beth Jehudah (known as Bais Yehudah) on Milwau-

**The Twerski Family**
kee's West Side, to which the center of the Jewish community had begun to shift from the North Side of the city. At some point, he asked Rabbi Chaim Chaskel Wrona, a *meshulach* for the Lomza Yeshiva, who had learned in Radin under the Chofetz Chaim, to open a *cheder* in the shul. The *cheder* differed from the Talmud Torahs in the other Orthodox congregations in that it also provided a least some introduction to Gemara learning for the older students.

Prior to his bar mitzvah, Stanley transferred from the Talmud Torah in which he had been enrolled to Bais Yehudah. He later told Seth Mandell, one of those whom he picked up at the Kotel and with whom he became very close, that he had been doing "lousy" in his previous Talmud Torah and feared that he would not be ready for his bar mitzvah. Reb Shea Twerski provided his bar mitzvah training; no easy task, as Stanley was nearly tone deaf.

His class in the Bais Yehudah *cheder* was no more than six to ten boys, according to his closest childhood friend, Gerry Glazer, who also moved to the Bais Yehudah *cheder* around the same time. One of the teachers was Israeli, and invariably addressed Stanley as "Rabbi Schuster." Glazer thinks that they may have also been introduced to Gemara learning by Reb Mottel Twerski, the Rebbe's second son.

But by far the major influence on the young Stanley was Reb Shea

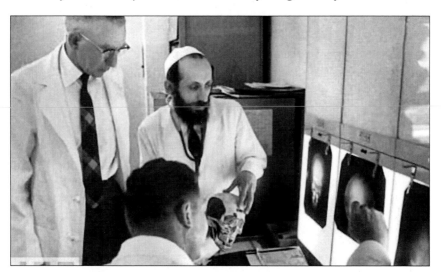

Shea Twerski as a young medical student with a stethoscope around his neck.

Twerski, then a 24-year-old pre-med student at Marquette University. Gerry Glazer, who went on to major in mathematics at the University of Chicago and become a college professor, describes Reb Shea as one of the most brilliant people he ever met. Rebbe Yaakov Yisrael did not enjoy speaking in public, and Reb Shea frequently delivered the *derashos*.[1] Glazer remembers them as masterful. But no less important for him was Reb Shea's ability "to discuss any subject under the sun," from evolution to history and everything in between.

Through the Bais Yehudah *cheder* and Reb Shea (the Twerski son most involved in the *cheder* at that time), Stanley became attached to the Bais Yehudah shul and its leader, Rebbe Yaakov Yisrael Twerski. He became a regular at the Rebbe's Leil Shabbos *tisch* and a frequent visitor in the Twerski home.

Rebbe Yaakov Yisrael Twerski arrived in America from the region around Kiev in 1927, and in Milwaukee about a year later, after a period of time in New York. He was the great-grandson of the founder of the Hornisteipler chassidic dynasty, the original Rebbe Yaakov Yisrael, who was himself the third son of the Chernobyler Maggid, Rebbe Mordechai Twerski.

Rebbe Yaakov Yisrael's original plan was to settle in Chicago, which had a large population of observant Jews.[2] But a first cousin had already established a *shtiebel* in Chicago, and Rebbe Yaakov Yisrael had no wish to compete.

Despite speaking only a very broken English, the Rebbe earned a stellar reputation in the city for his keen intelligence. Judges and attorneys would bring him their more challenging cases to hear his analysis. But his greatest strength was his warmth and ability to relate to individuals.

The warmth of the Twerski home is reflected in the manner in which each of Rebbe Yaakov Yisrael's five sons held fast to his chassidic *derech*, despite most of their formal yeshivah learning having been in non-chassidic yeshivos, and, in the case of two of his sons, reaching the pinnacle of academic success. The oldest son, Rebbe Shlomo Twerski (b. 1923), established a Hornisteipler *shtiebel* in Denver, Colorado. Reb Mottel, the second son, became a CPA, and moved to Brooklyn. He has sons who are *maggidei shiur* and communal rabbis. Rebbe Michel Twerski has,

---

1. Reb Shea was officially listed as the rav of the shul so that he would not be drafted during the Korean War.

2. Rabbi Berel Wein, a Chicago native, writes of 100,000 Chicago Jews performing Tashlich on Rosh Hashanah.

Rebbe Yaakov Yisrael Twerski

together with his wife Feige, expanded Bais Yehudah dramatically and turned it into a magnet for all those seeking a warm, personal atmosphere, including many baalei teshuvah.

Rebbe Michel's twin brother, Aaron, a law professor, is a recognized national expert in products liability, and served as Dean of Hofstra Law School. Finally, Rabbi Avraham Yehoshua Heschel (Shea) Twerski MD, a psychiatrist and the first of the brothers born in America, founded one of America's leading centers for the treatment of addictions in Pittsburgh, Pennsylvania. He has written 85 books for both religious audiences and the general public, and for both specialists in addictions and laymen. Yet the three brothers who entered the learned professions are scarcely distinguishable in their appearance from their brothers who led branches of Hornisteipler *chassidus*.

THUS FAR, WE HAVE DESCRIBED THE SKETCHIEST OUTLINE OF THE young Stanley Schuster's life, the religious environment in which he

**A Shy Youngster** came of age, and some of the influences on him, but have said little of his own personality at a young age.

Gerry Glazer's family moved to the West Side, near Bais Yehudah, at about the same time as the Schusters. From the age of 11

Bar mitzvah photo of Gerry Glazer

to 14, he and Stanley were inseparable. They attended the same public school, hung around Bais Yehudah, and attended its *cheder*. Both came from non-*shomer Shabbos* families (though Glazer's parents would later become *shomer Shabbos*), and were in the process of becoming more religiously observant.

They had a few friends who were from *shomer Shabbos* homes, including Yitzchak Meir Rube, the son of the local kosher butcher. One Shabbos, Stanley and Gerry were visiting the Rube home and apparently making too much noise for the father to take his Shabbos nap. As they heard Mr. Rube approaching the room in which they were playing, Yitzchak Meir told Stanley to jump out the first-floor window and Gerry to hide in the closest.

Sandy Aronin was a couple of years older than Stanley. After graduating high school at 16, he left for Hebrew Theological College (HTC) in Chicago. Yaakov Yeshaya (Jack) Anton was a role model who was much older — by ten years — who had left Milwaukee to learn both at HTC and subsequently at Ner Israel. As a boy, Rabbi Anton loved to attend Bais Yehudah with his European-born grandfather, and after bar mitzvah shocked his parents by expressing a desire to go to yeshivah. When he returned to Milwaukee from Baltimore, Stanley and Gerry would visit him on Shabbos.

Glazer remembers his tall, gangly friend, with wavy dark hair, as one of the shyest and least articulate people he had ever met. Initiating a conversation with someone he did not know was torture.

At around 14, Gerry and Stanley ceased to be inseparable. "All Stanley wanted to do was to learn Torah all the time. He had limitless zeal, and pushed himself extremely hard." Still, the two remained friendly, and when Stanley left Milwaukee for yeshivah in Chicago, he invited his boyhood friend to visit, which the latter did at least once. But as Stanley immersed himself in learning, they spent less and less time together.

Both the youthful shyness and the drive remained lifelong traits of

Stanley. What few at the time grasped, however, was that the latter would ultimately trump the former.

Rabbi Shea Twerski had one dominant memory of Stanley from those days. Stanley used to tell him that he heard Hashem speaking to him. At the time, Rabbi Twerski found that a bit strange. And later, when he was studying psychiatry, he would have found such a statement from a patient indicative of a serious psychological problem.

But in later years, when he would run into Rabbi Schuster at the Kotel and watch him in action, it began to dawn on Reb Shea that Stanley really had heard Hashem speaking to him.

*Chapter Two*

# YESHIVAH

B Y THE END OF HIS TENTH-GRADE YEAR IN PUBLIC HIGH
school, Stanley had convinced his parents to allow him to realize his dream and attend yeshivah in Chicago. Though his parents gave him permission, they told him that they would
not pay his tuition.[1]

**Chicago**

In 1958, Hebrew Theological College (HTC) was the only prominent
post-high school yeshivah west of Telshe Yeshiva in Cleveland, and the
logical destination for a young man from Milwaukee. Every yeshivah
student with whom Stanley would have come into contact growing up,
including the Twerski twins, Aaron and Michel, and Reb Shea before
them, passed through Chicago at some point.

HTC did not yet have a high school, though it had already moved
from its original location on Chicago's West Side to its present campus
in Skokie. High school students, such as Stanley, attended Chicago
Jewish Academy, which was still located on the West Side. Mornings
in the Academy were devoted to *limudei kodesh*, primarily Gemara.
The twelfth-grade boys in the Academy were bused to yeshivah, where
their rebbi was Rabbi Herzl Kaplan, the older brother of Rabbi Yisrael
Mendel Kaplan. Reb Mendel, as he was universally known, joined his

---

1. Gerry Glazer. How he paid tuition and for his room in the dorm is unknown.

brother in Chicago, after spending the War in Shanghai with the Mirrer Yeshiva, and taught the next highest *shiur*.[2]

After lunch the boys and girls were brought together for the secular studies classes.[3] Students at the Academy from outside Chicago slept in the Skokie dorms of HTC and learned in the *beis medrash* at night.

Who Stanley's Gemara rebbeim were at the Academy, and whether he was in the same *shiur* as his class for Gemara or started in a lower *shiur* because of his weak background, is information lost with the passage of time. In the words of one classmate, he "stood out only for not standing out in any way," except for the fact that he always learned in the *beis medrash* wearing a jacket and hat.[4]

Rabbi Yehudah Silver, whose father, Rabbi Dovid Silver, taught the tenth-grade *shiur* in the Academy, also roomed in the Skokie dorms, despite living in Chicago. He and Stanley would meet again in Jerusalem a quarter of a century later. In 1983 Rabbi Silver, after a career as a congregational rabbi and school principal, was invited by Rabbi Noach Weinberg to join the *hanhalah* (senior administration) of Aish HaTorah.

Rabbi Silver describes the contrast between the Stanley he knew in Chicago and the Rabbi Meir Tzvi Schuster he watched bringing young backpackers from the Kotel to Aish HaTorah every day as "the most amazing transformation I have witnessed in my life." In Chicago, "he was a very shy and withdrawn teenager, who found it almost painfully difficult to communicate or to make connections with people." And now, he was approaching dozens of complete strangers every day.

STANLEY ARRIVED AT THE GARRISON AVENUE CAMPUS OF NER ISRAEL Rabbinical College in time for the Elul *zeman* of 5719 (1960), and

**Ner Israel Rabbinical College**

the transformation from Stanley Martin to Rabbi Meir Tzvi Schuster began. He would remain in Ner Israel for the next eight years, until his marriage, leaving with *semichah* from the Rosh

---

2. The two brothers had a well-rehearsed routine. When a *bachur* in Rav Herzl's *shiur* would ask a good question, he would send him to his brother with the *kashe*, adding, "He knows everything." But when Rav Mendel learned that the student posing the question was from his brother's *shiur*, he would send him back to his own rebbi, with the admonition: "He only wants to hear what I'll say so that he can *upshlug* (refute) it."

3. There were not yet any non-coed high schools in Chicago. Rabbi Berel Wein, for instance, kibbitzes about sitting in class next to the future Novominsker Rebbetzin Yehudis Eichenstein Perlow, *a"h*.

4. Levi Van Leuwen.

Rabbi Schuster's *Semichah* from Ner Israel Rabbinical College

Yeshivah Rabbi Yaakov Yitzchok Ruderman and a teaching certificate from Torah Umesorah.

Again, nothing is known of his reasons for leaving Chicago or going to Baltimore, other than that he was following a path already hewn by a number of other Milwaukee natives, including Michel and Aaron Twerski and Yaakov Yeshayahu Anton.

Rabbi Naftali Kaplan, today rosh yeshivah of one of the premier yeshivos in Eretz Yisrael (known colloquially as "Kaplan's") and already a *maggid shiur* in the Ner Israel high school during Meir Tzvi's years in the yeshivah, describes him as a "*tayerer* (precious) *bachur*." But like everyone else who knew him in those years, he admits that he would have considered him the least likely person in the *beis medrash* to have a major impact on the world. His shy and withdrawn nature had not changed.

But Meir Tzvi clearly felt that he had found his place in Ner Israel, and in particular under the guidance of the Mashgiach, Rabbi Dovid Kronglas. On visits to Milwaukee, he would speak to Shlomo Porter, a Milwaukee native four years his junior, about coming to a "real yeshivah" in Baltimore. (Porter had followed his path in going to Hebrew Theological College in Chicago for high school.[5]) Something of his enthusiasm must have gotten through. Rabbi Porter arrived in Baltimore in 1964 and remained at Ner Israel for the next thirteen years — nine years in *beis medrash* and four years in the kollel.

If Meir Tzvi stood out among his peers, it was for two qualities: exceptional piety and great *hasmadah* (diligence) in learning. Dovid Greenblatt came to Baltimore from Memphis as a high school student. He liked to go to the main *beis medrash* very late at night to observe the action. Between 1:00 a.m. and 2:00 a.m., he would find many of those who went on to become *roshei yeshivah* or *maggidei shiur*: Rabbi Moshe Brown, Rabbi Yosef Kalatsky, the Nekritz brothers. But also to be found was Meir Tzvi Schuster.

---

5. By the time Rabbi Porter arrived at HTC it already had its own all-boys high school.

Nor did the late nights of learning prevent Meir Tzvi from serving as the *vekker* in his dorm, for at least part of his time in the yeshivah. He would make the rounds in the morning waking the *bachurim* for davening: "*Shtei oif! Shtei oif l'avodas haBorei* — Arise! Arise to the service of the Creator."

Perhaps his longest-standing *chavrusa* (study partner) in the yeshivah was Rabbi Sheftel Neuberger, who would eventually succeed his father, Rabbi Naftali (Herman) Neuberger, as the executive director of Ner Israel Rabbinical College. He and Meir Tzvi learned together every afternoon for three or four years, going through tractate after tractate together.

Rabbi Kalman Rosenbaum, subsequently a highly respected day school principal, learned with Reb Meir Tzvi for nearly three-quarters of a year prior to his wedding. Reflecting back on that *chavrusashaft* (learning partnership), what struck him most was that there was absolutely no extraneous talk. He knew nothing more about Reb Meir Tzvi — his past, his aspirations — at the end of the nine months than when they first sat down.

The Ozerover Rebbe of Bnei Brak, Rabbi Tanchum Becker, grew up in Milwaukee and was about six years younger than Meir Tzvi. After the latter's passing, he wrote to Mrs. Schuster of his impressions of Reb Meir Tzvi on the latter's return trips to Milwaukee to visit his family during *bein hazemanim* (intersession): "I still remember at a distance of more than a *yovel* [fifty years], when I was still a young *bachur* ... how during those visits Reb Meir was fully involved in his Torah learning. Even then he was an image for me of a *yeshivah bachur* immersed in learning, who exemplified refinement and *ahavas Yisrael*...."

In the *beis medrash*, Reb Meir stood out for the fervor of his davening. His *Yehei Shemei Rabbah* was by far the loudest. Rabbi Porter says with a smile, "He was the furthest thing from wanting to look cool. He could not even restrain himself to look normal."

On Shabbos, when the other *bachurim* went out to the homes of their rebbeim for meals, Reb Meir remained behind. After eating, he would head to the *beis medrash*, with a box of Stella D'oro cookies and a bag of dates by his side. When *bachurim* would return from their meals, he would motion them over to partake of a date or a cookie, but at a price: a *dvar Torah*. The barter all took place with sign language, as Reb Meir made a *taanis dibbur* (literally, a fast of speech) for everything but *divrei Torah* every Shabbos.

Rabbi Sheftel Neuberger, however, finds something more in the dates and cookies: Reb Meir's thoughtfulness and concern for others. Chaim Kass, who came to the Ner Israel high school after a year of public high school in Los Angeles, describes Reb Meir as always looking for opportunities to help, and "laughing a lot."

In general, the younger *bachurim* were more likely to gravitate toward him — particularly if they were lonely or came from weaker backgrounds, as Reb Meir himself had. Perhaps he felt more comfortable with the younger *bachurim* than with his peers, foreshadowing his life work with Jewish youth.

Chaim Kass felt himself to be considerably behind in his learning. But he quickly learned that if he brought a problem in learning to Reb Meir, the latter would sit with him and patiently work through the Gemara. That happened at least twenty or thirty times.

Yossi Nussbaum came to Ner Israel high school from Detroit, and did not know a single person in the yeshivah. But Reb Meir had been assigned as the older *bachur* in his room. The two became close, though they spent little time together. Reb Meir arrived back in the room at night long after the younger *bachurim* had gone to sleep. The two did, however, learn together during *mussar seder* for a time. But the biggest influence of Reb Meir came from "just watching him," he recalls. "I respected him tremendously."

Sammy Kassin was another younger roommate. He came to the Ner Israel high school from a traditional, but not fully observant, Syrian Jewish family in Miami. When he first arrived, he decided to take in such sights as Baltimore had to offer, and did not arrive back in the dorm until late in the evening. As he was sleeping peacefully the next morning, the bunk bed started to shake violently. Only later would he discover that it was Reb Meir getting dressed under the covers. Next, a pair of long, thin legs appeared, as Reb Meir prepared to jump down from the top bunk. Sammy, today Rabbi Shlomo Kassin, the founder and director of the World Sephardi Center in the Old City of Jerusalem, still recalls his first thought upon seeing the disembodied legs followed by Reb Meir: "This guy will never amount to anything."

But over the next months, Reb Meir took it upon himself to instruct his new charge in mitzvah observance, up to and including how to dress under the covers. The first time Reb Meir mentioned *negel vasser*, Sammy had no idea what he was speaking about. Not only did he have no familiarity with Yiddish, but the ritual was also entirely new to him.

Rabbi Shlomo Kassin and Rabbi Schuster in later years

He still remembers his shock one Shabbos morning when he was trying to pick out a tie, and Reb Meir mentioned to him that such a routine action might fall into the forbidden category of *borer* (selecting) on Shabbos. Still, says Rabbi Kassin, "he pointed out things I should be doing, but he never insisted or fought about it."

THE SINGLE INDIVIDUAL WHO EXERCISED THE GREATEST INFLUENCE on Meir Tzvi not only during his eight years in Ner Israel, but for the rest of his life, was Rabbi Dovid Kronglas, who **Rabbi Dovid** was both the Mashgiach at Ner Israel and gave the **Kronglas** highest daily *shiur*. Meir Tzvi was in Reb Dovid's Gemara *shiur* for four years.[6]

Rabbi Yaakov Yitzchok Ruderman, the Rosh Yeshivah, afforded great latitude to the rebbeim in the yeshivah with regard to how they developed their relationships with the *bachurim*. As a consequence, there were multiple centers of influence in the yeshivah. But Reb Meir Tzvi was definitely one of Reb Dovid's *bachurim*.[7]

Reb Dovid's style of intense *mussar* and constant spiritual striving reinforced Reb Meir Tzvi's natural tendencies from the moment he

---

6. Rabbi Yissocher Frand.
7. Rabbi Naftali Kaplan.

started on the path of religious observance. Reb Dovid took on multiple personal *chumros* (stringencies) — e.g., he fasted every day between Rosh Hashanah and Yom Kippur.[8] And he made little effort to hide the intensity of his *avodah*. *Bachurim* in the yeshivah did not need a calendar to tell them that it was Elul; it was enough to look at Reb Dovid's face to know. *"Ki heim chayeinu* — they [*divrei Torah*] are our lives" became a living reality for the Ner Israel *bachurim* when they saw the joy that radiated from Reb Dovid when he learned.[9]

The clarity of Reb Dovid's presentation of issues, whether in his Gemara *shiur* or in a *mussar shmuess*, would have also appealed to Reb Meir Tzvi, who was always very straightforward in his thinking and eager to find practical applications for what he learned.

Rabbi Gershon Weiss, one of Reb Dovid's closest disciples, who went on to serve as the Mashgiach of the Yeshiva of Staten Island, entitled his appreciation of Reb Dovid in *The Jewish Observer*, "A European Mashgiach in an American Yeshivah."[10] And indeed Reb Dovid's background was far removed from that of the *bachurim* in Ner Israel. He used to speak of how in his hometown of Kobrin there were sixty to eighty men learning in the *beis medrash* at every minute of the day and night.

Reb Dovid was nearly 40 when he arrived in America, after the War. But he had prior exposure to American *bachurim* in the pre-War Mirrer Yeshiva. Mrs. Batsheva Leshinsky, who served the American *bachurim* dinner, wanted to ensure that her dinner table not become "too American," and therefore invited Reb Dovid to eat at her table for free.[11] Besides the time Reb Dovid spent with American *bachurim*, the great Mirrer Mashgiach, Rabbi Yerucham Levovitz, appointed him as the "older *bachur*," or spiritual guide, for some of the German *bachurim* who came to the Mir.

Reb Dovid's relationship with one such German *bachur* — Naftali (Herman) Neuberger, who arrived in Mir in 1935 from Wurzberg — would have immense implications for Reb Dovid and Ner Israel. When Naftali reached America in 1938, he immediately went to work trying to obtain visas for relatives in Europe. And he persuaded Rabbi Ruderman to invite Reb Dovid to serve as Mashgiach in Ner Israel, which allowed

---

8. Rabbi Kalman Rosenbaum.

9. Rabbi Gershon Weiss, "A European Mashgiach in an American Yeshivah," *The Jewish Observer*, March 1975, pp. 10, 11.

10. *Jewish Observer*, March 1975.

11. Rabbi Shmuel Bloom.

him to secure a U.S. entry visa for Reb Dovid.[12]

Unfortunately, the visa that Rabbi Neuberger obtained arrived only after the Nazi invasion of Poland, and Reb Dovid ended up spending the War in Shanghai with the Mirrer Yeshiva.[13] The visa papers, however, proved useful after the War, and he was one of the first of the Mirrer *bachurim* to arrive in the United States. Before taking the position of Mashgiach in Ner Israel, Reb Dovid told Rabbi Ruderman that he would have to give a Gemara *shiur* as well or he would never command the respect of American *bachurim*.

He was no less qualified for the role of *maggid shiur* than he was for that of Mashgiach. His roommate in Shanghai related that he could never determine when Reb Dovid slept. Like most of the Mirrer *bachurim*, he lost almost his entire family in the War, and non-stop learning was the means of retaining his sanity. His *sefer Divrei Dovid* on *Zeraim* was a product of that period of remaining nearly around the clock in the *beis medrash* in Shanghai with his *chavrusa*.

Inevitably, there was an adjustment period for Reb Dovid to the standards of American *bachurim* upon his arrival in Baltimore. He was dismayed to discover sports magazines in the dorms, and delivered his next *shmuess* on the importance of one's choice of whom he looks up to — *ish l'fi mehallelo*, "a man according to his [or, whom he] praises" (*Mishlei* 27:21).[14]

---

12. Rabbi Sheftel Neuberger.

13. . Not only was Reb Dovid left without a usable visa to America, but he almost missed receiving the Japanese transit papers that a group of Mirrer *bachurim* had procured from the Japanese consul in Kovno, Chiune ("Sempo") Sugihara. Reb Dovid had a gall bladder attack on the day the transit papers were distributed. Fortunately, one *bachur* had procured two sets of transit papers, and agreed to sell his extra set to Reb Dovid.

He had previously offered the papers to Yonah Karpilov (known as Yonah Minsker), one of the shining lights of the pre-World War II yeshivah world and known for *sefer Yonas Eilem*, a collection of his writings. But he hesitated to purchase them and tragically perished in the War.

Obtaining the papers was not the end of Reb Dovid's adventures prior to reaching Shanghai. Riding on the Trans-Siberian railroad to Vladivostok with the Mirrer Mashgiach, Rabbi Yechezkel (Chatzkel) Levenstein, the latter told Reb Dovid to get off at one stop, without explanation, and to take the next train.

When they met again in Vladivostok, Reb Chatzkel asked him, again without explanation, whether he was afraid. Only when their ship had sailed from Vladivostok to Kobe, Japan, did Reb Chatzkel tell him that the danger had passed. Until then, he had feared that the Japanese would deny them transit through Japan because the end visas to the West Indian island of Curacao in the Caribbean, stamped by the Dutch honorary counsel in Kovno, would not be honored by Curacao. But had that been the case, Japanese officials would not have allowed them to board the ship.

14. Rabbi Shmuel Bloom.

The *bachurim* had to adjust to his rigorous standards as well. But many were soon attracted by his exceptional refinement. On days of heavy snow, for instance, Reb Dovid refused to have the driver assigned to pick him up attempt to pull into his driveway, but chose to trudge to the road to meet him there. On his final trip to the hospital in an ambulance, he requested that the ambulance driver not sound his siren on the Ner Israel campus so as not to cause concern to the *bachurim* and rebbeim. Even though his time in the hospital was relatively brief, hardened doctors and nurses were seen with tears in their eyes upon his passing. "That was a human being," said one doctor.

As demanding as he was upon himself, Reb Dovid was always available to discuss practical matters with the *bachurim*, and was heavily involved in *shidduchim*, including Reb Meir Tzvi's. As a consequence, writes Rabbi Weiss, "many a youngster who came to the yeshivah determined to become a professional in later life dropped those ambitions to concentrate instead on attaining *sheleimus* (perfection) in *avodas Hashem* (service of G-d), and eventually devoted his adult life to dissemination of Torah."

Reb Dovid persuaded Shmuel Bloom to remain in Ner Israel rather than return to New York to utilize his state scholarship to study mathematics in college, in combination with yeshivah learning. Reb Dovid lived to see Rabbi Bloom as a rebbi in Ner Israel's high school, though not long enough to witness his becoming the chief executive officer of Agudath Israel of America.

Whether in his Gemara *shiur* or in his weekly *mussar shmuess* given after *shalosh seudos*, Reb Dovid began by citing the basic texts in Gemara and Rishonim and patiently building his theme step by step from there. His Gemara *shiur* went faster than any of the other *shiurim* in the yeshivah to ensure that a student who missed a day would have to work hard to catch up. Reb Dovid himself almost never missed a *shiur*, even in the pain-racked final weeks of his life.

One of Reb Dovid's main themes in his *mussar shmuessen* was the need for each Jew to discover his unique life mission. In Mussaf of Rosh Hashanah, each person is described as passing before HaKadosh Baruch Hu and being judged on *maaseh ish u'fekudaso* — according to his deeds and his specific mission. Each person comes into the world with an assignment to be *mekadesh Sheim Shamayim* in a unique way that no one else has ever done or ever will do, Reb Dovid taught.

The Gemara in *Moed Kattan*, for instance, says that one's length of days, number of children, and material prosperity are not a function of merit but of *mazal*. And the Gemara proves the point with reference to Rabbah and Rav Chisda, two great *Amoraim*. Rav Chisda lived a long life, with many children, and enjoyed material plenty, while Rabbah lived a brief life, buried many children, and suffered perpetual want. Each, however, in Reb Dovid's explanation, was given precisely what he needed for his unique mission.

We shall see how important that need to discover one's personal mission in life and to fulfill it to the maximum would prove in the life of Rabbi Meir Tzvi Schuster.

# Chapter Three
# MARRIAGE

**M**EIR TZVI SCHUSTER MARRIED ESTHER GARFINKEL OF Monsey on 17 Kislev 5758 (December 18, 1967) at the Broadway Central Hotel in Manhattan. Rabbi Yaakov Yitzchok Ruderman, Reb Meir's Rosh Yeshivah, was the *mesader kiddushin*, and Rabbi Dovid Kronglas read the *kesubah*. Meir Tzvi did the artwork for the *kesubah* himself, and his friend Chaim Kass was the *sofer*.

All the relevant negotiations concerning support for the young couple while Reb Meir learned were conducted by Rabbi Kronglas.

At one level, it was a match of opposites. Esther was outgoing, bright, and possessed of a strong personality. Reb Meir Tzvi was quiet and seemed to do everything possible to avoid standing out, except when davening. Esther

The Schusters' *kesubah*.
Rabbi Schuster did the artwork framing it.

came from a well-established family on both her father and mother's sides. Both her parents were American-born. Yet despite having long been in America, both the Garfinkel and Kramer families had remained firm in their religious observance. Finally, there was an over-four-year difference in age: She was still under 20 at the time of their engagement on Rosh Chodesh Elul, and he was nearly 25.

Rabbi Schuster at his *chasunah*

The *shidduch* was suggested by Eli Gibber, Esther's first cousin, who learned at Ner Israel together with Reb Meir, though he was five years younger and did not know him well. What he did know, however, was that his cousin was looking for a "serious boy," and Reb Meir certainly fit the bill. He was one of the few Ner Israel *bachurim* of his day who did not attend college at night.

Rabbi Dovid Kronglas reading the *kesubah* at the wedding of Rabbi Meir Schuster and Esther Garfinkel. Rabbi Yaakov Yitzchok Ruderman is to Rabbi Kronglas's left.

Despite the obvious differences between Meir Tzvi and Esther, the *shidduch* proceeded smoothly, and the couple was engaged within three weeks of their first meeting. Meir Tzvi's conversation during the dating process consisted primarily of *divrei Torah*, and he never spoke about his personal history. But he was not a complete stick-in-the-mud. On one of their dates, they went miniature golfing.

## The Garfinkel and Kramer Families

WHILE NEXT TO NOTHING IS KNOWN ABOUT RABBI SCHUSTER'S PARents or larger family, books have been written on Esther's grandfather, Reb Dovid Garfinkel, and her maternal great-grandfather, Moshe Eliezer Kramer, and his descendants. Reb Dovid Garfinkel was born in Antipola, near Brisk, in White Russia. After the local *melamed* told his father that he had nothing more to teach the boy before his bar mitzvah, he was sent to learn in Brisk under Rabbi Chaim Soloveitchik. When he left Brisk to go to the United States at the age of 16, Reb Chaim Brisker gave him a letter of recommendation.

Though the departure from Brisk marked the end of his formal yeshivah training, he continued to learn for hours each day and to teach Torah in every place he lived, while refusing all offers of rabbinic positions. It was said that there were more *sefarim* (Torah books) than chickens on the chicken farm he ran with his youngest son in Monticello in the Catskills.

Rabbi Nachman Bulman, then a young rabbi in Fallsburg, wrote an article for Torah Umesorah in 1961 in which he described Reb Dovid without naming him:

> There was one family, however, in the city of Monticello, with a father who was a *talmid chacham,* a simple Jew, not a "professional" Jew, but a scholar. Somehow this father, alone among these nine or ten communities, managed to hold on to all his sons and daughters. Each one of them married a shomer mitzvoth, an observant Jew, a minor miracle in itself. But what sort of observant Jew could their children have been if there was no yeshivah...

> [T]his one grandfather, looking at his 5- and 6-year-old grandchildren, began to say to his sons and sons-in-law: '*Es muz zein a yeshivah* — there must be a day school here....' [And] *es iz gevoren a yeshivah* — a day school came to the Catskills."

Reb Dovid lived in Monticello as if he were still in Antipola. On a trip to England for a son's *chasunah* in 1961, he declined to do any sightseeing. His explanation for remaining behind, "First, a person must thoroughly know himself," could have been taken from a classical *mussar sefer*. And indeed that is how he conducted his life.

He frequently quoted Rav Yisrael Salanter's statement, "One can judge a Jew's love for Hashem by his love for his fellow man," and lived accordingly. The Garfinkel home at 47 Liberty Avenue was always filled with guests. Reb Dovid's aversion to *lashon hara* was obvious from his conversation. The struggle to avoid *lashon hara* and any expression of anger is a recurrent subject in the spiritual diary he maintained, parts of which have been published. The entries read like those from the *mussar vaadim* in Kelm:

> March 23 — Today I had great pleasure to discuss words of halachah with a person greater than me in wisdom, and I learned very much....
>
> April 15 — *Baruch Hashem*, I was spared today from accepting *lashon hara*, as a bird who flees from a trap.
>
> June 9 — It is a mitzvah to bring joy to the soul of someone who lacks many friends, and to make him happy and act on his behalf....

Reb Dovid's honesty in business was legendary. When he sold his sales route to a non-Jew, the latter entered into the deal based on a handshake alone. Once he went to the local bank to repay a loan, only to be told that the bank had no record of any such loan. He refused to leave, however, until the documentation of the loan was found in archived files.

On another occasion, a fire engulfed his chicken house, destroying the entirety of a lot of six thousand chickens he had just purchased. Friends advised Reb Dovid to overstate the quantity because the insurance company would surely deduct for a certain number of chickens assumed to have died since delivery. Reb Dovid refused to do so, and told the insurance adjustor that he had purchased six thousand chickens but had no idea how many died subsequently. The insurance company covered the entire lot.

During Reb Dovid's lifetime, the larger Garfinkel family would gather at 47 Liberty in Monticello every Sunday. And even after his passing, his influence was strongly felt by the entire family. In his final ethical will, he enjoined his wife Anne not to cry too much (more than three days) after his passing, and expressed his confidence that she would follow his instructions, "as you are a wise and understanding person from the first day I saw you until the last day we were together." In an era where women covering their hair was still not the norm, he requested his female descendants to do so, and adjured his male descendants to be careful about refraining from speaking during the Torah reading.

Nor was Reb Dovid Garfinkel the only notable member of Esther's family tree. She was named after her great-grandmother, Esther Davidson, Anne's mother, who was universally known as Guta for her sparkling character. As a young woman, Guta Esther married a widower with three small children, Moshe Davidson, and raised his three children, together with three daughters of her own.

In both Europe and America, she would chop firewood to keep the family dwelling warm, and while thus engaged in Europe, she delivered a baby outside by herself, wrapped the newborn infant in blankets, and brought her into the house. After the death of her husband, Guta Esther supported her family by running a chicken market on the Lower East Side.

Moshe Davidson, like David Garfinkel, was a native of Antipola, and thus it was natural for David, upon arriving in America, to find his way to the Davidson home, across from Yeshivas Yaakov Yosef (RJJ), in which Guta Esther ran an informal restaurant. Unlike Reb David, however, Moshe Davidson was of chassidic stock and known as the leader of Kobriner *chassidus* in America.

Guta herself had a thirst for Torah, and despite scant formal education taught herself to read *Tze'ena U're'ena*. In later years, she used to listen from the women's balcony as her son-in-law Reb Dovid gave an evening *shiur* in Mesivtha Tifereth Jerusalem to *baalei batim*, shortly after his and Anne's wedding.

On her mother's side, Esther was also descended from a well-known American Orthodox family. Ruth (Kramer) Garfinkel's grandfather, Moshe Eliezer Kramer, arrived in America in 1895, leaving his wife Rochel Elka and six children in Kurenitz in White Russia. Not until 1899 had Moshe Eliezer saved enough money to bring over his entire family, who endured a harrowing three-month trek by land and sea.

By 1917, however, Moshe Eliezer's business as a pants manufacturer had flourished, and he was one of the most prominent Jews in the United States, certainly one of the most prominent Orthodox Jews. Jacob Pfeffer describes him in *Distinguished Jews in America* (1917) as having gained his fortune in business in the most solid and conservative fashion. He eschewed all speculation, and bought only for cash and on ten-day terms. His firm rule was to never do business with more than half of his available cash. His philanthropic endeavors included serving as a founder and director of the Hebrew Immigrant Aid Society (HIAS).

Jacob Pfeffer noted that Moshe Eliezer remained a Sabbath observer and strictly Orthodox, which was very rare for one who had succeeded in business. Even more remarkable for the times, "his children remain devoted to their father, and all the principles and traditions of Jewish religion." Moshe Eliezer maintained a synagogue in the backyard of his private home in the Bensonhurst neighborhood of Brooklyn. Visitors to the shul were routinely invited to join the Kramer family for the entirety of Shabbos.

Moshe Eliezer not only remained strictly observant, but also thoroughly immersed in learning. He is believed to have been the first person to celebrate a Siyum HaShas in America, long before the introduction of the *daf hayomi* cycle. A family friend remembered watching him lay out fabric for cutting, with an open volume of Gemara in front of him as he worked.

His wife Rochel Elka involved all her daughters in *chesed*, such as delivering food packages to the needy. One daughter recalled that she and her sisters had attended every funeral of a poor Jew within a few miles' radius of their home.

Of Moshe Eliezer's many philanthropic activities, the one closest to his heart was Agudah Chasidei Chabad, which he founded in the early '20s at the behest of the Lubavitcher Rebbe, Rabbi Yosef Yitzchak Schneerson, for the purpose of uniting Chabad chassidim across America. When he passed away in 1935, his oldest son Hyman (Chaim Shneur Zalman HaLevi) — Ruth Garfinkel's father — succeeded him as head of the organization, and two other sons served as senior officers. Sam Kramer convinced the Joint Distribution Committee to secretly support the Rebbe's work in the Soviet Union to the tune of $75,000 a year, a huge sum in those days (1925-26).

When the Rebbe was imprisoned in 1927 by the Soviet authorities, the brothers were at the forefront of the worldwide campaign to secure his freedom. After his release in 1929, the Rebbe visited America. Hyman and his wife Fannie hosted a *melaveh malkah* in his honor, and Hyman accompanied the Rebbe to Washington, D.C., to meet President Hoover. The brothers were also involved in the complicated ransom negotiations that resulted in the Rebbe being allowed to leave Warsaw for the United States on March 19, 1940, after the Nazi takeover of Poland.

Esther's father, Mr. Herb Garfinkel, did not have the benefit of a yeshivah education growing up in the Catskills (where his father had moved due to his asthma). But he acquired a special expertise in several areas of practical halachah in which he helped his father, particularly the construction and maintenance of mikvaot.

Mr. Garfinkel was intent on providing the best possible Jewish education for his children. In order to do so he left Monticello for Monsey in 1955, when Esther was 8. His two sons, Moshe and Aaron, both learned in Telshe Yeshiva in Cleveland. Two nephews, Aaron and Harvey Gibber, sons of Herb's sister Ruth Gibber, also lived with the Garfinkels for several years so that they could benefit from the superior yeshivah education available in Monsey.

Esther was one of a small class of girls in Rebbetzin Shoshana Soloveitchik's Bais Yaakov High School in Monsey — the entire school consisted of just fourteen students. After high school, she joined three classmates in Rabbi Wolf's Seminary in Bnei Brak. Of the American girls who went to Rabbi Wolf's Seminary in 1965, Esther was the only one whose father was not a rosh yeshivah or communal rav.

It was still long before a post-high school year in seminary in Israel had become de rigueur for American Orthodox Jews. That year, no more than thirty American girls learned in Israel following high school — fifteen in Bnei Brak and fifteen at the Bais Yaakov Seminary of Yerushalayim (BJJ). The two groups had a great deal of contact, and many of Esther's closest lifelong friendships were formed during that year.

In the late 1960s, Rabbi Yaakov Kamenetsky moved next door to the Garfinkels, after retiring as Rosh Yeshivah of Torah Vodaath. Reb Yaakov always showed great respect for *ehrliche baalei batim*, like Mr. Garfinkel, who lived proudly as an Orthodox Jew, even as he racked up thousands of miles by car each year as a salesman for two furniture manufacturers based in North Carolina.

The Kamenetsky and Garfinkel families became very friendly. Reb Yaakov would frequently quote the verse "Better a good neighbor than a distant brother" (*Mishlei* 27:10) in reference to the Garfinkels. Herb Garfinkel translated documents for Reb Yaakov from time to time, and also took Rebbetzin Kamenetsky shopping almost every week. She in turn sent a home-baked challah to the Garfinkels for Shabbos weekly. In later years, Reb Yaakov and Mr. Garfinkel would winter near one another in Florida.

One of the *sheva berachos* for Reb Meir and Esther was held in the shul underneath Reb Yaakov's home, and on a visit to Israel in the early years of the Schusters' marriage, Reb Yaakov and his Rebbetzin came to visit the young couple at their apartment in Jerusalem's Sanhedria neighborhood.

MEIR AND ESTHER BEGAN MARRIED LIFE WITH FEW CONCRETE PLANS. Such plans as they had, Mrs. Schuster makes clear, bore no resemblance

**Newlyweds** to the life they would actually lead together. Though she was perfectly amenable to Reb Meir's desire to begin married life learning in Israel, she had no intention of living her entire life in Israel. While in *shidduchim*, she had rejected even meeting a young man who was determined to live there.

While Herb Garfinkel would help the young couple as long as he could, the Schusters had no real financial plan. Reb Meir hoped that he might be able to bring in at least some *parnassah* making hand-decorated *kesubos*.

The new couple remained in America for three months after their own *chasunah* in order to be there for the wedding of Esther's brother Moshe. But they were off to Israel as soon as possible after Moshe's wedding. They arrived with four suitcases, representing most of their worldly possessions, ten days before Purim.

Shortly thereafter, the young couple took a brief trip to Eilat. It may well have been the most frivolous thing Reb Meir ever did in his life. In later years, he would not allow himself even a day or two off during Chol HaMoed or summer vacation.

Examples of Reb Meir's decorative religious art

Fortunately, the Schusters had packed light, as they moved multiple times during their first year. They started in the post-1967 Mattersdorf neighborhood, which at that time consisted of only five buildings. They subsequently moved to Bayit Vegan, and after that to the older Sanhedria neighborhood, which had been the border during the 1948 War of Independence.

On Chol HaMoed Pesach of 1969, the Schusters' first child, Yocheved Faige Dina (universally known as Shatzi), was born. She was given the nickname Shatzi, which means beloved or very dear one in German, by a Swiss neighbor.

By early 1970, the couple purchased an apartment at 11 Rechov Even Ha'ezel in Ezras Torah, another post-1967 neighborhood, for all of $10,000, which was mostly paid for by a government mortgage, with some help from Esther's father. It would be their home for over thirty years. Among those living nearby was Rabbi Noach Weinberg, whose life would be intimately intertwined with Reb Meir's for the next thirty-five years. Rabbi Mordechai Pearlman, who had been about six years behind Reb Meir at Ner Israel and one of the group of English-speakers learning in the Mir when he arrived, introduced the two. They davened in the same minyan on Shabbos.

Upon arriving in Israel, Reb Meir followed the most frequently trod

path and went to learn in the Mirrer *beis medrash*. The entire *beis medrash* in 1968 consisted of little more than 100 students, as opposed to over 7,000 today spread over multiple *batei medrash*, and there was a high concentration of English-speakers. Among those learning at the Mir were a number of English-speakers who would soon find themselves teaching in the new yeshivos for baalei teshuvah: Rabbis Gedaliah Elfenbeim, Mordechai Pearlman, and Moshe Pindrus at Ohr Somayach; Rabbis Chaim Walkin, Dovid Affen, Shlomo Kaplan, and Zelig Pliskin at Aish HaTorah.

Reb Meir's first *chavrusa* at Mir Yeshiva was Rabbi Yehudah Samet, who was also a Mattersdorf neighbor. Rabbi Samet has been a fixture in the Ohr Somayach *beis medrash* for nearly half a century. The Samets, who had already been in Israel for about five years, hosted the Schusters for their first Seder in Israel. In the course of the conversation, it was discovered that Rabbi Samet's mother had taught Mrs. Schuster's mother in Shulamis, one of the first religious girls' schools in New York City. Mrs. Schuster's mother's family, the Kramers, had been major supporters of Shulamis.

From Mir, Reb Meir next went to learn in a kollel run by Rabbi Meir Malin and Rabbi Nechemia Malin. The brothers were cousins of Rabbi Aryeh Leib Malin, the shining light of pre-War Brisk and subsequently the founder of Yeshivas Bais HaTalmud in Brooklyn. It was a high-level kollel, according to Rabbi Yitzchak Berkovits, today rosh yeshivah of Aish HaTorah, which produced many leading rabbanim.[1] The Rabbis Malin were strict about *avreichim* (married students) being at their *shtender* (lectern) by 9:00 a.m., something that was not a challenge for Reb Meir, who almost always davened in the *haneitz* (sunrise) minyan. His *chavrusa* was a Rabbi Jungreis from Brooklyn, who went on to become a respected *posek*.[2]

Though Reb Meir always maintained regular *chavrusos* for his entire life, despite his frenetic pace, his last full-time kollel was in the rabbinic program of Machon Harry Fischel, a multi-year, extremely focused program. He asked Rabbi Dovid Refson, who was then learning at Machon Harry Fischel and would soon thereafter found Neve Yerushalayim, the largest of the seminaries for baalos teshuvah, to introduce him to Rabbi Leizer Kugel, who headed the program.[3]

Rabbi Kugel noted that Reb Meir was not exactly the "hail-fellow-well-met" type, and later asked Rabbi Refson, as his unofficial sponsor, what he envisioned him doing. Rabbi Refson was not prepared for the question and blurted out the first reply that came to his mind, "Oh, he'll

---

1. In time, the Malin brothers formed a host of educational institutions under the banner Knesses Yehudah, including a *cheder*, shuls, and kollelim. Rabbi Berkovits has lived across the street from the Knesses Yehudah building for approximately forty years. He serves as rav of a shul on the premises for the English-speaking community of Sanhedria Murchevet and also heads a large kollel on the premises, which prepares kolleleit for rabbinical careers in *chutz laAretz* in a three-year program.

2. Yonoson Israel, who learned together with Reb Meir in the kollel.

3. In those days, the number of English-speakers in Israeli yeshivos was still very small, and everyone knew everyone else. Rabbi Schuster and Rabbi Refson had overlapped in the Mirrer *beis medrash*.

do kiruv." No doubt Reb Dovid was proud of himself for that example of dry British humor, which was sure to go over the head of the distinguished older Israeli rav, who was married to the granddaughter of Rabbi Aryeh Levin and the niece of Rabbi Yosef Shalom Elyashiv.

But, in truth, he had prophesied without knowing what he prophesied.

# Part II

# SOUL-SEARCHER

*Chapter Four*
# GETTING STARTED

W HAT POSSESSED REB MEIR TO CONTEMPLATE GETTING involved in kiruv? Kiruv was not something that he and his wife had ever discussed during the *shidduch* process, or even after moving to Israel. Indeed the possibility that tens of thousands of Jews far removed from Torah observance might become fully observant was not even part of the communal discussion when they were married.

Not until the early 1970s were there any institutions in Israel designed for adults from non-Orthodox backgrounds to learn Torah. The first two such institutions for English-speakers, Dvar Yerushalayim and the Diaspora Yeshiva, opened at the beginning of the decade. Shema Yisrael, which would later split into Ohr Somayach and Aish HaTorah, began in 1972.

Rabbi Dovid Refson's offhand remark to Rabbi Kugel notwithstanding, kiruv was not an area anyone would have contemplated for Reb Meir, and especially not engaging complete strangers in conversation to convince them to go to a yeshivah. To initiate conversation one must, after all, be able to speak fluently and confidently — or so one could have been forgiven for assuming.

Fortunately, we do have an eyewitness to Reb Meir's earliest venture in kiruv: his younger friend from Ner Israel, Chaim Kass. After coming to Israel in 1968 to learn in ITRI Yeshiva, Chaim renewed his friendship with Reb Meir, and he was a frequent Shabbos guest at the Schusters' home. One Shabbos, Reb Meir told him that he was feeling low. He no longer had the *zitzfleish* (ability to sit for long) that Torah learning required. Though he had been learning with great diligence since he was first introduced to Gemara around the time of his bar mitzvah, he wondered now whether he was cut out for full-time learning.

Reb Meir's comment was totally out of character: He simply did not speak about himself or his feelings. In addition, Chaim had never seen him down before. One of his chief memories of Reb Meir from Ner Israel was the beauty of his full-throated laugh.

Chaim Kass responded by telling Reb Meir a well-known story about the Netziv (Rabbi Naftali Tzvi Yehudah Berlin).

Someone who had known the Netziv in his younger years once approached him in his later years, when he was universally recognized as one of the greatest *talmidei chachamim* of his generation, and asked him how he had become so great. The man recalled that as a youngster, Naftali Tzvi had been a wild child from whom nothing much was expected.

The Netziv responded with a story from well before his bar mitzvah. He described how, one day, after another run-in with the local *cheder* rebbi, he overheard his parents talking about him when they did not

The Netziv

know he was within earshot. His father told his mother, "There is nothing to be done with him. We have no choice but to apprentice him to learn some trade that will enable him to earn a livelihood."

The boy jumped out of bed and implored his parents for one more chance and promised them that henceforth he would apply himself. And he did. Not too many years later, he was married to the daughter of Rabbi Itzele of Volozhin, the son of Rabbi Chaim of Volozhin, and eventually he became the Rosh Yeshivah of Volozhin, the "mother" of all Lithuanian yeshivos.

After relating the story, the Netziv made a larger point. Had his parents carried out their original plan, in all likelihood he would have come to his final judgment, *Yom Hadin*, with a relatively clean slate, as someone who lived from the fruit of his labor and always dealt honestly with customers. But, said the Netziv, besides the *Yom Hadin*, there is a *Yom Tochachah* [the Vilna Gaon makes a point of the twofold judgment] at which point a person is judged by what he could have been. And that judgment would have been a harsh one. All the *sefarim* he was destined to write — *Haamek Davar, Haamek She'eilos, Meishiv Davar, Meromei Sadeh,* and the commentary of *Mechilta* — would have come forward to testify against him.

Had Chaim told the story during a *mussar shmuess* in a yeshivah, his intention would likely have been to spur his friend to a renewed commitment to full-time learning so as not to be judged for all he could have achieved as a *talmid chacham* and did not. That is how the story, and a similar story told about Rabbi Yitzchak Elchonon Spector of Kovno, are usually cited in yeshivos.

But that does not seem to have been Chaim's intent. Nor is it how Reb Meir understood the story. Reb Meir appears to have understood the meaning of the story to be that each Jew comes into the world with a special mission and will be judged on the *Yom Tochachah* in accord with how he fulfilled the mission.

A week later, Reb Meir called Chaim. "I've been thinking a lot about the story of the Netziv," he began. "I feel I'm chosen for something, and that learning alone will not be enough." They agreed to meet at the Kotel to talk more and to daven.

The first thing they saw when they reached the Kotel was a backpacker close to the Wall crying. Chaim approached him and initiated a conversation:

"It really affects you, doesn't it?" he began. "That we got it [the Kotel] back after so many centuries." (This incident took place in 1971, four years after Israeli forces had recaptured the Old City of Jerusalem in the Six Day War.)

Rabbi Chaim Kass

Then he made his pitch. "Something touched you very deeply here. But one time is not enough."

At that point, Reb Meir invited the backpacker for Shabbos, and the young man accepted.

For the next three or four days, the two went back to the Kotel every day. And each day a similar scenario played itself out, where they were able to interest a young man who had obviously had a highly emotional experience at the Kotel in learning more about his Judaism.

In each case, it was Chaim who initiated the conversation and Reb Meir who held back. But before they could go again, Chaim called up Reb Meir and told him that he would not be able to go for the next couple of days, as he had to take care of arrangements for his upcoming *chasunah*.

"Do you think you can do this yourself?" he asked his older friend. Chaim had his doubts on that score: "Meir was so *eidel* (soft-spoken) and often tongue-tied."

But Meir was eager to try. He went back that day and every day after that for the next fourteen years, until it became necessary, with the opening of Heritage House, to start traveling abroad periodically for fundraising.[1]

BY THE TIME REB MEIR BEGAN VISITING THE KOTEL REGULARLY IN search of young Jews to introduce to their heritage, three yeshivos for

**The Time Was Right**  baalei teshuvah, adult male beginners to Torah learning, already existed: Diaspora Yeshiva, located on Har Tzion, and headed by Rabbi Mordechai Goldstein,

---

1. Heritage House opened in late 1984. Until then, Rabbi Schuster had not once left Israel since his arrival shortly after marriage in 1968.

Rabbi Noach Weinberg teaching in the early Aish HaTorah

a product of Chofetz Chaim Yeshiva in Queens; Dvar Yerushalayim, headed by Rabbi Baruch Horowitz, formerly of Manchester, England; and Shappell's, under the leadership of Rabbi Chaim Brovender, a *musmach* of Rabbi Yitzchok Elchanan Theological Seminary (RIETS).

But of most relevance to Reb Meir's life's mission was Shema Yisrael, founded by Rabbi Noach Weinberg in 1972, in partnership with Rabbi Mendel Weinbach, Rabbi Nota Schiller, and Rabbi Yaakov Rosenberg. Almost from the inception of Shema Yisrael, Rabbi Schuster became the exclusive recruiter.

In addition, he taught a *shiur* to the newcomers on the daily life of a committed Jew. It was he who would take them to buy tefillin from his friend Chaim Kass for $175 and into Meah Shearim to purchase their first tzitzis, which he taught them how to knot.

The early Shema Yisrael was on fire, remembers Rabbi Avraham Rockmill, head of the intermediate program at Ohr Somayach today and a member of the *hanhalah*. Young men, with the world at their feet by the standards of American society, were making huge life decisions: Beryl Gershenfeld turned down his place in Yale Law School; Ze'ev Kraines dropped out of the Telluride Scholars Program at Cornell; Yaakov Fried had dropped out of Harvard and rarely left the *beis medrash*, while sleeping on a bed without a mattress and eating a minimal diet. Avraham Rockmill himself had been accepted to Georgetown Medical School, but elected to stay at Shema Israel. Each of them would in time leave their mark on the Torah world.

The ferment and intensity was unlike anything that anyone had ever experienced before. Rabbi Noach Weinberg's introductory 48 Ways class was a raucous affair, filled with argument and confrontation. "Finally, I've found what I've been looking for my whole life," Avraham Rockmill thought to himself when he began to learn Gemara. One student — albeit only one — fled in the middle of the night, leaving a note behind. He knew that he would never be able to face his friends if he tried to leave during the day.

The sheer excitement of those days can still bring tears to the eyes of those who lived through them. And Reb Meir kept the cauldron boiling by bringing in new students on a daily basis.

Like most idylls, this one too came to an end. By June 1974, the original partners of Shema Yisrael had agreed to split. Their views on the proper methodology and order of learning for adult beginners and visions for the place of baalei teshuvah in the larger Torah society were too divergent to be encompassed by one institution. Shema Yisrael broke off into two institutions: Ohr Somayach, under the leadership of Rabbis Weinbach, Schiller, and Rosenberg,[2] and Aish HaTorah, headed by Rabbi Noach Weinberg. Aish HaTorah opened in Elul of 1974 with six unmarried students and a small kollel.

The break-up of Shema Yisrael was traumatic for the students. Most were close to the leading figures on both sides, and felt like children in a divorce custody suit, forced to choose between parents.

The division also placed Rabbi Schuster in a quandary. He had been on the payroll of Shema Yisrael, and subsequently of Ohr Somayach for a period of time. But he also realized that the very different vision of the two yeshivos meant that one might be a better fit for one potential student and the other a better fit for a second student. The dispute was not a matter of personalities but of philosophy. The two yeshivos were not carbon copies of each other.

Reb Meir would not compromise his independence in making the decision where to bring a potential student. His sole criterion was the best interest of the young man in question.

There were also practical factors that weighed in each decision. The greatest concentration of young Jews who might be interested in exploring their Judaism was at the Kotel, and Aish HaTorah was located in the Old City. If those whom Rabbi Schuster approached at the Kotel

---

2. Rabbi Rosenberg subsequently left Ohr Somayach to found Machon Shlomo.

appeared ambivalent about following him to hear a class in a yeshivah — as most were — it was simply easier to convince them to come to Aish HaTorah, which was just up a couple of flights of steps from the Kotel, than to get into a car or on a bus to go to Ohr Somayach.

Moreover, Reb Noach's 48 Ways class, given daily, was both accessible to those with no prior Torah background and a practical demonstration of the relevance of Torah for most life issues. And Reb Noach was always available to talk to newcomers at length.

There was also an ethical consideration. Although the principals of Ohr Somayach agreed that the interest of the potential student must be paramount, was it proper for Ohr Somayach to pay the salary of someone who was devoting most of his efforts to another yeshivah? At some point, Rabbi Mendel Weinbach told Rabbi Schuster that Ohr Somayach could not justify paying him a salary if he was also going to be bringing potential students to a different institution. Rabbi Schuster understood the dilemma, but he could not commit himself to recruiting exclusively for Ohr Somayach. His first obligation lay with the *neshamos* (souls) of those he met and attempted to interest in learning more about Torah. Rabbi Weinbach understood, but both rabbis agreed that Rabbi Schuster could not continue to be employed by Ohr Somayach.

By that time, the Schuster family had grown to three children, and Reb Meir had no other source of income. Still, he was no more willing to work exclusively for Aish HaTorah than for Ohr Somayach.

A few months earlier, Mrs. Schuster's brother Moshe and his wife had come to Israel for a visit, on the proceeds of an Irish Sweepstakes ticket sold to them by their Irish neighbor. Reb Meir asked his brother-in-law to join him for a walk and engaged him in probably the longest conversation they ever had. Reb Meir told him that he had begun to enjoy some success in his kiruv work and was contemplating leaving kollel to expand his activities.

He offered his brother-in-law a Yissachar-Zevulun relationship, in which in return for Moshe's

Rabbi Mendel Weinbach

financial support the two would share in the Divine reward of the mitzvah. Moshe Garfinkel pointed out that he was barely feeding his own family, and certainly in no position to support two.

But apart from that, Reb Meir's plan shocked his brother-in-law. The whole concept of kiruv was then virtually unknown in America. "Who does that besides Chabad?" he challenged Reb Meir. He added that in leaving kollel for kiruv work, Reb Meir was violating the halachic principle of *ein safek motzi miy'dei vadai*. The mitzvah of learning in kollel is a certainty (*vadai*), said Reb Meir's brother-in-law. But whether he would be successful in his kiruv efforts was very much in doubt (*safek*). In that situation, better to remain with the sure reward of full-time learning.[3]

In the end it was Rabbi Weinbach himself who worked out a solution whereby Rabbi Schuster could retain his independence and still earn enough to cover his spartan family budget. Reb Mendel suggested that perhaps American P'eylim would be willing to support Reb Meir's work. The Israeli P'eylim began in the early 1950s as a group of yeshivah activists determined to rescue the children of immigrants from Arab lands from the efforts of the Jewish Agency, and in many cases the Israeli government, to separate them from their religious parents and deny them any religious education. American P'eylim came into existence originally as an effort by American yeshivah students to serve as a fundraising adjunct for the Israeli organization.

The American P'eylim office was run by Rabbi Avraham Hirsch in New York and Rabbi Aaron Bleich in Yerushalayim. Rabbi Bleich had been a *chavrusa* of Reb Meir's in Ner Israel. And for that reason, he could not imagine Reb Meir succeeding in what he was doing: "He was the shyest person on earth," Rabbi Bleich remembered.

Fortunately, Rabbi Weinbach, who had been active in P'eylim in New York as a *bachur*, was able to assure the heads of P'eylim that Reb Meir had been phenomenally successful over the preceding two years. Not only did American P'eylim support Rav Schuster's work for over a decade, but eventually it took on the support of a full office staff under the direction of Mrs. Bracha Zaret, who began working as Rabbi Schuster's assistant at the Kotel.

Prior to moving to Los Angeles with her husband to establish a campus kiruv organization, Mrs. Zaret built a team of twelve people

---

3. Ten years later, at the bar mitzvah of the Schusters' son Duvie, Reb Moshe Garfinkel told the story and added, "This proves that no one should consult me for career advice."

combing the Central Bus Station, kibbutzim, and university campuses for young Jews interested in enriching their Jewish knowledge. Every Leil Shabbos, the Zarets would host a "Fabulous Friday Night" for fifty students in their Ezras Torah home.

Bracha Zaret is a human dynamo, almost the exact opposite of Rabbi Schuster in personality. But as Rabbi Bleich came to realize, they shared one crucial quality in common: They both were "pure *l'sheim Shamayim*, and such people are successful."

## Chapter Five

# A MAN AND THE MOMENT WELL MET

THE IMPACT OF EACH PERSON'S LIFE IS INTIMATELY BOUND UP with the times in which he lives. With few historical figures is that interrelationship so clear as with Rabbi Meir Schuster.

He came to the peak of his powers precisely when a unique window of opportunity opened to reach tens of thousands of Jews with little knowledge of Torah or traditional Jewish life — perhaps for the last time.

Without Rabbi Meir Schuster operating from his lonely perch at the Kotel, the potential of that historical moment, extending from the Six Day War in 1967 to the outbreak of the Second Intifada in late 2000, might have gone largely untapped. At the same time, it is impossible to conceive of Rabbi Schuster having had the impact he did on the collective Jewish world but for the tens of thousands of Jewish backpackers wending their way to the Kotel during the three-decade period of his greatest activity.

A concatenation of many factors created the magical era of *kiruv* between 1967 and the start of the new millennium. The Six Day War in June 1967 is frequently described as the beginning of the teshuvah movement in Israel. In the period leading up to the War, prominent

Arab spokesmen proclaimed daily their intent to drive the Jews of Israel into the sea. The tens of thousands of graves dug in public parks in Tel Aviv to receive the expected war casualties attest to the seriousness with which those threats were received.

The pre-War pessimism and dark foreboding quickly gave way to euphoria as Israel recaptured the Old City of Jerusalem, including the Temple Mount, the West Bank, Gaza, the Sinai, and the Golan Heights in a matter of days. The scope and rapidity of the Israeli victory seemed to many an open miracle on a Biblical scale.

In the Diaspora, Israel's victory against enemies on three fronts spurred Jewish pride among many who had given scant previous thought to their Judaism or Israel. Jewish tourism spiked dramatically, as Jews from abroad came to view the Kotel and tour the newly recaptured territories.

In the United States, the first cohort of baby-boomers came of age in an era of extended economic prosperity. They assumed as a matter of course that they would be better off than their parents. Nor did they graduate from college saddled with tens of thousands of dollars in accumulated debt, as do many graduates today.

As a consequence, they thought little of taking a year or two in their early 20s to travel the globe in search of new experiences and greater self-understanding. Nor were they deterred from spending time in the yeshivos or seminaries for newcomers to traditional Judaism that opened their doors in the early '70s by the fear that they would be left behind in the quest for economic security.

Alex Haley's *Roots*, tracing the history of his family from Africa through slavery, was published in 1976, and triggered an interest in family history among many American ethnic groups, including Jews, most of whom had arrived on American shores only one or two generations earlier. *The First Jewish Catalogue*, published in 1973, which came out of the Boston *chavurah* movement, transformed many aspects of traditional Jewish life into something vaguely countercultural and hip.

Finally, most young Jews in the early '70s, when Rabbi Schuster began his work, still came from families with two Jewish parents. By today's standards — 71% of non-Orthodox Jews currently intermarry — the intermarriage rate of their parents' generation was comparatively low. If the backpackers had an ethnic identity it was Jewish, not some admixture of various nationalities and religions. The parents of young Jews arriving at the Kotel were still likely to be involved in some form of

Jewish charity or volunteer work. The Holocaust and birth of the State of Israel, not to mention the Six Day War, were relatively recent events.

In short, the Jewish story still resonated with many young Jews, and was one to which they could attach themselves. Israel was still looked upon, even in liberal circles, as a doughty underdog, which had triumphed against overwhelming odds. Jewish students were not subjected on campus to nonstop descriptions of Israel as an apartheid, genocidal regime born in sin, though after the Arab oil boycott of 1973, Israel began to be subjected to harsher criticism. Being Jewish was not yet something of which to be ashamed for many young Jews.

The late '60s counterculture pursuit of authenticity was another key factor opening up many young Jews circumnavigating the globe to new experiences and cultures. The affluence of the post-World War II years provided the seekers of the late '60s and '70s with the luxury of questioning the assumptions of traditional institutions, in the search for a more authentic alternative to their bourgeois values.

The generational distrust of anyone over 30 and of traditional institutions had many negative consequences, including undermining marriage. Drugs took their toll on many young lives. Young Jews were disproportionately drawn to various cults and exotic quasi-religions. But openness to new experiences and cultures — and traditional Torah society was certainly a foreign culture as far as the backpackers were concerned — had an upside as well.

When Rabbi Schuster tapped a young Jew on the back and asked him whether he (or she) was interested in "talking to a wise man," "hearing a class on Jewish philosophy," or "experiencing a traditional Jewish meal," many answered, "Why not?" After all, they had already meditated with Buddhist monks in Thailand and learned mantras in Nepal. What reason could they offer for being less receptive to their own religion?

## Tom and Rafi's Journeys

TOM STEINBERG AND RAFI SIMON[1] PROVIDE TWO EXAMPLES OF THE ways in which the pursuit of new experiences made youthful Jews vulnerable to Rabbi Schuster's offer to learn more about their own religion. Tom graduated from Yale in 1978 and Rafi from Harvard in 1982. Prior to embarking on their journeys of self-discovery both had already been accepted at leading professional schools.

---

1. Not his real name.

**Tom and Rafi's Journeys**
nerable to Rabbi Schuster's offer to learn more about their own religion. Tom graduated from Yale in 1978 and Rafi from Harvard in 1982. Prior to embarking on their journeys of self-discovery both had already been accepted at leading professional schools.

---

Refugee encampment near the Laos border a few days before it was overrun
and destroyed by the Pathet Lao

But both felt that they needed a year off. As Tom pictured his future, he was going to "work really, really hard, until I retire. Then I'm going to die. What a boring life." Rafi was thinking about getting married and starting a family, and felt it important to develop his own value system before doing so. That would be easier to do at a remove from the Western culture in which he had grown up. The distance, he decided, would make it easier to determine what was essential to him.

Tom's journey did not get off to a good start, He had intended traveling with a cousin, who was himself starting medical school the next year. But in Borneo, his cousin became violently ill and had to return to the United States. Tom was now on his own, 8,000 miles from home, and (in those pre-cellphone days) almost totally incommunicado.

Within the first few months of his journey, he went through five life-threatening experiences. On a river boat from Bangkok, the captain suddenly took out a machete and gestured to the money pouch around his neck. Tom considered himself fortunate to get away with a payment of only $15, even after he was unceremoniously dumped in a jungle alongside the river.

Subsequently, near the border between Thailand and Laos, Tom came across a group of refugees fleeing the Pathet Lao guerillas in neighboring Laos and spent some time in their encampment. Two days after his departure, the encampment was overrun by the Pathet Lao and many of the refugees were killed.

Tom with a group of Buddhist monks

Much of the explorative aspect of the journey had to do with exposure to Far Eastern religion. In Bangkok, Tom was approached by a stranger who took him to a Buddhist monastery; in Nepal, another stranger offered to teach him to chant a mantra for $5, an offer he refused because it was above his $3 per day budget. And in xenophobic Burma (today Myanmar), he watched villagers slaughtering pigs to their harvest gods from inside a bamboo hut.

The cumulative effect of all these encounters was "to open [him] up to look at new cultures without being judgmental." That willing suspension of disbelief would leave him without a defense when he first met Rabbi Schuster, who asked him if he wanted to learn about his own heritage.

Rafi's journey also included a heavy dose of Eastern religion. At a Bangkok guest house, he noticed a Westerner meditating and was fascinated. When he asked the fellow where he too could learn to meditate, the latter directed him to a local monastery where he was advised that there were too many distractions in Bangkok. But there was a Buddhist monastery in the forests of eastern Thailand built for monks from Western countries.

Armed with only two phrases in Thai — the name of the train station nearest the monastery and of the monastery itself — Rafi set off on the overnight train journey, passing an endless stream of water buffaloes

Ubiquitous water buffaloes seen by Rafi on his train trip

working in rice paddies on the way. When he alighted from the train, no one seemed to recognize the name of the monastery, until a stranger on a motorcycle motioned for him to hop aboard. The motorcyclist proceeded to take him on an off-road journey through the forests, until they at last came upon the monastery through a break in the trees.

Rafi explained to the one in charge of admissions that he wished to learn to meditate. He was told that he could either agree to shave his shoulder-length locks or be limited to a three-day stay in the monastery. He took the three-day option. The regimen consisted of long hours of meditation from well before sunrise. Once a day, the monks would walk in procession through the neighboring villages with bowls in hand, which the villagers were supposed to fill with rice or other foodstuffs.

Near the end of his second day, Rafi was informed that the head monk wanted to see him privately. The chief monk asked him where he was from, what he was doing, and where he was going. Rafi responded that he was from New York, and was traveling around the world, with Israel as his ultimate destination. The chief monk told him, "I'm also a Jew from New York, who was traveling around the world with Israel as the goal."

Rafi mentioned that he was interested in trying both a kibbutz and a yeshivah. At the mention of a yeshivah, the head monk perked up, and he mentioned that one of the other monks had a magazine with the address and information about a yeshivah. The other monk was summoned, and he gave Rafi the famous 1977 *Rolling Stone* article "Next Year in Jerusalem," by Ellen Willis, about her attempt to rescue her younger brother Mike Willis from Aish HaTorah. (See p. 113.) An outspoken feminist, she wrote with great sensitivity and honesty of her many discussions with her brother and Rabbi Noach and Rebbetzin Denah Weinberg over the course of a number of months spent in Jerusalem.

At the end of his conversation with the head monk, Rafi asked him how was it that the other monk had the *Rolling Stone* piece. He responded, "His mother sent it to him, and wrote that if he had to be a religious fanatic, couldn't he at least be a fanatic in his own religion?"

By the time he finished the article. Rafi knew he wanted to spend some time in Aish HaTorah and meet Reb Noach. The realization that he had learned of Aish HaTorah in a Buddhist monastery in a remote area of Thailand caused him to think to himself, "Wow, not only is there a G-d, but what a sense of humor."

Years later Rafi read a short tale by Rebbe Nachman of Breslov, "The Treasure," that captured precisely what had happened to him. Rebbe Nachman relates how a chassid had a dream of a great treasure buried under a bridge in Vienna. He travels to Vienna and locates the bridge, but is too afraid to start digging in broad daylight. A policeman comes along and asks why he is loitering under that bridge, and the chassid can think of no alternative to telling him the truth, in the hope that the policeman will agree to split the treasure with him.

Instead the policeman laughs at the Jew and tells him that he also had a dream of a treasure buried under the cellar of a poor hovel. From his description, the chassid recognizes his own town and house. He rushes home and finds the treasure just where the policeman had seen it in his dream. "I had the treasure all along. But in order to find it I had to travel to Vienna."

Similarly, Rafi felt, the treasure he had been looking for was close by, but he had to go to Thailand to discover it.

TOM HAD BEEN ENTICED BY OFFERS OF SPIRITUAL TREASURES IN Bangkok, Katmandu, and Bombay. So when Rabbi Schuster approached

**The End of the Journey in Jerusalem** him on his first-ever visit to the Kotel and asked him whether he would be interested in a class in Jewish philosophy, his natural response was, "Why not?" The class was Tom Meyer's *Pirkei Avos* class at Aish HaTorah. One line still remains fresh over forty years later:

"Nations have always tried to conquer one another; one nation — the Jews — have devoted themselves to conquering wisdom."

Every day that week, Tom returned to the *Pirkei Avos* class. And every day, he met Rabbi Schuster at the Kotel. On Thursday, Rabbi Schuster invited him for Shabbos, something with which Tom had no familiarity.

That Friday night, Tom joined Rabbi Schuster with another forty young people whom the latter was placing for Shabbos dinner. They walked for what seemed like an hour and a half, dropping off members of the group at their hosts along the way, until only Tom and one other young man were left. Rabbi Schuster informed them that they would be joining his family. Everything about the meal was new for Tom, and at the end of the meal, Rabbi Schuster rolled out two cots from behind the sofa for the two visitors to sleep on.

The next morning Rabbi Schuster announced that they were going to shul. He handed Tom a copy of Rabbi Mayer Schiller's *The Road Back* to keep him occupied during the davening. Tom did not pay much attention until it came time for the *duchaning* (priestly blessings), which struck him as spooky, with the Kohanim swiveling from side to side, hooded by their *tallesim*.

The next week Rabbi Schuster took Tom to the home of Rabbi Noach Weinberg. Tom was astounded to find Reb Noach busy changing a baby's diaper. Tom shared with Reb Noach some of his near-death experiences. Getting in touch with the spiritual aspect of life, Reb Noach suggested, is itself a form of near-death experience. He used the metaphor of being on a conveyor belt headed toward a buzz saw. As one comes closer and closer to death, much of what formerly seemed important fades into insignificance.

During his second week at Aish HaTorah, Tom noticed something fascinating. He had been a two-pack-a-day smoker since the age of 14. But now the desire to smoke disappeared completely. And it would never return. As he describes it, "Though I would not have yet described myself as consciously believing in Hashem at that point, the connection to my *neshamah* had been opened, and with it the desire to live and relate to Hashem. Smoking is literally killing oneself."

That second week Tom continued to run into Rabbi Schuster almost every single day, and was eventually convinced to move from the Arab hostel in which he was staying to the Aish dorm. To his surprise, his dorm, known as the Arc, housed at that moment seven out of eight present or former Yale students like himself. That second Shabbos, Rabbi Schuster once again claimed Tom as his Shabbos guest.

By the end of the summer, Tom knew he wanted to stay at Aish HaTorah, but felt he could not petition Stanford Business School for a deferment without speaking with his parents, with whom he had had very scant contact over the course of the year. He flew to Lake Tahoe, Nevada, to meet with them, and over the course of a very intense week, his parents eventually prevailed upon him to start business school by "calling in all their chips," in his father's words.[2]

But the brief time at Aish had its effect. After his first year in business school, Tom returned to Aish for part of the summer, and the following summer, between business school and assuming a position at Goldman Sachs, he studied in Ohr Somayach for a month.

In some ways, Rabbi Schuster's involvement with Rafi was even more crucial because Rafi did not have a smooth entry into the world of baalei teshuvah yeshivos. He arrived in Jerusalem already determined to go to Aish HaTorah. When he asked a relative by marriage how to find Aish HaTorah, he was told, "Just go stand at the Kotel. Someone will come up to you. That person is Meir Schuster, and he will take you to Aish HaTorah."

And that's just what happened. Rafi stood in front of the Kotel until Rabbi Schuster approached and asked him, "Are you Jewish?" Rafi replied, "Are you Rabbi Schuster?" But despite the anticipation with which Rafi came to Aish HaTorah, after two days, he felt it was not a fit for him.

He walked out of Aish, and over the next few days decided to head to Kibbutz Degania. But before he could do so, he once again bumped into Reb Meir. To his query, "How's it going?" Rafi responded sharply, "I'm finished," and indicated he was going to a kibbutz.

Unfazed, Reb Meir did what he always did in such situations. He did not argue with Rafi or attempt to dissuade him. He simply offered him an alternative plan: Instead of going to Kibbutz Degania, why not take a week in Tzefat, where Reb Meir would arrange housing.

---

2. Tom's father, "Goody" Steinberg, was a prize-winning architect and one of the founders of the local Reform temple, Beit Am. He was very eager to win the commission to do the temple, and, as he writes in his autobiography, found himself praying for the first time in his life. He pleaded that if he won the commission, he would not even complain if one of his sons became a rabbi. When Tom called from Israel to say he was learning in a yeshivah and wanted to stay, his father's first reaction was, "G-d is seeking payment of my promise."

Rafi accepted the offer. But the next time they met in Jerusalem, he told Reb Meir that he was still intent on going to a kibbutz. Again, Reb Meir started bargaining. Just come with me to Ohr Somayach for an hour, he urged.

And Rafi did — this time meeting with Rabbi Nota Schiller, who offered him a room in the yeshivah, with no strings attached, to come and go as he pleased. Reb Nota suggested, however, that as a philosophically inclined person, he would enjoy the class of Rabbi Dr. Dovid Gottlieb, the former chairman of the Johns Hopkins philosophy department. Rafi went to the class, but still decided to go to Degania, as he had planned.

The very first night on the kibbutz, however, his roommate had sweats and chills all night. At an emergency meeting of the entire kibbutz the next day, Rafi learned that the kibbutz would be entering into quarantine because of a case of hepatitis — his roommate. Before the imposition of the quarantine, Rafi left the kibbutz, and had himself checked into a hospital in Haifa. He then headed back to Jerusalem, where, naturally, he once again met Rabbi Schuster.

This time everything went smoothly, and Rafi spent a very interesting week at Ohr Somayach before entering law school. For his second year of law school, he devised an independent study program comparing secular and religious law, which basically allowed him to spend the entire year learning at Ohr Somayach.

But his need for Rabbi Schuster was not over. At one point, Rafi approached Rav Schuster and told him that he was corresponding with a very bright woman he had met in New York, and she felt that his current path was, as she put in bluntly, "nuts." "Is there anything we can do?" he asked Rabbi Schuster.

Reb Meir did not hesitate. He told Rafi that he would offer her a ticket and housing at Neve Yerushalayim if she would agree to attend at least one class a day for a month. Her response to Rafi: "Let me get this straight: You want me to spend a month at some kind of Jewish nunnery."

But come she did, and she even stayed after Rafi had returned to law school. They were married before his final semester in law school.

The relationship with Rabbi Schuster for both Tom and Rafi lasted until the end of his life. Both went on to great success in their respective fields, Tom (now more frequently known as Yaakov) as an investment advisor and Rafi as an attorney.

And their talents were put
to use on behalf of the Jewish
community. Tom was cofounder
of the Meor campus outreach
initiative, which presently has
branches on twenty campuses
and a budget approaching ten
million dollars annually. Rafi
has frequently put his legal talents to use *pro bono* on behalf of
the Torah community.

Rabbi Schuster and Yaakov Steinberg

While both Tom and Rafi did
take off at certain points in their
careers to immerse themselves in learning for between sixteen and
twenty-four months, neither was able to spend as much time in full-
time learning as they would have wanted. Both, however, have numerous sons and sons-in-law learning and teaching Torah.

Until the Steinbergs made aliyah, Rabbi Schuster would stay with
them in Passaic for four days every year, and they would make a parlor
meeting for Heritage House. That parlor meeting always featured a
well-known speaker, since Rabbi Schuster would never speak for more
than ninety seconds at the most. Rafi and his wife also hosted Rabbi
Schuster frequently when he was in Monsey and made contacts for him
in the community.

Both Tom and Rafi first encountered Rabbi Schuster in the midst of
circumnavigating the globe, just as they reached the center of the world,
the Kotel adjacent to the Temple Mount. In their minds, his crucial role
in the dramatic life changes they made could never be fully repaid. But
in Rabbi Schuster's mind it had been repaid many times over in the
vibrant Torah families each built.

*Chapter Six*

# THE WILLIE MAYS
# OF THE KOTEL

I
N EVERY SPORT, IT IS COMMONPLACE TO SPEAK OF THE HOME court or the home field advantage. The Kotel and the large plaza in front of it was Rabbi Schuster's turf, his home, the area where he operated with the greatest confidence and the scene of many, if not most, of his greatest successes.

The emotional impact of viewing the Kotel for the first time, even on Jews who considered themselves completely estranged from the Jewish religion, provided Rabbi Schuster with a "home court advantage" whenever he operated within its precincts.

For decades, he patrolled the area around the Kotel like a sentry, his eyes expertly surveying the scene in front of him (or below, when he stood on the steps leading down to the Kotel Plaza) in search of young Jews who might be open to what he was offering.

June 1975, Jeff H. stood in front of the Kotel on what was supposed to be his last Friday night in Israel. He was due to enter Harvard Business School in three months, and he was on his first trip to Israel. His plans for the summer included trips to Greece, Switzerland, and Paris to meet three different women with whom he had become friendly in Boston, two of them non-Jewish.

Raised in a Reform home, Jeff was not an atheist, just agnostic about G-d's existence. But he had always been interested in Judaism, and had read a great deal of modern Jewish thought — mostly Martin Buber and Abraham Joshua Heschel — in college.

In his jeans and cardboard kippah (yarmulke), he asked G-d to let him know in what direction his life should go. As he backed up from the Kotel, something inside him told him, "You are going in the wrong direction." A few seconds later, he felt a tap on the shoulder. When he turned around, surprised but not angry, he did so to find Rabbi Meir Schuster. The latter asked him his name, if he was Jewish, and if he was interested in learning about G-d.

Jeff found it uncanny that within seconds of his entreaty to G-d for direction, here was someone asking whether he wanted to learn more about G-d, not to mention that he had had such a powerful feeling that he was headed in the wrong direction.

Rabbi Schuster did nothing more than hand Jeff off to Kalman Packouz, one of the six original students at Aish HaTorah, which had at that point been open for less than a year.[1] Kalman invited him to dinner at Aish HaTorah and for a walk around Jerusalem the next day. He also took him to visit Rabbi Moshe Lazarus, one of the rabbis at the fledgling yeshivah. Over the course of two days, Kalman persuaded Jeff to postpone his planned trip to Greece and to stay at Aish HaTorah for a few

---

1. Kalman — by that time Rabbi Kalman — would go on to establish, together with Rabbi Chaim (Mike) Willis, the first Aish branch, in St. Louis. He passed away in November 2019.

weeks. Those few weeks eventually extended until the end of summer vacation. At one point, Jeff even considered deferring Harvard Business School for a year and remaining at Aish.

But over the summer, the Bostoner Rebbe, Rabbi Levi Yitzchok Horowitz, had visited Aish HaTorah, and told Jeff that there was at least an option of continuing on his new path in Boston. Rabbi Noach Weinberg did not push him hard either way, likely out of recognition of how complicated it would be to delay his studies at Harvard. The most powerful thing he said, in Jeff's view, was: "Whatever path you choose, G-d loves you."

A measure of overt *siyata d'Shmaya* often attached to those connected to Rabbi Schuster. And so it was with Jeff. On his next to last evening in Jerusalem, he went to visit Rabbi Lazarus at his home in Rechavia. As he waited at the bus stop to take him back to the Old City, waiting at the same bus stop was a beautiful and modestly attired young woman. He said to himself, "I would like to marry someone as beautiful as this woman, who also shares the powerful Jewish feelings that I've developed over the summer."

The next day, he was at a library where he occasionally went for a respite from his studies at Aish HaTorah, and she was there again. Before he could figure out how to initiate a conversation, she had departed. He was so disappointed that he mentioned the encounter to both his parents and his roommate at the yeshivah.

After returning to Boston, Jeff went to Friday night services at a local *chavurah*, and to his surprise and delight, in equal measure, there she was again. This time he made sure that he did not miss the opportunity to speak to her. He found out that his presence had not gone unnoticed by Minna (for that was her name) in Jerusalem, and that she, like him, had a premonition that they would marry. The next summer, Jeff was back in Jerusalem, working as a management consultant at the Jewish Agency by day and learning at Aish HaTorah at night. He and Minna were engaged that summer, and married not long after that.

Reflecting on the amazing series of events that took place from the time that Rabbi Schuster first tapped him on the shoulder, Jeff took to referring to Reb Meir as "the Willie Mays of the Kotel." Just as the great centerfielder Willie Mays knew how to play each ball as it caromed off the centerfield wall, so Reb Meir knew how to play young Jews as they backed away from the Kotel.

Just how many young men Reb Meir caught bouncing off the Kotel can be gleaned from the following story. In April 1989, the editor[2] of the then-new English *Yated Ne'eman* commissioned an article on Rabbi Schuster from Rabbi Menachem Nissel. The article concludes with the following story:

> A young Jewish traveler is standing at the Kotel. As he stares at the ancient stones and contemplates the meaning of Jewish history, he feels, for the first time in his life, a need to address his Creator: "Dear G-d. I don't know if You exist, but if you do, please give me a sign." At that moment, he feels a tap on his shoulder. It is Rabbi Meir Schuster about to offer him a "real Shabbos meal."

The week that article appeared, the editor was driving with a friend in the back seat and handed him the article on Rabbi Schuster. Sometime later, at a stoplight, he looked into the rearview mirror and saw that his friend was crying. He asked his friend what was wrong, and the latter responded that he was the subject of the last story in the article. The editor, however, knew that the author of the piece and his friend did not know each other. In other words, that story happened at least twice, and likely dozens of times.

Something about the Kotel opened emotional floodgates and stirred feelings of being connected to Jewish history. At the very least, going to the Kotel constituted engaging in a positive Jewish experience. As a consequence, those standing in front of the Kotel were naturally more open to what Reb Meir was offering.

Baruch Mytelka took off from the second semester of his college year abroad at Oxford University to travel. After arriving in Jerusalem, he followed the advice of the travel bible in 1978, "Let's Go Europe," to go down to the Kotel on Friday night to "watch the Hassidim dance and sing in accepting the Sabbath."

His first glimpse of the Kotel affected him in a way for which he was totally unprepared, and he began crying, without knowing why. As he stood there observing the rush of different types of people all around, and feeling somewhat of an outsider, Reb Meir approached with an offer for a Shabbos meal. Had he already eaten, he would likely have demurred, but he was hungry and more than happy to accept that offer. While he was standing around waiting to be brought to his Shabbos host, a group of Aish students came over and told him about Reb Noach Weinberg's 48 Ways class on Sunday morning.

---

2. I was that editor.

The Shabbos meal was an eye-opener, and on Sunday morning, Baruch decided to try out the 48 Ways class. But Reb Noach was out of the country, and Baruch was not impressed with his student replacement. He left the class planning to travel south to Eilat. But as he exited the class, he came face

my name is yisrael Shraga
I go to yeshivas Chelen D' Mansey,
I love doing mitsvas, my zeidy is
m.r Baruch mytelka, I appreciat
that your late husband R' meir Shuster a"h
tapped my zeidy On his Shoulder and
helped him become frum.
I am sorry I couln't come tonight, but
I feel פיך הכרת for what you did.

Handwritten note from Baruch Mytelka's grandson to Mrs. Schuster after Rabbi Schuster's *petirah*

to face with Reb Meir, who would not hear of his going to Eilat.

Reb Meir insisted that Baruch try out Ohr Somayach. Baruch resisted and told Reb Meir that he had to go check out of the Arab hostel where he was staying just inside the Jaffa Gate. Unfazed, Reb Meir hailed a taxi to the youth hostel, from which the two headed to Ohr Somayach, where Baruch ended up staying for several years.

Not always was the vulnerability of those at the Kotel the result of some inexplicable emotional connection to the place. Rabbi Noach Weinberg enjoyed telling the story of a young man from an American Jewish family who was openly disdainful of religion. But while in Israel, he went to the Kotel, as one would visit any tourist attraction. He was irritated to be told by a guard to don a cardboard yarmulke, and even more so at the sight of Jews davening fervently around him. To express his scorn, he threw down his cardboard yarmulke. At just that moment, one of those pigeons that proliferate at the Kotel flew overhead and, in Reb Noach's words, "did its business on the young man's head."

As he was looking up to see what hit him, Reb Meir sidled over to ask him whether he'd like to visit a yeshivah. At that point, said Reb Noach with a big smile, the young man was "too afraid to say no."

NOR WERE ALL THOSE JEWS WHO BOUNCED OF THE WALL MEN. TOBY Levy grew up in a Yiddishist/socialist culture. Her parents did not even make a Seder. While still in high school she came to Israel with a Yiddishist camp. From her first visit to Jerusalem, the city aroused special feelings in her. Watching the stores closing on Rechov Yaffo before Shabbos and seeing an old man already dressed for Shabbos, she thought to herself, "I know about Eskimos [from her mother's anthropologist friends], but I have no idea what this old man is thinking."

**Women Too**

Toby returned to volunteer on a HaShomer HaTzair kibbutz after the 1973 (Yom Kippur) War. After six months, she was headed to pick grapes in France and go ice-fishing in Iceland, when she decided to visit Jerusalem once again. At the Kotel, she felt the same frustration as two years earlier: "All these people know what to say, and I don't know." Those feelings led to an impromptu prayer:

> I don't know if You are out there, but if You are, let me know about it, because I invested a lot of time and energy to come to Israel. I came to find out what it is to be Jewish and where does this fit with socialism and feminism.
>
> If You want me to know anything about Judaism, let me know now.

As she reached the edge of the women's section, Rabbi Schuster was there to answer her prayer, and asked her if she was interested in going to a family for Shabbos. She said she was, but she was scheduled to fly on Saturday morning.

He looked at his watch and told her, "You know what, I can change the ticket. Do you want to learn about Judaism?

"But I'm not religious," Toby said.

"You don't have to be religious."

"But I don't speak Hebrew."

Rabbi Schuster assured her that was no prerequisite either. It was the days before he had a car, and Rabbi Schuster gave her the address of Neve Yerushalayim.

Toby went back to her kibbutz, gathered her belongings, and came back to Jerusalem for Shabbos, getting into an argument with her Shabbos host. Sunday morning, she was in Neve.

WHILE THE KOTEL WAS THE MOST LIKELY SPOT FOR ONE OF REB MEIR'S taps on the shoulder to coincide with a just-expressed request for Heavenly guidance, such cases were not limited to the Kotel. Risa C. was walking down the steps of the Arab shuk of the Old City one day in the early '80s when the thought popped into her mind that she should really invest some time in learning more about her Judaism one day. At that moment, Rabbi Schuster approached her out of nowhere and asked whether she would like to go to a seminary.

**Not Just the Kotel**

Though she was struck by the way her thought was apparently answered almost instantaneously, she hesitated to follow Rabbi

Schuster. Seeing her hesitation, Rabbi Schuster suggested that she come to speak to his friends Michael and Marcia Kaufman,[3] who lived nearby. She took him up on that offer, and the meeting with the eminently respectable and normal Kaufmans, in their elegant Old City apartment, put her at ease. From the Kaufmans, she went with Rabbi Schuster to Neve. Today, Risa is a Chabad shaliach, together with her husband, on the East Coast of the United States.

Chaim Harris came to Israel shortly after completing his tour of duty in the Naval Reserves. In the navy, he was engaged in intelligence gathering while stationed in the Aleutian Islands off the coast of Alaska. He was the only Jew among about 4,000 sailors, marines, and coast guard members stationed together with him.

After completing his service, Chaim came to Israel hoping to find Zionism and socialism combined on a kibbutz. Instead he spent much of his time fielding questions from young kibbutz members about how they could obtain green cards to work in the United States. Disillusioned, he left the kibbutz for a long weekend and came to Jerusalem to look for a yeshivah. After four hours of searching on his first Sunday morning, he gave up, and decided to go to the Central Bus Station and purchase a ticket for Ein Gedi.

At the bus station, he uttered a prayer: "G-d, I've just spent four hours walking around Your Holy City seeking to connect. I probably don't deserve it, and maybe I'm too late. But please give me a little help." He then purchased his ticket for Ein Gedi, and as he turned from the ticket counter, there was Rabbi Schuster. Reb Meir asked him whether he was Jewish, his name, and what he was doing. Chaim's answer that he was looking for a yeshivah must have left Reb Meir dumbfounded. It was decidedly not a common response to his queries.

Just then, however, the bus to Ein Gedi arrived, and Chaim ran to find his seat. As he settled in, he looked out the window to see Reb Meir looking up sadly at the bus. Chaim thought to himself, "What a dummy I am. I asked G-d for some help, and it arrived immediately. Then I didn't take it."

But he need not have worried. Reb Meir had gotten the name of the kibbutz where he was staying, and the next week, Chaim received a postcard inviting him to spend Shabbos in Jerusalem. This time he did

---

3. During the period that the Kaufmans lived in the Old City, he used the name Kaniel, an occasional nom de plume, and many people from that period remember his wife and him as the Kaniels. For simplicity's sake, we use the name Kaufman throughout the book.

Chaim Harris in an iconic recruiting
poster for Ohr Somayach

not pass up the opportunity. And the following Friday night, he was standing in the Gerrer *shtiebel* in Geulah wearing newly cleaned jeans, hiking boots, and a khaki shirt. Soon he was surrounded by a dozen or so young chassidishe *yingelach* staring intently at him. He realized that he must have looked as foreign to them as they did to him.

Eventually, Chaim returned to Cleveland, his hometown. One night, he was watching the nightly news with his family, and Walter Cronkite had a segment on prospects for peace between Israel and her Arab neighbors. "What will bring peace?" Cronkite intoned, as the camera panned the Kotel Plaza.

Suddenly, Chaim's eye caught sight of Rabbi Meir Schuster, followed by two long-haired young men leaving the Kotel Plaza. He jumped from the living room sofa and yelled out, "That's what is going to bring peace."

Not long after that, he was back in Israel and learning at Ohr Somayach. He has lived and raised a large family in Israel over the last forty-five years.

Nor is that the only example of Rabbi Schuster's ability to summon young Jews back to Israel via the TV screen. Rabbi Avraham Edelstein, the long-time director of Heritage House, related in his eulogy of Rabbi Schuster the story of two young South Africans who stayed for a while at Heritage House. They attended an occasional class at nearby Aish HaTorah during their stay, but showed no more than a lukewarm interest.

Eventually, they decided to continue their travels and left. Then one day a few months later, one of the young men was back in Jerusalem and learning full time at Aish HaTorah. Rabbi Edelstein ran into him and asked him what had happened.

He recounted that they had been in Egypt and had turned on the TV in their hotel room. The story was about Jerusalem, and included live footage from the Kotel. The two young men caught sight of Rabbi Schuster, and he appeared to be summoning them.

Their next stop was Turkey. They turned on the TV in their hotel room, and once again, there was footage from the Kotel and Reb Meir appeared. So they fled further from Jerusalem to Madrid. "I was waiting in the Madrid bus station," the young man told Rabbi Edelstein, "for a bus to another city, and I had a few hours on my hand to think. I started to reflect on everything that had happened. In any event, I never got on the bus. I went to the airport instead, purchased a ticket for Israel, and went straight to Aish HaTorah."

## He Was Always There

"HE WAS THERE EVERY TIME I NEEDED HIM" IS ONE OF MOST FREQUENTly heard remarks about Rabbi Schuster. Nachum (Jon) Braverman decided to take some time off midway through his studies at Yale as a philosophy major, and came to Israel to study socialism in action on a kibbutz.

On a visit to Jerusalem, in the middle of Jon's time on a kibbutz, Rabbi Schuster succeeded in getting him to a 48 Ways class with Reb Noach and to a family for a Friday night meal. He got into an argument with Reb Noach in the class, and ended up walking out on his Shabbos hosts in the middle of the meal — something the host said had never happened before.

Despite that unpromising beginning, when his time on the kibbutz was over, Nachum returned to Jerusalem to visit a friend before returning to Yale. The friend left the next day, and Nachum still had a few days left on his ticket. He stood in a phone booth contemplating what to do next, and when he turned around, Rabbi Schuster was standing right there.

This time, Nachum did not resist when Rabbi Schuster took him to Aish HaTorah. After a few days, he came to the realization that there really is *chochmah* (wisdom) in the Torah, and for him to leave at that point would be an admission that he was not really interested in wisdom.

Nachum never returned to Yale, and within two years of arriving at Aish, he was running the Beginner's Gemara program. After marrying his wife Emuna, Nachum became the first teacher in the fledgling Aish-LA branch. Together with his friend Irwin Katsoff, who convinced

Nachum to join him in Los Angeles, they built one of Aish's largest and most successful branches.

Feivel (Phil) Wartel decided to visit Israel while traveling in Europe after college. He stayed in a hostel in Tel Aviv his first week, and even spent his first Shabbos at the home of a young Israeli he met. The next week he came to Jerusalem, and like every tourist in the '70s, Phil went to the Kotel, though he had only the faintest idea of what it was or why its capture in 1967 had ignited such excitement among Jews around the world.

As he stood at the Kotel, he wondered why it was such a magnet for Jews. At that moment, he felt a tap on the shoulder. Rabbi Schuster set him up for Shabbos with Mordechai Schiller, the younger brother of Rabbi Nota Schiller, the rosh yeshivah of Ohr Somayach. Everything was new, especially the davening at the Amshinover *shtiebel* in Bayit Vegan. At one point, Eliezer Shapiro, then an Ohr Somayach *bachur*, but one who had attended yeshivos all his life, leaned over to him and said, "Pretty weird, heh?"

Still, as he began packing his belongings after Shabbos, Phil had to admit that the experience had been a positive one. But when he headed out of his room to thank his hosts, he had a surprise. "Where are you going? It's Shavuos, and no buses are running," he was informed.

After the *Chag*, and with the resumption of bus service, he headed for the Kotel, as if drawn. He once again met Rabbi Schuster, who persuaded him to come to one class at Ohr Somayach. That class on *Shir HaShirim*, given by Rabbi Nachman Bulman, Feivel remembers until today as a "verbal tapestry as if painted on the wall."

Though he had told Rabbi Schuster in advance of the class that there was no more than a one in a million chance that he would stay for more than one class, he ended up remaining at Ohr Somayach for five weeks, with one week off in the middle to try to clarify the dramatic changes in his life.

His sister was getting married soon in the United States, and Phil still hoped to squeeze in a bit more travel in Europe before the wedding. On his last day in Israel, he once again went to the Kotel, and once again, he met Rabbi Schuster. This time Rabbi Schuster urged him to come speak with Rabbi Noach Weinberg at Aish HaTorah. Reb Noach began the conversation by asking him whether he viewed himself as primarily a spiritual or material person. Phil answered, "Spiritual."

Reb Noach then asked him whether he would forgo Europe for

$20,000, and Phil said that he would. Reb Noach then delivered the *coup de grace*: "You told me that you are more spiritual than materialistic. Yet for $20,000, you would forgo your trip to Europe. I'm offering wisdom for life; shouldn't you be willing to do the same for that?"

Phil knew he had been bested. This time, however, Reb Meir was not there when he left Reb Noach's office, and he left as planned for Athens. Already on the plane, however, he felt that he had made a serious mistake. That Shabbos in Athens, he went to shul, and tried to keep Shabbos as much as he knew. No one invited him for a meal after the Leil Shabbos davening, but he was saved from starvation the next day by two older Israeli women he met who had lots of extra kosher food.

For the rest of his trip in Europe, he kept Shabbos in every city. And when he went back to the States, he enrolled in a new Ohr Somayach branch that had been established in Yonkers. Rabbi Ezriel Tauber, one of the great pioneers of kiruv, came to speak in Yonkers shortly thereafter. He and Phil developed a close relationship, and eventually Rabbi Tauber provided him with a ticket to return to Israel. On the plane back, Feivel thought to himself, "I'm not fighting anymore."

He has been learning full time ever since he landed back in Israel over forty years ago, and today leads a *chaburah* (study group) in the Mirrer Yeshiva.

Dr. Pesach Ostroy dates his religious journey to a visit to the Altneu Shul in Prague in 1975, in the midst of an around-the-world trip after finishing his residency. An old man approached him on Shabbos and showed him his arm bearing his tattooed concentration camp number. "The Germans destroyed our lives," the man told Pesach. "But you know, I still believe in G-d."

Three years later, in July, 1978, the U.S. Army offered Dr. Ostroy a position in their Center for Infectious Diseases in Frederick, Maryland. Pesach was then in Israel visiting family members, and for reasons not entirely clear to him, he told the U.S. Army that he had to be in Jerusalem for Rosh Hashanah and Yom Kippur, even though he had only the sketchiest knowledge of the two Holy Days

Sometime thereafter, on a bus from Tel Aviv to Jerusalem, he saw a sign at the entrance to Jerusalem that read: "If you have not been to a yeshivah, you haven't seen Eretz Yisrael." He naturally went first to the Kotel, and, as he was heading down from the Temple Mount, he ran into Rabbi Schuster, who asked him about his background, as a prelude to inquiring, "Would you like to meet a rabbi who is also a philosopher?"

Pesach went to meet Reb Noach, and when he came out of the meeting Rabbi Schuster was waiting for him. Pesach told him that he was planning a trip to Eilat and the Sinai. Reb Meir protested that Rosh Hashanah was fast approaching. To which Pesach replied nonchalantly that it would be no problem, as he could spend Rosh Hashanah in Eilat.

At that point, Rabbi Schuster lifted Dr. Ostroy, who is well over six feet tall and a former college swimmer in a top-ranked program, up by his collar and informed him, "You are not spending Rosh Hashanah in Eilat. You'll be right here." Pesach agreed, and went with Rabbi Schuster to Aish.

He had been reading a great deal about the Holocaust ever since that meeting with the elderly survivor in Prague, and was deeply affected by the reading of the curses of *Ki Savo* before Rosh Hashanah. When Dr. Ostroy left after two weeks to assume his new position, he was fully observant. He returned to Aish the next year for a much longer period. In subsequent years, whenever he met Rabbi Schuster in Jerusalem, he would tell him, "I must have been your easiest case."

Sometimes, the crucial meetings with Rabbi Schuster took place months, or even years, apart. Not many stories were as simple as: He walked into yeshivah and lived happily ever after.

Yirmi C. had already been accepted to a graduate program in energy planning at the University of Pennsylvania when he came to Israel in 1977 after having been inspired by a feature on Israel that appeared in *The New York Times Magazine*. He met Rabbi Schuster at that time, and Rabbi Schuster brought him to meet Rabbi Noach Weinberg. Based on that meeting, Yirmi promised that he would return, and remarkably he did, three years later, after completing his graduate program and before starting work. His first stop was at Aish HaTorah for a month, and then he joined a group of Aish students who went to learn in Beth-El in the West Bank.

Yirmi was still not fully mitzvah observant, and he decided to spend one Shabbos at the Dead Sea. On the way to catch a bus to the Dead Sea, he ran into Rabbi Schuster. When Reb Meir heard of Yirmi's Shabbos plan, he offered him a chance to spend a Shabbos instead with Rabbi Aryeh Carmell. He knew that Yirmi had a background in science, and Rabbi Carmell was one of the founders of the Association of Jewish Scientists and had written extensively on scientific topics.[4]

---

4. Rabbi Carmell was also the moving force behind the publication of the works of his boyhood teacher Rabbi Eliyahu Eliezer Dessler in Hebrew, as the five-volume *Michtav MeEliyahu*, and in English translation as *Strive for Truth*.

Nearly a decade after that fateful Erev Shabbos meeting at the bus station, Yirmi, who had in the interim learned many years in yeshivah, began working for Rabbi Schuster as a night counselor at Heritage House. And in time, he set up Heritage House's first fledgling efforts to follow up with visitors after they returned to their native countries. That follow-up would prove crucial in the long term to the impact of Heritage House.

*Chapter Seven*

# MAN ON A MISSION

I SRU CHAG PESACH 5735 (1975), THE SCHUSTERS' FIRSTBORN CHILD, Shatzi, asked her mother for money so that she could run to the nearby *makolet* to buy gum. She never returned home. As she crossed the street to the *makolet,* she was hit by a truck and killed instantly.

Neighbors came to tell Mrs. Schuster of the tragedy and stayed with her. But Rabbi Schuster was well into his day by then. Neighbors of the Schusters from the adjacent building went to Shaare Zedek to identify the body. When Reb Meir was finally located and came into the hospital, his initial reaction was to feel sorry for his neighbors whose faces were contorted in pain, until he realized that it was for his own daughter they were crying.

Shatzi's parents were both devastated. But they reacted in different ways. Mrs. Schuster was able to find solace then, and over the years, by speaking about her daughter. Reb Meir, as was always the case, kept his feelings to himself, and was rarely able to speak about his daughter once *shivah* was over. Chaim Kass walked together with Rabbi Schuster at the *levayah* (funeral). He observed tears forming in Reb Meir's eyes and falling silently, but Reb Meir did not say a word.

Reb Meir was, in his wife's words, *"meshugah"* over his daughter. He had chosen the name Yocheved simply because he loved the name;

90 □ A TAP ON THE SHOULDER

Faige Dina was after Mrs. Schuster's maternal grandmother. (In any event, Yochevel Faige Dina was universally known as Shatzi.)

By all accounts, Shatzi was an unusually *bacheint* (charming) child. Dr. Shimon Friedman and his wife Chani spent six weeks one summer in Ezras Torah, in the building in which the Schusters lived. Mrs. Friedman remembers Shatzi as "mesmerizing everyone." On the way back from Israel, after a packed vacation, she and her husband spoke primarily about Shatzi. "There was something unique about her," she explains.

Though only 6 at the time of her death, the entire street (of six buildings, in 1975) knew her by name. *Bachurim* who ate at the Schusters' regularly remember her as a very bright child, who had inherited her mother's outgoing nature.[1]

Reverberations from her tragic death were felt far beyond the confines of Rechov Even Ha'ezel, particularly in the as-yet small English-speaking Torah community. Someone who was in the home of Rabbi Noach Weinberg when the news of the accident arrived remembers how Rebbetzin Denah Weinberg burst out crying.

For the *bachurim* in Ohr Somayach, Shatzi's death was traumatic. Even forty-five years later, when they speak about Rabbi Schuster, they inevitably mention Shatzi's passing. In those days, many of the *bachurim* davened on Leil Shabbos at the Kotel, and there was a large group who served as "runners" for Rabbi Schuster to bring those gathered at the Kotel to their Shabbos hosts. Rabbi Schuster had been the one to bring most of the Ohr Somayach students to the yeshivah, and even those who did not know him personally saw him daily in the yeshivah as he escorted new recruits and checked on those whom he had brought to the yeshivah.

The *shivah* for Shatzi was notable for two reasons. The first was the large number of those who arrived to pay their condolences in jeans and ponytails. For many of the Ohr Somayach and Aish HaTorah talmidim who came, it was their first *shivah* house. The more advanced students in Ohr Somayach organized an ongoing rotation to say *Tehillim* in the *shivah* house for the entire week.[2]

The second notable aspect of the *shivah* house was the fact that Rabbi Yosef Shalom Elyashiv, then the foremost living *posek* in Israel, made a *shivah* call. True, Rabbi Schuster brought all his *she'eilos* to Rabbi

---

1. Rabbi Avraham Rockmill.
2. Ibid.

Elyashiv, who was still relatively accessible compared to later years. But the great sage almost never left his Meah Shearim neighborhood.

The story of how Rabbi Elyashiv came to make a *shivah* call perhaps more than any other brings out the overwhelming sense of mission with which Rabbi Schuster lived.

Not long after the beginning of *shivah*, Rabbi Schuster grew agitated at the thought of all the Jews who would visit the Kotel during the week of *shivah*, and for whom there would be nobody who could offer an introduction to Torah. That raised in his mind a halachic *she'eilah* as to whether he should return to the Kotel.

And what was that *she'eilah*? Is not the saving of a Jewish *neshamah* from a state of ignorance of Torah and mitzvos a matter of *pikuach nefesh*? And if it is *pikuach nefesh*, did the imperative of saving Jewish *neshamos* not mandate, or at least permit, Reb Meir to be at the Kotel to meet them, for who could know whether there would ever be another opportunity to bring them to a yeshivah or arrange a Shabbos meal for them?

The *she'eilah* was brought to Rabbi Elyashiv by Rabbi Yehudah Samet. Rabbi Elyashiv did not dismiss the *she'eilah* or refute Reb Meir's conclusion that his going to the Kotel was no different than any other form of *pikuach nefesh* about which the general rule is that *pikuach nefesh* supersedes all other mitzvos, with three exceptions — murder, idol worship, and forbidden relations.

Quite the opposite. Rabbi Elyashiv responded that Reb Meir was right and that the work that he did at the Kotel was indeed life-saving. But because few people, if any, possess the same clarity of vision (which is why there has been only one Meir Schuster), his failure to sit *shivah* in the normal fashion would not be understood. That failure might even undermine his work.

As if to prove Rabbi Elyashiv's point, among those who did not understand Reb Meir's desire to return to the Kotel was Mrs. Schuster. Even though she knew better than anyone her husband's intense love for his oldest daughter, it pained her that he could seemingly not give a week to mourning her loss.

In any event, Rabbi Elyashiv instructed him to continue sitting *shivah*.[3] But Rabbi Elyashiv did not leave matters there. The next day the *gadol hador* made a rare *shivah* call outside of Meah Shearim. If there

---

3. From a *hesped* given in Baltimore by Aaron Gibber on the *sheloshim* of Rabbi Schuster.

was a person in the world capable of putting aside his personal grief upon the loss of a child and think only about the *neshamos* of *Klal Yisrael*, Rabbi Elyashiv wanted to personally convey his *tanchumim* (condolences.)

On Leil Shabbos during *shivah*, when there is no mourning in public, Rabbi Schuster was back at the Kotel setting up Jews for Shabbos meals with religious families.

In the face of tragedy, he did the one thing that he knew how to do well: Keep going, move forward, and maintain a laser focus on his mission in life — connecting Jews with their Father in Heaven.

Many years after his personal tragedy, one of the Ohr Somayach *bachurim* to whom the entire Schuster family became very close lost a son to cancer. When the bereaved father was sitting *shivah* in America, Rabbi Schuster called and offered him the only advice he could because it was the one that got him through the darkest moments of his life: "Be strong, be strong."

RABBI SCHUSTER'S DEDICATION TO HIS MISSION WAS ESTABLISHED not only in the extraordinary moments, such as in the aftermath of

## Neither Rain Nor Sleet Nor Snow

the death of his beloved daughter, but also in his consistency over decades. Reuven Eliyahu,[4] one of those closest to Rabbi Schuster over the years, once asked him where he derived the ability to go to the Kotel day after day, week after week, year after year, in the freezing rain and the scorching sun, without any slackening of effort. He replied, "Excellence, excellence, excellence, that's what the Ribbono shel Olam demands from us."

Reuven recalls being at the Schusters' for a Leil Shabbos on a nasty, rainy winter night. Rabbi Schuster had sprained his ankle on the way home from the Kotel, and spent the entire meal with his leg elevated on a chair to relieve the pain. But he had committed to meeting some of those whom he brought to hosts after the meal, and was still determined to go out again in order to do so. Mrs. Schuster insisted, "Meir, you are not going out in this rain with a sprained ankle." But she knew her words would prove futile. And so they did.

The same question that Reuven Eliyahu had asked Rabbi Schuster — How do you do this 24/7? How can you always be "on duty"? — was

---

4. Not his full name.

Rabbi Schuster at the Kotel on a snowy day
escorting two new "finds"

once posed to him by one of the counselors at the women's hostel, as they were driving back from bringing a young woman to Neve Yerushalayim. He was quiet for a moment, and then taking his hands off the wheel for added emphasis, he replied, "There's a house on fire. When a house is on fire, you don't decide you are 'off duty.'"[5]

Rabbi Schuster was never off duty. He and Reb Asher Israel once went to daven Maariv at the Bobov minyan on 15th Avenue in Boro Park around 11:00 p.m. As they were entering the building, Reb Asher saw a tall, secular-appearing fellow looking at a poster. He half-jokingly remarked to Reb Meir, "Looks like a client for you." When he came out after davening, he found Reb Meir speaking earnestly to the young man. And when Rabbi Schuster finished davening, he told Reb Asher that he had convinced his "client" to come to Israel to learn.

Just as the U.S. Postal Service used to boast that neither rain nor sleet nor snow could keep the mailman away, so it was that nothing could keep Rabbi Schuster away from his perch by the Kotel. Rebbetzin Lori (Zelcer) Palatnik gives an example. Lori's younger sister had become religious on a trip to Israel, and upon returning to Canada, invited her older sister to a Shabbos meal at which a number of rabbis were present. The Shabbos did not do that much for Lori, but she did decide to come to Israel shortly thereafter.

She was staying in an Arab hostel near the Damascus Gate when she suddenly felt unsafe — not without reason — and decided to leave. She passed through the Damascus Gate and by the Kotel. It was a bitter,

---

5. Estrin, Dena, *It Happened at Heritage House*, p. 27. The book includes numerous stories of those whose lives were changed by their time at Heritage House.

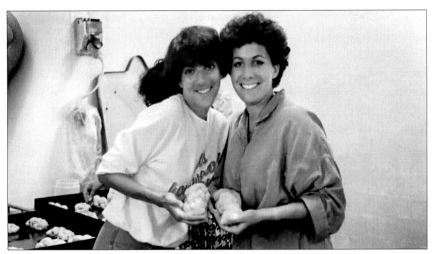

Lori (Zelcer) Palatnik (left) a year after she met Rabbi Schuster on a rainy night at the Kotel.

rainy night, and there was not a soul at the Kotel. Just then Lori spied a solitary figure, standing sentry even on that cold, rainy night, waiting for any Jew who might happen by for any reason.

Lori was that Jew. She recognized Rabbi Schuster as one of those rabbis who had been at the Shabbos meal hosted by her sister, and approached him. He convinced her to go with him to Neve Yerushalayim, where she could at least be assured safety and a warm bed. She stayed for a few weeks, and returned to Israel the following summer on the first-ever Aish HaTorah-sponsored Jerusalem Fellowships program. At the end of the summer, Lori and five other women from the program decided to attend Rebbetzin Denah Weinberg's EYAHT Seminary.

Rabbi Schuster's presence near the Kotel that night would have made no sense to anyone besides him. The chance of anyone passing by, much less being amenable to any kind of conversation, was slight. And even if someone chanced by, the odds were always against his or her agreeing to follow Rabbi Schuster to a yeshivah or seminary. Against those minuscule odds there was his own physical discomfort standing in the rain.

Yet, over time Lori Palatnik would have as great an impact on the Jewish world as anyone of her generation. She and her husband Rabbi Yaakov Palatnik were the founding rabbinic couple of Toronto's Village Shul, which at its inception could accurately be described as "an Orthodox shul for non-Orthodox Jews." Her weekly videos for Aish. com, *Lori Almost Live*, were extremely popular. And in 2013, she founded Jewish Women's Renaissance Project, sometimes known as Birthright for Moms, which has to date brought over 20,000 non-Orthodox women to Israel for a more than week-long trip of bonding with other Jewish women and developing a deeper commitment to their crucial role as wives and mothers in bringing Judaism into their homes.

RABBI SCHUSTER LIVED WITH A CONSTANT SENSE OF URGENCY THAT never waned. Rabbi Avraham Edelstein, probably the person who

### Living With Urgency

worked most closely with him over decades, attests that he would sooner take a longer route and drive around the block than stop at a red light. Nothing was more abhorrent to him than standing still. He viewed what he was doing as the most important work possible in the world, and so anything connected to that work took on its own urgency.

When he would come to the Heritage House office and tell the long-time administrative secretary Suzanne Lieberman that he needed something immediately, she would not even look up, while responding, "Just put it in the urgent pile." As far as anyone can remember, there was no corresponding non-urgent pile.

That same sense of urgency was expressed in the pace with which he moved. Mrs. Dahlia Fried worked at the Kotel for two years at the turn of the millennium for the governmental body charged with oversight of Holy Sites, and found herself transfixed by watching Rabbi Schuster in action. He ran after every potential young Jew, she says, like a prospector in the 1849 California Gold Rush chasing after gold.

Rabbi Hillel Goldberg captured nicely the impression Rabbi Schuster made in his constant search for Jews to interest in their heritage: "Like a darting shadow, he is often sensed rather than seen. Out of the corner of your eye, you catch sight of him moving through open-air markets, lingering at the Western Wall or striding along isolated or busy streets in Jerusalem."[6]

Reuven Eliyahu was not too many years removed from being an all-state high school basketball player, recruited by several major college basketball programs, when he first met Rabbi Schuster in Jerusalem. Yet he struggled to keep up with Rabbi Schuster the first time he was invited to come to his home for a Shabbos meal.

---

6. Goldberg, Rabbi Hillel, "The Teshuvah Solicitors," *The Jewish Observer*, May-June, 1980, p. 10.

One time, Reuven Eliyahu challenged Rabbi Schuster to a footrace through the Old City to a particular bus stop. Reuven was an athlete, twenty-five years younger, and wearing gym shoes, while Rabbi Schuster was in leather dress shoes. Still Rabbi Schuster beat him handily, leaving Reuven Eliyahu to make excuses about Rabbi Schuster's greater knowledge of the streets of the Old City. After an event for Rabbi Schuster's *sheloshim* in Baltimore, someone came up to Rabbi Moshe Garfinkel, Mrs. Schuster's brother, and told him that he was a long-distance runner, but he had had great difficulty keeping up with Reb Meir in the Old City.

The very speed with which he moved could sometimes allay fears of young women who agreed to follow him. Gavriella was in Israel on a one-semester program at Tel Aviv University when she first met Rabbi Schuster at the Kotel Plaza. After a brief conversation, he determined that Michael Kaufman, who lived in the Old City, would be ideally suited to speak to her, and offered to bring her to his apartment.

She was leery of taking him up on the offer, until it started to rain hard, and Rabbi Schuster pointed out that she would be better off sitting in the Kaufmans' beautiful apartment with a panoramic view of the Kotel than standing out in the rain. She agreed, though her concerns were not completely allayed. But when Rabbi Schuster took off at breakneck speed at least fifteen feet in front of her, with her struggling to maintain the gap, and made no effort at conversation whatsoever, she quickly realized that she had nothing to worry about.

Once Rabbi Schuster had a prospect in his sights, escape was impossible. Skip Rose had dropped out of law school to study at Aish HaTorah, and was staying at a Lutheran Youth Hostel in the interim. One morning, as he set off to open a bank account, he saw Rabbi Schuster, whom he recognized from a prior trip to Israel. Determined to open the bank account, he tried to avoid Rabbi Schuster, changing direction three times, and each time, when he looked up, Rabbi Schuster was still right in front of him. Finally, Skip had no choice but to tell him, "I know who you are and what you want, and I'm going to Aish. But first I'd like to open a bank account." Still, when Rabbi Schuster ascertained he was staying at a Christian hostel, he insisted on first picking up his belongings and taking him straight to Aish.

YAD ELIEZER IS ONE OF THE MAJOR CHESED ORGANIZATIONS IN THE world, with an annual budget approaching one hundred million dollars

## Keeping Sight of the Goal

a year. The current CEO, Dov Vizel, shares a lesson that he learned from his father Rabbi Yaakov Vizel, who together with his mother Hadassah founded the organization. One day Dov was meeting with a group of wealthy donors when a poor man came to the door of the office in which the meeting was taking place. Dov asked him to come back later, as he was in a meeting. At that point, his father took him aside and told him, "Never forget that this organization exists for that poor man. He is the important one. The donors are only important insofar as they enable us to help him."

Rabbi Schuster would never have needed such a lecture; it was intuitive with him. He often struggled to remember the names of large donors, even those who had contributed generously for years. But his memory for the young Jews with whom he interacted was uncanny. Rabbi Shlomo (Steven) Goldberg, today the principal of Ohr Eliyahu educational institutions in Los Angeles, first came to Israel as part of a college class on Fascism and the Rise of Nazi Germany.

On his first visit to the Kotel, he was overwhelmed with emotion and cried for a long time, even though he did not even know what the Kotel was or what it represented. "I felt I had come home and connected to something I had been searching for, even though I did not know I was missing it," he would remember later.

On that occasion, together with another Jewish student in his class, he met Rabbi Schuster and was set up for Shabbos with Rabbi and Mrs. Aharon Feinhandler in Meah Shearim. The house, as he describes it, "was beyond simple, and the children were beyond pure." Rabbi Feinhandler heads a yeshivah that caters exclusively to those who have spent some time in prison. His wife, Sarah, who was stricken with polio as a child, which left her permanently disabled, runs a seminary for young women from disadvantaged backgrounds.

Rabbi Feinhandler sang only *niggunim* without words during the meal so that Shlomo and his friend Bennett could join in the singing. The experience was "a deep immersion in *kedushah* (holiness)," but Shlomo was honest enough to admit that he was relieved when it was over, as it was too intense for his as yet "underdeveloped *kedushah* sensors."

But after that Shabbos, Shlomo donned a yarmulke for the rest of his

Rabbi Shlomo Goldberg with his first Shabbos host, Rabbi Aharon Feinhandler

trip, which was a source of some amusement to the passengers on the Arab buses he rode on Shabbos. At the end of that trip, Shlomo knew he would return to Israel, and that when he did, Rabbi Schuster would take care of him.

When he did return nine months later, the first time he ran into Rabbi Schuster, the latter said, "Steve from Texas," followed by the question, "Where's your friend Bennett?" In the interim, Rabbi Schuster had interacted with at least a thousand new people, and his initial contact with Shlomo/Steve was relatively brief. Yet he remembered both his name and the name of the friend he had been with when they last met. And once again he took Shlomo to the Feinhandlers for a Shabbos meal, where he was greeted like a long-lost cousin.

Michael Kaufman writes of Rabbi Schuster, with whom he worked closely for decades and with whom he had a daily *chavrusashaft*, "I've known many people who were deeply devoted to causes. But *never* before — or since — did I meet anyone as single-mindedly devoted as Reb Meir to *kiruv rechokim*. It was his life."

Mr. Kaufman did not have to wait long to learn this about Reb Meir. In 1981, he and his wife purchased a beautiful apartment in the Old City with an unimpeded view of the Kotel. Shortly after moving in, he went down to the Kotel to offer Reb Meir, about whom he had heard a great deal, his assistance and the use of his apartment in any way that would be helpful.

Michael Kaufman

Reb Meir did not reply. Before Mr. Kaufman had even finished speaking, he was gone. "He had pivoted on one foot and spun away like a top, speeding off in the direction of the Kotel, without so much as a 'goodbye' or an 'excuse me.'" Mr. Kaufman stood there in astonishment, mouth agape, as Reb Meir made a beeline for a young man with a backpack, whom he engaged in animated conversation. A short time later, he was escorting the young man up the steps from the Kotel. He passed by Mr. Kaufman, slowing just long enough to say matter-of-factly that they were going to Aish HaTorah, without further explanation or apology.

Rabbi Yirmiyahu Abramov once expended considerable energy arranging a meeting for Reb Meir with a chareidi representative on the Jerusalem City Council, whose assistance was needed to secure a vital zoning waiver for Heritage House. The councilman even came to the Old City specifically to view the premises and to speak with Reb Meir. But while they were talking, Reb Meir spied a young couple and was off, never to return, leaving Rabbi Abramov on his own to smooth over things with the councilman.

Many people found it disconcerting to carry on a conversation with Reb Meir, especially in the vicinity of the Kotel, because his eyes were continually darting about in search of new targets. Sam Friedland was speaking to him one day near the Kotel when a young traveler walked by. Reb Meir hooked his arm through the young man's, and asked whether he was Jewish. The traveler struggled to free himself from Reb Meir's grasp and told him, "You don't have to be Jewish to go to the Kotel." But Reb Meir neither desisted nor returned to the young man exclusive possession of his arm, until the traveler admitted that he was Jewish. Next Reb Meir inquired where he was staying, and was told that the young man was staying at a Christian hostel in the Armenian Quarter of the Old City — a response that always put Reb Meir into paroxysms of anguish. In the end, Reb Meir was unable to persuade the traveler to change his accommodations.

Yet when Sam found Reb Meir the next morning preparing himself a cup of coffee in the kitchen of the apartment the Friedlands had rented, as he did every morning after davening in the *haneitz* minyan, he was in an exceptionally elevated mood.

He started to tell Sam about the young man he had met the previous day, seemingly oblivious to the fact that Sam had been there as the young man attempted to disentangle himself from Reb Meir.

That morning on his way to the Kotel for the early minyan, Reb Meir had been a few minutes early and decided to recite a few chapters of *Tehillim* by the Armenian Quarter

Rabbi Schuster with a huge smile

hostel. Just then the young man came out and saw Reb Meir reading out of a book.

In retelling the story, Rabbi Schuster then let out a huge belly laugh and his face broke into a wide grin: "He thought I had been there all night praying."

Reb Meir had already brought the young man for breakfast and an early-morning class at Aish HaTorah.

## Chapter Eight
# SUPER SALESMAN

"RABBI SCHUSTER POSSESSED ALL THE KEY INGREDIENTS OF a successful salesman," comments Reuven Eliyahu, the Rabbi Schuster "catch" who remained closest to the Schuster family over the years and who is himself a veteran salesman. "He believed in his product, he overcame any fear of rejection, he was persistent, and he followed up." Notably, Reuven Eliyahu does not list verbal fluency or social graces among the qualities of a super salesperson. And Rabbi Schuster could be his proof case.

About his belief in the product he was offering — Torah and mitzvos — there could be no doubt, and that was instantly ascertained by all those with whom he interacted, even if they had no knowledge of what he was selling. Belief in his "product" rendered him immune to fear of rejection. Even open mockery rolled off his back and did not deter him.

Seth Mandell and his friend Micas were in Jerusalem for what Seth assumed would be the last time ever. Seth had spent most of the previous two years in Israel, including six months working at a community center in Afula, and he had decided that he did not want to live in Israel forever. Now he and Micas were embarked on a farewell tour of Israel before Seth went back to the United States to join the Peace Corps and serve in Senegal.

After visiting the Kotel on a dark and chilly night, Seth and Micas realized that they had no idea where their car might be. At the first parking lot they checked, they brushed against a tall, silhouetted figure, with his trench coat draped over his shoulders.

Seth recognized Rabbi Schuster from earlier trips to Jerusalem, and for some inexplicable reason taunted him, "You can't get me."

Puzzled, Reb Meir asked him what he meant. Seth told him, "Well I've met you several times over the past couple of years, and each time you asked me if I wanted to go to a class or a Shabbos meal,

Seth Mandell around the time he first met Rabbi Schuster.

and each time I said I didn't have time. So I just wanted you to know that you can't catch me anymore."

"Why not?" said Reb Meir, smiling.

"Because tonight I'm going back to Tel Aviv, then I'm going to the beach, and then I'm flying back to America. Then I've been accepted for the Peace Corps in Africa. So you can't get me anymore."

Reb Meir most likely understood that taunt as the plea of a Jewish *neshamah* that he should redouble his efforts. And that is what he did.

"How would you like to meet a rabbi?" he asked. Seth replied that they had to find their car because they had someone to meet in Tel Aviv.

"How can you not be interested in learning something about your own religion?" Reb Meir said, trying a new tack.

Seth did not have a ready answer to that question. "Be open to everything" had been his motto over his two years of travel. "If the purpose of my travels was really to learn as much as I can, how could I not be open to learning something about my own religion?" he thought to himself. He tried to divert Reb Meir's query by asking how old the rabbi mentioned was, and when told that he was 50, Seth asserted that he could not possibly have anything to learn from a boring, old rabbi.

Undeterred, Reb Meir told them that he just had to run one quick errand and then he would help them find their car. And that's what he did. During the entire time that they walked through every parking lot in the Old City, including the Arab Quarter, he did not speak, other than to say that his name was Meir.

Eventually the car was found outside the Old City, and in gratitude to Reb Meir for his efforts, the two young men agreed to meet Rabbi Nachman Bulman. Most of their conversation centered on Yom Kippur at their kibbutz. They told Rabbi Bulman that no one had fasted, and they had driven to Gaza to drink tea, and then amused themselves by driving back going the wrong way on the deserted highway.

During this account, Rabbi Bulman clutched the table hard, obviously furious. But the only thing he said to the two young men was, "It's not your fault, boys; it's not your fault."

By the time they left Rabbi Bulman's, it was already 11:00 p.m., and Rabbi Schuster pointed out that it was late and offered to find them a room for the night. Seth still wanted to return to Tel Aviv, but only Micas was insured to drive the car, and he was tired. Reb Meir took them to the Ohr Somayach dorms, which were still under construction, and went room to room until he found two empty beds.

It was past midnight when Micas and Seth went to bed, but Reb Meir was back early the next morning offering them a class in Jewish philosophy from Rabbi Nota Schiller. Rabbi Schiller's three-piece suit marked him as "the enemy" in Seth's mind, but he had to admit that he was brilliant. When the class was over, Reb Meir was at the door to

Rabbi Nota Schiller, Rosh Yeshivah of Ohr Somayach

take them to a private meeting with Rabbi Schiller. In the course of the meeting, Rabbi Schiller assured them that if Seth was concerned about his ticket back to the States, arrangements could be made.

Seth was still not ready to commit, and went to the beach to think things over. He was afraid of being brainwashed, but came to the conclusion that if he could be brainwashed after 27 years of living as a secular Jew, he did not have much of a brain to begin with.

When he walked back into Ohr Somayach after five days, Rabbi Bulman kissed him in greeting. Over the next several years, Seth became one of the Ohr Somayach *bachurim* closest to Reb Meir and his family.[1]

## Fearless

NOT ONLY DID RABBI SCHUSTER'S BELIEF IN HIS PRODUCT IMMUNIZE him to all manner of taunts and rejection, it made him fearless in general. He did not hesitate to interject himself between Arab merchants and their young Jewish customers in the shuk leading down to the Kotel from the Jaffa Gate or to enter into any number of Arab or Christian hostels to remove Jewish backpackers. On more than one occasion, he was attacked by Arabs as he passed through the Damascus Gate.

Reuven Eliyahu, who had been a star high school basketball player, was learning at Ohr Somayach when he met some members of Tel Aviv Maccabee, Israel's perennial championship basketball team, while playing in a pick-up game. Reuven could no longer play at a top-flight level due to an injury, but Tel Aviv Maccabee viewed him as a possible coach for the club's under-18 women's team. One day, three very tall Maccabee representatives entered the Ohr Somayach *beis medrash* in search of Reuven Eliyahu. Rabbi Schuster happened to be in the *beis medrash* at that moment, and he quickly ushered the interlopers out before they could speak to Reuven Eliyahu.

Michael Kaufman relates a fascinating story of how far he and Reb Meir were willing to go to rescue a single Jew. Lucy, who was raised as a Reform Jew, came to Israel with a church group, which she found to be warmer and more welcoming than the temple in which she grew up.

---

1. Micas also became religious and lives in Jerusalem today. After learning at Ohr Somayach and marrying, Seth became a Hillel director at Penn State University and the University of Maryland. He and his wife Sherri subsequently made aliyah. Today they direct the Koby Mandell Foundation, named after their son Koby, who together with a friend was brutally murdered by Arab terrorists in a cave near the family home in Tekoa, May 8, 2001.

At Yad Vashem, however, something snapped and she began sobbing. The tour guide, David, was puzzled by the strength of her reaction and questioned one of the group members, who replied innocently, "Lucy used to be Jewish."

David had learned at Aish HaTorah for a couple of years, and knew that there is no such category as "used to be Jewish." As he was leading the group through the Old City, he prayed that he would run into Reb Meir and could introduce him to Lucy. And as always seemed to happen in such situations, Reb Meir soon appeared on Rechov Tiferes Israel walking in the direction of the group. David made a hasty introduction to Reb Meir, and told Lucy that Reb Meir would take her to see places that were more Jewish than those the group was interested in visiting.

Instead, Reb Meir brought her to Michael Kaufman's house, and Mr. Kaufman spent two and a half hours speaking to her. At the end of their conversation, she agreed to remain in Israel and not return with her church group, which was scheduled to be picked up at their hotel on Har HaZeisim a little after 6:00 a.m. the following morning.

Around 2:30 a.m. Mr. Kaufman called Reb Meir. He realized that their plan was too susceptible to reversal, and urged Reb Meir to pick him up in his car for a nocturnal visit to Lucy's hotel. When they arrived, the door was locked, and the Arab night clerk was asleep at the front desk. They managed, however, to rouse him and to convince him to let them in. Michael got Lucy's room number from the clerk and called her room to urge her to meet them in the lobby.

Michael's premonition proved to have been correct. Lucy related how her decision to remain in Israel had not been well received: Her closest friend in the group and their pastor had soon appeared at her door and urged her to kneel with them in prayer. At the end of that session, Lucy agreed to forsake her plan of studying in Israel. But she was not at peace with her decision, and in her heart hoped that somehow she would still be able to stay. That's when Michael Kaufman and Reb Meir showed up.

By 6:00 a.m. the church group was milling around the lobby, and casting very uncongenial looks in the direction of Mr. Kaufman and Reb Meir, whom Lucy had agreed to accompany. When she went to her room to get her bags, however, she found that they had been removed and packed on the bus. Reb Meir and Mr. Kaufman quickly moved Reb Meir's car so that it blocked the only exit wide enough for the bus to pass through. They refused to budge until the luggage was unpacked and Lucy's bags restored to her. Fearful of missing their flight, the group complied. Lucy's luggage had been deliberately placed at the very back.

The middle-of-the-night rescue proved to have been well worth the risk. Lucy attended Rebbetzin Denah Weinberg's EYAHT Seminary for a number of years, and eventually married a fellow baal teshuvah.

CERTAINLY, REB MEIR WAS PERSISTENT. HE NEVER TOOK A REBUFF AS final, and his automatic response to any rejection was to keep bargain-

## Persistent

ing and making counter-offers. A "no" was never final as far as he was concerned.

Mitch Mandel was standing at the Kotel, with a cardboard kippah perched on his bright red "afro," when Rabbi Schuster first spotted him. He first asked Mitch whether he wanted to listen to a class on Judaism, to which the latter replied, "No thanks." A class on Judaism was soon amended to a meeting with a Jewish philosopher, but elicited the same response.[2]

Mandel began to pick up his pace as he headed for the nearest bus stop, but Rabbi Schuster easily kept abreast. At some point, Mitch realized that if he got on the bus, Rabbi Schuster would also get on the bus. To forestall that nightmare scenario, Mandel turned to Rabbi Schuster and told him that he might have an hour for one class after all.

Instead of a class, Reb Meir took him to meet Reb Noach Weinberg. Mitch ended up studying at Aish HaTorah for almost four years, prior to being chosen as one of the group of five couples who opened the Toronto branch of Aish HaTorah, which created an upheaval in the Toronto Jewish community. Mitch has remained in Toronto for almost forty years, and has been the Executive Director of Aish-Toronto for many years. All three of his sons are rabbis, and his three daughters are each involved in spreading Torah.

Shalom Schwartz's story provides a good example of Reb Meir's strategy of keeping the initial conversation going as long as possible. One could never know from where the winning argument might emerge, especially since it might have nothing to do with a sudden desire to learn about Torah.

---

2. Rabbi Zelig Pliskin, who has taught at Aish HaTorah almost since its inception, remembers Mitch telling him at the time that Rabbi Schuster grabbed his wrists at that point, and fairly pleaded, "Why don't you want to speak with a Jewish philosopher?" Mandel, however, does not recall that part of the exchange.

Shalom Schwartz on
Kibbutz Ein Dor

Shalom was near the end of a six-month stint on a kibbutz ulpan (Hebrew language course) when the group from the ulpan came to Jerusalem. As the group boarded the bus, after a stop at the Kotel, Shalom realized his "buddy" was not there and went back to the Kotel to fetch him. He found his friend engaged in conversation with a tall man in a black hat.

He signaled to his friend that the bus was waiting and he should break off the conversation. At that point, Reb Meir, whose back had been to Shalom, suddenly turned around, and started to throw out questions at Shalom: "Where are you from? Have you ever heard of Yeshiva Ner Israel's Toronto branch? Do you know where Fitch Avenue is?"

"Excuse me, we have a bus waiting for us; sorry, no time to talk," Shalom answered curtly.

And to the question about Fitch Avenue: "Yes, I do know where Fitch Avenue is, but that doesn't make me any more interested in what you are selling."

"I'm not selling anything," Rabbi Schuster responded. "I was just telling your friend that if he's planning to be in Jerusalem for a few days, he can stay in a yeshivah for free and listen to a class or two on Jewish philosophy."

Now, he had caught Shalom's attention. Shalom was planning to stay in Jerusalem for another few days, and had been told that morning that another group was scheduled to arrive at the hostel where he was staying and there would be no room for him.

"What's the catch?" Shalom wanted to know.

"No catch. Just a chance to learn something about Judaism."

Shalom still hesitated, but Reb Meir wrote out a note with his name and phone number and handed it to him. That evening, after every hostel he called turned out to be full, Shalom had no choice but to contemplate Reb Meir's offer. And the offer itself triggered a series of reflections in his mind. "One of the reasons I came to Israel in the first place," he thought to himself, "was to figure out this Jewish thing.

What is my relationship to the empty religious identity that has been such a confusing burden until now? Do I want to jettison the whole thing?"

Reluctantly, he called Reb Meir, and arranged to meet him at the Damascus Gate the next morning at 8:45. Fifteen minutes later, he was at Shema Yisrael, listening to Rabbi Noach Weinberg's 48 Ways class and hearing "inspiring wisdom I never knew existed in Judaism."

After three days, he went to his kibbutz to complete the ulpan, but with the intention of returning to the yeshivah for a couple of weeks once the ulpan concluded. While on the kibbutz, he received a letter from Rabbi Schuster reminding him of his commitment to return.

In the end, those two weeks at Shema Yisrael extended to three months. Shalom was one of the handful of students who followed Reb Noach from Shema Yisrael to Aish HaTorah. He remained at Aish for seven years, only leaving to head the group that started the extraordinarily successful Aish branch in his native Toronto. And after that, he directed Aish HaTorah's kiruv efforts in the former Soviet Union for nearly a decade.

By all rights, Gila Manolson should have been an even tougher nut to crack than Shalom Schwartz, for her feminism was bound to make her suspicious of Orthodox Judaism. And indeed her first visit to the Kotel got off to a bad start for that reason. She noticed that the section for the men's prayers seemed to be larger, and resolutely marched toward the Kotel on the men's side before being stopped by a guard and evicted.

Rabbi Schuster came up to her while she was still seething from that experience. When he asked her whether she was Jewish, she could barely get out, "Yes," between gritted teeth. When he inquired whether she would be interested in classes on Judaism, she told him, "I just graduated college, and I have never felt happier in my life now that I don't have to go to classes. So, no thanks."

At that response, she recalls, he looked so sad that she felt sorry for him.

That evening Gila returned to the Kotel, and this time went to the

Gila Manolson in Israel
shortly after graduating Yale

women's side. When she exited the prayer pavilion, Bracha Zaret approached her. Only years later did she learn that Rabbi Schuster had told Bracha, "I got nowhere with her; why don't you try?"

Mrs. Zaret opened the conversation by asking Gila whether she had a map of the Old City — apparently her equivalent of Rabbi Schuster's, "Do you have the time?" — before asking Gila whether she would be interested in some classes on Judaism or a Shabbos meal with an Orthodox family.

But Gila's mind was elsewhere: "What is that partition doing here?" she demanded to know. Bracha spoke to her in language she could understand. "Imagine a really cute guy was standing next to you. Wouldn't it be hard to concentrate on your prayers?" she asked. Not only did Gila have to admit that made sense, she made the next inference: Perhaps other things in Judaism make sense.

Bracha ended the conversation by handing Gila a card with her phone number and an invitation to come and stay with her. Gila, however, went to a kibbutz, as she had planned. But a month later, she was back in Jerusalem and called the number Bracha had given her, which turned out to be that of the P'eylim office. The person on the other end told her that Bracha was not there, but would return shortly, and invited her to the office. Instead of Bracha, however, it was Rabbi Schuster who arrived to take her to Neve Yerushalayim "to meet Bracha."

Bracha Zaret was not at Neve either, but someone suggested that Gila attend a class while she waited. The class on Mashiach was not one for which she was ready. But by the time it was over, Bracha had arrived. Though she was happy to bring Gila home with her, she suggested that she would be better off staying in the dorm with young women her age.

Gila did stay overnight, but then went traveling to the South for a week. At the end of the week, however, she returned to Neve and started going to classes. When she heard Rebbetzin Tzipporah Heller[3] teach or Rabbi Nathan Lopes-Cardoza speak of "being and not having," she felt as if she had discovered a "3,000-year-old counterculture, emphasizing spiritual rather than material values."

Still, Gila had a looming deadline. Her round-the-world ticket was set to expire. Rabbi Schuster told her to give him her passport and he would take care of the ticket when she wanted to return to the United

---

3. Recently Rebbetzin Heller, a widow for many years, married Rabbi Dr. Dovid Gottlieb. But because she was Rebbetzin Heller throughout Rabbi Schuster's active period, I have chosen to refer to her as she was known in that period.

States to visit her parents. By the time she did, nine months later, her guitar had already arrived in Israel, and she knew that she would live her life in Israel.

Since then Mrs. Manolson has written six books, several of them, like *The Magic Touch*, major bestsellers, and has lectured internationally on all the feminist concerns that she brought with her to the Kotel that first time she met Rabbi Schuster — modesty and the sanctity of marriage among them.

In many cases, it took multiple interactions before Reb Meir's efforts bore any fruit. That's where his persistence proved so crucial. Baruch and Sandy provide a good example. They came to Israel on their honeymoon, after backpacking through Europe. They started off on a kibbutz founded by some relatives of Baruch, but were soon dismayed to find that among the volunteers they were part of a distinct minority who were Jewish.

Their first meeting with Rabbi Schuster took place on a Friday evening at the Kotel, where they had gone to meet Sandy's sister. They enjoyed the Shabbos meal, along with forty guests or so, at the home of Michael and Marcia Kaufman, but had to leave before the meal was over because the Arab hostel at which they were staying was closing for the evening.

The next time they met Rabbi Schuster was after returning from a trip to Egypt. He saw them at the Central Bus Station negotiating with the owner of an Arab hostel, offering to work in return for free lodgings. Rabbi Schuster hurried over and offered them free accommodations with Rabbi Asa and Chana Wittow in Jerusalem's Mattersdorf neighborhood.

Baruch and Sandy very much enjoyed their stay with the Wittows, particularly the Shabbos meals and conversations with Reb Asa, who combined wit and wisdom. One could feel the "*orah v'simchah*" of Shabbos, Baruch remembered later, in the shining faces of the Wittow children.

Still, when Reb Asa pressed them to spend some time in a yeshivah and seminary, they politely declined on the grounds that they were in the midst of a once-in-a-lifetime worldwide tour. They had donned their backpacks and were out the door when Reb Asa called out that they had a phone call. (Reb Asa had called Reb Meir as soon as he realized that they were leaving.)

On the line was Rabbi Schuster, the only person who knew where they were. He had another offer: an unoccupied apartment in the Old City where they could stay indefinitely, with no strings attached. He pointed out that with the money they saved on a hotel while they toured Israel, they would have more left to spend on the rest of their journey. Eventually, out of gratitude to both the Wittows and Rabbi Schuster, Baruch and Sandy decided that the least they could do was to try several classes. With Rabbi Schuster's guidance both found learning frameworks that suited them, though many times over that period they had their backpacks packed and ready to go. But each time, Reb Meir would appear, as if to rescue them from their own impetuosity.

Had Reb Meir not continually gone the extra mile for them, Baruch would not be on the staff of one of Jerusalem's major baal teshuvah yeshivos today nor would Sandy be making a name for herself as a teacher of Torah.

ON AT LEAST ONE OCCASION, REB MEIR ENGAGED IN PRECISELY THE type of bargaining that he so frequently observed in the Arab shuk of

## He Bet His Hat

the Old City. Beth had been living at Heritage House for some time. She would occasionally attend classes at Neve Yerushalayim, and she always went for Shabbos meals. But she did not want to move into the seminary dorms.

Beth on a trip to the Sinai

One day, Rabbi Schuster said to her, "It's time to get serious and go to learn at Neve for six months."

Beth shook her head and countered, "One month."

"Five months," insisted Rabbi Schuster, pointing his finger emphatically. Beth loved Rabbi Schuster — she called him "her second Abba" — so she melted and gave in. "Okay, Abba, two months." Rabbi Schuster's eyes opened intently, as they did when he meant business. "Four months!" he demanded with a soft twinkle in his widened eyes.

Finally, they agreed on three months, but Beth added one condition: If she fulfilled her commitment Reb Meir would give her his hat. At the end of three months, she approached Reb Meir and asked him whether

Mrs. Beth Wenger holding the "hat" she earned from Rabbi Schuster

he knew what day it was. Without saying a word, he took off his gray, faded hat and handed it to her.

Later, while examining her prize, she pulled away the band of the hat a bit and was astonished to discover that the hat was actually *black* and had been bleached gray by countless hours under the sun.

Beth went back to the U.S. after those three months, committed to return to Neve for further study, but was soon swept up in her previous life. Months later, while on a fundraising trip to the States, Rabbi Schuster contacted Beth and invited her to spend Shabbos at the home of Dov Wolowitz, one of Heritage House's major donors.

Beth accepted the invitation, even though it meant a two-hour drive to Lawrence, Long Island, where the Wolowitzes lived. On Motzaei Shabbos, Rabbi Schuster and Mr. Wolowitz offered Beth a ride back to where she had parked her car, at the home of Mr. Wolowitz's son. It was raining hard.

As soon as she was seated in the car, Reb Meir asked when she was going to come back to Neve. Beth shrugged. There was a lot going on, she explained, and it just did not seem the right time.

Mr. Wolowitz drove Beth around and around various side streets, while he and Rabbi Schuster tried to convince her to return to Neve. They refused to take her to her car until she agreed to go back to study for six more months. Rabbi Schuster told her, "You're half-baked, Beth, you need to return to Neve."

She protested, "This is kidnaping! This is blackmail, Abba! Seriously! Bring me back to my car!"

Finally, Dov Wolowitz pulled the car over to the side of the road. "When you agree to go back to Neve, we will bring you to your car."

Beth sighed, "But I can't afford a ticket."

Without hesitation, Mr. Wolowitz responded, "I'll pay for your ticket."

Checkmate. Beth was stuck. But she didn't want to accept such a gift. Rabbi Schuster held up his hands, "*Nu?*"

Beth protested, "Abba!"

But Rabbi Schuster just repeated, "*Nu!*"

Though Beth agreed, "Okay, okay! I'll go," her words masked the excitement she felt. She thanked Mr. Wolowitz profusely as he returned her to her car.

IN MANY CASES, AS WE HAVE SEEN, RABBI SCHUSTER SUCCEEDED IN bringing one of those whom he met to a yeshivah or seminary only after

## He's Here; He's There; He's Everywhere

multiple interactions. Fortunately, his apparent ability to be in many places at one time or to travel at supersonic speed made those multiple encounters likely.

Chaim (Mike) Willis is a good example. Mike had been living and working in the Far East for several years, prior to arriving in Israel on his way home to New York. He first ran into Rabbi Schuster at the Kotel, and brushed him off. Later he met him at the Central Bus Station, and once again he pushed aside his offer to attend a class at a yeshivah. But the third time he ran into Rabbi Schuster that same day — this time in the Machane Yehuda shuk — he finally gave up and said yes, when Rabbi Schuster asked him, "Would you like to see a yeshivah?"

Willis's "yes" would end up being a major factor in the growth of the baal teshuvah movement. He, together with Rabbi Kalman Packouz, opened the first Aish HaTorah branch in America in 1979. But of even greater importance was the appearance in the April 21, 1977 *Rolling Stone Magazine* of a long feature by his sister Ellen Willis entitled "Next Year in Jerusalem." Willis's highly sympathetic portrayal of Rabbi Noach Weinberg and Rebbetzin Denah Weinberg, in the bible of the 1970s counterculture, put the teshuvah movement on the map and provided it with legitimacy in the eyes of many young Jews.

Though initially appalled by her brother becoming an Orthodox Jew, after spending a few months in Jerusalem, Ellen Willis describes how she herself felt the pull of Torah, despite her hardcore feminism. Even though she did not, in the end, take the plunge, at no point did she claim to have refuted the claims of Torah or the attraction of a Torah life.

Sara Karan first met Rabbi Schuster several weeks before her marriage when her *chassan* Bennett introduced her to him at the Kotel Plaza. But she had heard of him from young women he brought to Neve Yerushalayim, where she was studying, and friends had pointed him out at the Kotel. That first meeting, however, would not be the last of the day.

Sara and Ben had multiple errands to take care of, and treated themselves to cabs to get through their list. The first stop was the office of the Eidah Hachareidis in Jerusalem's Geulah neighborhood. As they exited their cab, there was Rabbi Schuster. Next stop: Shaare Zedek hospital to speak to the *mashgiach* (kashrus supervisor) of the hospital, who would also be the *mashgiach* for their wedding. As they entered the hospital, Rabbi Schuster was leaving and greeted them. After their meeting with the *mashgiach*, Ben took Sara back to Neve Yerushalayim, and there again was Rabbi Schuster bringing a young woman to the Bayit Vegan campus. At that point, Sara turned to her *chassan* and commented, "This man clearly is a beneficiary of *kefitzas haderech*" (a miraculous shortening of the time taken to traverse the distance between places).

After their *chasunah* — Ben was the first Aish HaTorah student to marry — Sara would learn much more about Rabbi Schuster in addition to his apparent ubiquity. The young couple chose to live in the Old City, and Rabbi Schuster would show up at their door every Friday to ask how many guests they could take that Shabbos. Sometimes he would supply a bit of information about the guests he hoped to send, but he rarely stayed for more than a minute or two. With the passage of time, Sara realized that Rabbi Schuster always brought two more guests than she had bargained for.

RABBI BERYL GERSHENFELD WAS ONE OF THOSE CLOSEST TO RABBI Schuster in the early days of Shema Yisrael. He went to the Kotel to

**A No Is Not a No**

help with the assignment of those looking for Shabbos placements nearly every Leil Shabbos, and frequently joined the Schusters for the Shabbos meal after the group had all been placed with their respective hosts. After he married the daughter of Rabbi Yaakov Rosenberg, one of the original founders of Shema Yisrael, he and his wife Gila often took Friday night guests sent by Rabbi Schuster.

Above all, Rabbi Gershenfeld shared Reb Meir's passion for kiruv from his earliest days in Shema Yisrael.[4] By 1983, he was teaching Torah regularly at the Hebrew University Overseas Program, and the Shabbatons he and his wife ran during the year were a crucial part of the success of the program. He knew exactly how many people his none-too-large apartment could seat — 21 — and how many sleeping spaces he could provide for those coming.

So when Reb Meir called on Erev Shabbos of one of the Shabbatons and said that he had met a student who would be perfect for Rabbi Gershenfeld, the latter had no choice but to say he could not take him: Every available spot was already filled. Never one to take no for an answer, even from someone to whom he was so close, Reb Meir called back again half an hour later to once again plead the case of the young man he had met. Beryl told him no again, in a firm tone that left no room for interpretation.

Nevertheless, at 3:30 p.m., not long before the onset of a winter Shabbos, a young man showed up at the door and told Rabbi Gershenfeld that Meir Schuster had sent him. Though Rabbi Gershenfeld was careful not to take out his anger on his unwanted guest, he did not show him his usual warmth. And he gave the guest no individual attention over Shabbos, as he already had private meetings scheduled with each of his Hebrew University students. The best he could do was to take his unexpected guest to a *vort* (engagement party) at Ohr Somayach on Motzaei Shabbos.

A few days later, Rabbi Gershenfeld received a call from his father-in-law, Rabbi Rosenberg, who was in the States recruiting for the summer program he ran for prospective baalei teshuvah. He told him that something extraordinary had just happened. A young man had called up, unsolicited, and asked whether he could come to the summer program and insisted on paying full tuition. Such a thing was unprecedented.

That young man was the very Shabbos guest whom Rabbi Schuster had sent, despite Rabbi Gershenfeld's explicit instructions. He went on to learn in Machon Shlomo for two years, and for four years after

---

4. Today he serves as the CEO of the Meor Campus Outreach Initiative that has placed rabbis on close to twenty campuses, and as Rosh Yeshivah of Machon Shlomo and Machon Yaakov.

that at Mercaz HaTorah. Today he is the menahel of a respected yeshivah in Israel for post-high school young men from the United States.

THERE EXISTS A MYTH THAT RABBI MEIR SCHUSTER WAS A ONE-TRICK pony; all he ever did was tap people on the shoulder and ask them: "Do

**Following Up** you have the time?" followed by "Are you Jewish?" Thus an old joke had it that someone gave Meir Schuster a watch and thereby destroyed the teshuvah movement by taking away Reb Meir's opening line.[5]

But like most myths, that one bears no relationship to reality. Yes, he tapped thousands upon thousands upon the shoulder. But he also had clearly thought-out strategies and possessed a surfeit of certain skills that made it possible for him to achieve what he did.

And chief among those skills was organization. In the early days, prior to the ubiquitous personal computer, his information was all "filed" in the black book filled with names and numbers that he always kept with him.

If Reb Meir succeeded in obtaining a name and address of one of the young Jews he encountered, that person was nearly guaranteed to hear from him again. After their marriage in 1975, Shragi and Sharon Weimer were neighbors of the Schusters in Ezras Torah, and became close friends. Reb Meir stayed in their apartment when his wife and children were in the States visiting parents and grandparents so that the Schusters could rent out their own apartment for the summer. One night, Shragi got up around 3:00 a.m. to attend to one of his children. At that hour, Rabbi Schuster was bent over the dining room table writing letters to those who had returned to the kibbutzim on which they were volunteering or even to the States.

The sheer volume of that correspondence, especially given how packed his day was and the amount of physical energy he expended, is astounding. Seth Mandell once mentioned that he was going to the post office and asked Rabbi Schuster whether there was anything he could purchase for him. Rabbi Schuster asked for 150 aerogrammes.

The impact of those aerogrammes was twofold. For one thing, it was a clear demonstration of how important the recipient was to Rabbi Schuster. But in addition, they almost always contained a tangible suggestion, such as a reminder that Chanukah was approaching; the festival would be an ideal time to come to yeshivah or seminary.

---

5. In fact, Rabbi Schuster used the question "Do you have the time?" even while wearing a watch.

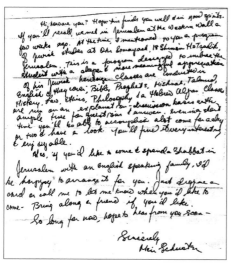

A letter from Rabbi Schuster to a young man whom he had met briefly, exhorting him to try a few days at Ohr Somayach

To receive mail from Rabbi Schuster required no previous show of interest on the recipient's part. David, for instance, was on a HaShomer HaTzair kibbutz on the Lebanese border when he took the advice of an old friend from Los Angeles to visit Jerusalem as soon as possible after coming to Israel. Standing at the Kotel, reading Biblical passages that had always been meaningful to him, he felt a tug from his left. After the usual questions — Do you have the time? Where are you from? What are you doing in Israel? — Rabbi Schuster inquired whether he would be interested in meeting a wise man. David told him that he had just graduated college, and was taking a break from professors, lectures, and seminars.

At that point, Rabbi Schuster disappeared, only to return some time later with the offer of a Shabbos meal. But David once again demurred on the grounds that he and his friend had already made arrangements for dinner. It was getting late, so Reb Meir contented himself with securing the name of David's kibbutz. Several weeks later, David received a postcard at his kibbutz inviting him to come to Jerusalem for Chanukah. Rabbi Schuster informed him that a place had been arranged for him at Aish HaTorah, and that he could "enjoy the *chag* in the city where the Maccabees reclaimed the Temple and the miracle of the Menorah occurred."

David decided to take up Reb Meir on the offer for a few days and called the number he had listed on the postcard. Rabbi Schuster told him what buses to take to the Old City, and walked him to Aish HaTorah. He also brought him to Reb Noach's home for a conversation. Though David found his time in Aish HaTorah "interesting," he was still determined to finish his program on the kibbutz. Three weeks before his program ended, however, David and a group of his fellow volunteers decided to head to the beaches of the Sinai.

Hitchhiking back from Nueba in the Sinai, David was picked up by an

Israeli family headed home to Jerusalem. At some point in the journey, he noticed a copy of *Shema Yisrael*, a magazine produced by Ohr Somayach, on the back seat next to him. David had intended to get off in Arad to check out a World Union of Jewish Students (WUJS) program that placed social workers (which he was thinking of becoming) in development towns. But before they reached Arad, David had been sufficiently intrigued by the magazine to ask his hosts whether they could drop him off at Ohr Somayach instead. They agreed.

Ze'ev Kraines
as high school valedictorian

Arriving at Ohr Somayach, David was fortunate that the first person to whom he was introduced was Ze'ev Kraines, a fellow Angelino, who had attended a cross-city rival high school at the same time as David. Ze'ev regaled him with the story of how he had been detained by the security guards at his high school graduation, held in the Hollywood Bowl, because the school authorities suspected him of planning to deliver an incendiary address as class valedictorian.

David's introduction to yeshivah provides a good example of how disorienting the experience was for newcomers. When he asked Ze'ev

Reuven Eliyahu with Rabbi Schuster after role-playing him
in the Ohr Somayach Purim *shpiel*

about lunch, he was told that it was Taanis Esther, a fast day. "Do you have many of those?" he inquired. Ze'ev was able to reassure him that there were no more than half a dozen a year. Instead of lunch, Ze'ev took David shopping in Meah Shearim to purchase *mishloach manos*, something of which David had never heard.

But all this was a mere prelude to Purim itself. David enjoyed what he could understand of the Purim *shpiel*, and the inevitable inside jokes. But he was totally unprepared for the pandemonium that erupted on Purim day, and the general drunkenness. Whatever he had thought a yeshivah was, it was certainly not the raucous behavior he witnessed.

As interesting as the experience had been, David still returned to his kibbutz for the last two weeks of his program, with plans of traveling in Europe thereafter. But Ze'ev Kraines had urged him to return to Ohr Somayach for Pesach, and he did. David ended up staying at Ohr Somayach, and various branches in northern Israel, from Pesach of 1976 until November 1978.

During that time, he frequently volunteered to help Rabbi Schuster, as he made his rounds between the Kotel, the Central Bus Station, and various youth hostels. Though their conversations were primarily logistical, David was always struck by Rabbi Schuster's firm belief that his efforts would be greeted with *siyata d'Shmaya*. Even when those he approached slipped through his fingers, as many inevitably did, that only increased his motivation to "try harder, work smarter, and always leave a lasting good impression, like planting a seed to blossom at the right moment."

Mordechai (Mitchell) Dubin with his grandfather in Jerusalem

At the *shivah* house for Rabbi Schuster, one of those who came to offer his condolences related that Rabbi Schuster had written to him three times at the kibbutz, and each time he had ripped up his postcard as soon as he saw the name Meir Schuster. On a subsequent trip to Jerusalem, Reb Meir saw him and immediately rushed over to embrace him, adding, "I've been waiting so much to hear from you." He is an observant Jew today.

Mordechai Dubin was in Israel

on a kibbutz during the 1973 Yom Kippur War. He had come to Israel filled with enthusiasm and intending to stay, but had become disillusioned. He was near the Kotel, reading, when Reb Meir first approached him and asked him whether he was interested in a Jewish experience. Mordechai told him that he was too tired just then.

Reb Meir said he would return in an hour, but in the interim Mordechai left. When he arrived at his youth hostel that night, the clerk asked him whether he was Mitchell Dubin, because someone had been calling for him. At first he panicked. His father had passed away suddenly when he was in high school, and he feared more bad news. But then he remembered that he had given Rabbi Schuster the name of the hostel where he was staying.

Around 9:00 p.m., Rabbi Schuster called and invited Mordechai to Shema Yisrael. Mordechai decided that if he did not at least check out a yeshivah he would not be confronting his own Judaism honestly. Not long thereafter, Ze'ev Kraines, one of the young stars in the Shema *Yisrael beis medrash*, appeared to escort Mordechai to the yeshivah, where he remained for two years. While he was in Ohr Somayach, Mordechai's European-born grandparents came to visit him in Israel. One evening, he took them to see the place where he had first met Rabbi Schuster, and there was Rabbi Schuster pacing back and forth in the rain waiting for the next Mordechai Dubin.

For over forty years, Mordechai has been a beloved elementary school rebbi in Los Angeles, and has produced many popular albums and music videos on Torah themes. He is a recipient of a Miliken Foundation award for excellence in Jewish education.[6]

Miriam Gold (formerly Debby Gross) was another beneficiary of Rabbi Schuster's intense follow-up. She was on a worldwide architectural tour, in the midst of her architecture degree program in Australia, when she decided, on the spur of the moment, to stop in Israel as well. She was standing in front of the Kotel, with no idea of what to do, when Rabbi Schuster asked her, "What are you doing here?"

Australians, she attests, are friendly people, and in the course of the ensuing conversation, Rabbi Schuster learned that she was staying at a youth hostel on Kikar Tzion. When she arrived back at the hostel, after midnight that night, the desk clerk asked her, "Are you Debby? This rabbi is calling every five minutes, and he's driving me crazy."

---

6. One final irony: He discovered as he became close to Rabbi Schuster that Mrs. Schuster's great-uncle, the brother of Reb Dovid Garfinkel, was married to his grandmother's sister.

Soon Rabbi Schuster called again, and told Debby that he had set her up for a Shabbos meal the next evening, and told her where to go. Australians are also very polite and respectful, says Mrs. Gold, and she felt obligated to go. Her host turned out to be Uri Kaploun, a well-known Lubavitch writer, who is originally from Melbourne.

It was her first real taste of Shabbos, and she was extremely impressed. Every moment was a learning experience, as, for instance, when she offered to help with the dishes and was told that the family did not do dishes on Shabbos.

But by far the biggest surprise of the Shabbos was a conversation with a *bachur* at the table wearing a long black coat and long *peyos*. He too was from Melbourne. Debby said that was impossible, as she had been active in the Jewish radio station and knew almost every Jew her age.

"I did not always look or dress like this," the young man said. That statement stunned Debby: "It was a bombshell that someone who was born into a certain type of home could become something else."

That realization opened Debby up to going to Neve Yerushalayim. She had always been a big questioner, and had frequently challenged authority by asking, "Why?" That practice had gotten her into no small amount of trouble in school, despite being a good student. At Neve, she found she could ask as many questions as she wanted, and Rebbetzin Heller and Rabbi Cardoza had the answers.

Today, Miriam Gold heads the architecture program in three Bais Yaakov seminaries in Jerusalem and maintains a private architecture practice that employs many Bais Yaakov graduates, in addition to being a mother and grandmother many times over.

At least one recipient of multiple aerogrammes from Rabbi Schuster had the foresight to retain the correspondence: Herschel Arno. He had met Rabbi Schuster in Jerusalem, and even went to Aish HaTorah for a bit, before returning to work in his family shoe store in Schenectady, New York, a job he detested. During the time he was back in the States, he and Rabbi Schuster both spoke on the phone and corresponded. The remaining letters from Rabbi Schuster show how much effort he put into his correspondence. They were not brief two-line postcards, but full-fledged letters.

In the first letter, Reb Meir brings Herschel up-to-date on developments at Aish HaTorah and expresses his "hope" to see him very soon:

> ...The Yeshiva is coming along very nicely. We have a new Beis Midrash, a lot more spacious than our old one. We are still trying

to get a new dining room and things are looking good. Another thing that's looking good here is the weather. You would be smart to get out of that freezing New York and come over to sunny Israel real fast.

The second letter was more of a pep talk. Reb Meir clearly knew that Herschel did not consider himself a happy person at that stage in his life:

> I received your letter the other day and was indeed very happy to hear from you — especially that your return to the Holy Land is close at hand.... You will be welcomed at Aish HaTorah with open arms. It was at Aish HaTorah that you first began to discover your 'roots,' and it will be at Aish HaTorah that you will continue to grow in your newly discovered identity.... The more you find out about your heritage the more you will find out about yourself. At Aish HaTorah you will be afforded an opportunity to grow spiritually, strengthen yourself mentally and become a genuinely happy person. We're all 'rootin' for you, Herschel! .... Looking forward to seeing you.
>
> Love,
>
> Meir Schuster

In the third letter, Reb Meir encourages Herschel to strengthen his resolve to return to Israel, and addresses fears that he will develop cold feet:

> ... It was good speaking to you over the phone and nice receiving your letter. It is very apropos that this coming Shabbat is the reading of *Lech Lecha*, in which G-d tells Avraham to go from his birthplace and from his father's house to a land which he will be shown.... The L-rd is also telling you to leave your birthplace and the house of your parents to go to the land of Israel. If life were easy there wouldn't be much meaning to live for at all. It's at times like these that we have to draw on the inner strength that our *neshamah*, or soul, provides us and use it to carry ourselves through.
>
> You're doing the right thing, Herschel, that's what counts. I'll sign off now with the words of encouragement that Moses gave to Joshua as he was about to lead the people of Israel into the land of Israel. "Be strong and fortified." I am eagerly waiting to see you here in the Old City. With deep friendship I remain,
>
> Meir

A lack of response or a negative response did not deter Rabbi

Schuster from continuing to write to young Jews whom he had met and who were currently in kibbutz programs. But when asked to cease and desist, he would. Shlomo Goldberg returned to Israel after finishing his college work, and went to a kibbutz to ascertain whether there was truth in socialism. On trips to Jerusalem, he relied on Rabbi Schuster to take care of him, and always ended up returning to Rabbi Aharon Feinhandler and his wife Sarah, the family with whom Rabbi Schuster had originally set him up, for his Shabbos meals,[7] after which Rabbi Schuster would bring him to Ohr Somayach to sleep.

In between visits to Jerusalem, he received a constant stream of letters, postcards and phone calls from Rabbi Schuster urging him to leave the kibbutz for yeshivah. The pressure grew too much, and at one point, Shlomo told Rabbi Schuster that his constant importuning was only pushing him further away from coming to yeshivah. And that if he were to come to yeshivah it would have to be when he decided he was ready, and not at the urging of anyone else. The calls and letters stopped.

But after a year or so on a kibbutz, Shlomo determined that he needed to give "real Judaism" a chance. He decided to go to Aish HaTorah because he was not yet excited about learning what happens when two men appear in *beis din*, each one holding on to the end of a tallis and each one claiming the tallis as his own, as he had on his visits to Ohr Somayach.

When he walked into the Aish HaTorah office to register, who should be standing there but Rabbi Schuster. Shlomo held out his arms in front of him, as though he were about to be handcuffed by a police officer, and said, "Here I am. Take me away." Rabbi Schuster's face lit up, and he put his arm warmly around Shlomo.[8]

---

7. See above, Chapter Six, pp. 98-99.

8. From that day, Shlomo would spend three years at Aish HaTorah, half a year at Yeshivas Torah Ore, and then five years at the Israeli branch of Yeshivas Chofetz Chaim before returning to the United States to serve as a communal rav and then educator.

*Chapter Nine*
# PIED PIPER

"**E**VERY GIRL WHO WALKED IN SAID THE SAME THING: 'I would never get into a car with a strange man,'" says Rabbi Eli Liff, long-time head of the beginner's program at Neve Yerushalayim. So why did they?

That question is compounded when one considers that almost every outside observer of Rabbi Schuster in action — people with proven intrapersonal skills — felt that they could improve his performance with a few helpful hints. Rabbi Yom Tov Glaser, the famous "surfer rabbi," used to watch Reb Meir walking at breakneck speed through the Old City, with a young Jew in his wake struggling to keep up, and think to himself, "Talk to them. Carry on a conversation." But Reb Meir's only priority seemed to be to get to Aish HaTorah or to his Heritage House hostel as soon as possible.

Beryl (Bob) Gershenfeld joined Reb Meir at the Kotel almost every Friday night from his early days in Shema Yisrael. He had turned down Yale Law School to come to Jerusalem to learn Torah, and thought that Rabbi Schuster could benefit from the presence of someone articulate and possessing a level of worldly sophistication to speak to those gathering to be assigned Shabbos hosts.

Anyone watching Reb Meir in action would likely have thought exactly as Rabbis Glaser and Gershenfeld did. Charles LeBeau, who ran kiruv programs at the Hebrew University under the auspices of

Heritage House, was at the Kotel one Friday night trying to convince a couple to go for a Shabbos meal with a religious family. "The guy was interested, but she wanted to go back to their hotel," he remembers. "Despite all my efforts, I struck out. Then Rabbi Schuster walked over and said, 'So you want to go for a Friday night dinner?' This time, it was the woman who said yes, and off they went."

JOSH EPSTEIN, WHO RAN THE HERITAGE HOUSE MEN'S HOSTEL FOR more than three years, once had the opportunity to run a con-

### "What's He So Excited About?"

trolled experiment to ascertain the basis for Rabbi Schuster's success. Adam arrived at the Heritage House just before Rosh Hashanah of 2000. The Second Intifada had just broken out and Heritage House was almost empty, so the staff had plenty of time to devote to Adam, who described himself as a devout atheist. Adam was both very smart and more than happy to engage in debate.

He turned down all suggestions that he go for a class or two in a yeshivah — or one of those "lame establishments," in his lexicon. The next morning, Yaakov, whom Josh describes as "the most cheerful positive Jew on the face of the planet," again encouraged Adam to attend a lecture or two. But the latter told him that he was not interested and was headed to the Israel Museum for the day.

Adam was sitting downstairs near the front gate with Josh when Rabbi

Josh Epstein in his office in the Heritage House men's hostel

Schuster walked in. Rabbi Schuster asked him where he was going for the day. Adam said that he was thinking of going to the Israel Museum. "No, you should go and check out a class at the yeshivah," Reb Meir told him. To which Adam responded meekly, "OK, that sounds like a good idea."

When Adam returned that evening, he was filled with excitement. The yeshivah was, in his words, "awesome. I had a blast, and I'm going back tomorrow."

At least three different staff members had made the same suggestion without stirring a trace of interest. How had Rabbi Schuster turned Adam around in the space of a one-minute conversation? Josh put the question directly to Adam, and the latter was able to clearly articulate Rabbi Schuster's power: "I have never met anyone in my life with such a passion for something, such a love. I have to find out what this guy is so excited about."

Rabbi Sender Chachamovits headed a Spanish-speaking program at Aish HaTorah for a number of years. One day, Rabbi Schuster came bounding up the stairs from the Kotel looking for him. Breathless, Reb Meir told him that he had met a Jewish group from Mexico at the Kotel, but they didn't speak English and he could not speak Spanish. Reb Meir told them to wait there, and he would find someone to speak to them in Spanish.

Reb Sender tried to convince him that it was pointless for him to go down to the Kotel, as the group had surely departed by then. But Reb Meir was importunate.. At some point, Rabbi Chachamovits decided that it would take him less time to walk down to the Kotel and back than to stand there arguing with Reb Meir.

But to his amazement, when he reached the Kotel the group was still standing exactly where Reb Meir had left them. Reb Sender could not contain his curiosity, and asked the leader of the group why they had stopped everything to wait for him.

The leader replied, "We really have no idea. But it seemed so urgent to him [i.e., Rabbi Schuster] that we could not leave."

## The Most Authentic, Pure Person

BUT RABBI SCHUSTER'S BELIEF IN THE PRODUCT HE WAS SELLING WAS only part of his ability to move people in a way that those far more articulate or charismatic were not. Not only did he care deeply about the Torah; he cared deeply about each Jewish *neshamah*, and those he met felt that.

Rabbi Schuster once called his brother-in-law

Moshe Garfinkel about a young woman from Philadelphia whom he wanted Reb Moshe to invite for Shabbos. When she came for Shabbos, Reb Moshe asked her why she had responded so positively to Reb Meir. Her response: "He was the first person in my life I felt truly cared about me."

Toby Levy was just out of high school and would not talk to any man she did not know. Yet when Reb Meir spoke to her for the first time at the Kotel, she "looked into his face and saw the most sincere person I had ever met. This man is so pure, in a way I have never seen before. I'm absolutely safe," she thought to herself.

An American backpacker once told Rabbi Avraham Edelstein, "I broke all the rules. I went in a car, in a strange country, with a strange man, to a place I never heard of. But I trusted him. He radiated authenticity."

Rabbi Moshe Chaim Eade teaches today at Aish HaTorah. He was raised in a Reform home, but was always a spiritual seeker. Arriving in Israel on a Birthright trip, he kissed the ground at the airport. After the trip was over, he stayed in Israel walking the Israel trail from the top to the bottom of the country, sleeping outside at night in avocado orchards and meditating. He first met Rabbi Schuster at the Kotel.

"I can still feel the sensation of him tapping me on the shoulder. He had an angelic presence. I felt that he was somehow my grandfather and thought to myself, 'This person cares about me and I can trust him!'" Rabbi Eade remembers.

As soon as he confirmed that he was Jewish, Rabbi Schuster told him, "You should go to yeshivah." He then went with him to gather his belongings from the Arab hostel where he was staying to bring him to Heritage House and from there to meet Rabbi Yom Tov Glaser. It was an inspired match. They are both musicians, still performing regularly, and like Rabbi Glaser, Rabbi Eade became a chassid in time.

"It seemed like the most natural thing in the world to follow him," says Rabbi Eade.

Rabbi Schuster found Alana Rubin on the steps from the Kotel up to the Old City, and asked her if she had a place to stay. "He was so gentle and shy," she remembers, "that I could not help thinking about how painful it must be for him to approach complete strangers in this fashion." And that realization led her to another: "How much he must care about me to subject himself to such torture."

Mordechai R. had much the same reaction as Alana. He spent a year on a kibbutz in 1979. Three times in the course of that year, at intervals of a few months, he ran into Rabbi Schuster near the Kotel. Each time, he expressed interest in going to yeshivah in response to Rabbi Schuster's entreaties, but in each case deferred doing so because he had to return to his kibbutz program. On the third such encounter, Rabbi Schuster asked him, "Were you really honest with me when you said at our previous meetings that you'd go to yeshivah but did not yet have time?"

With the question put so bluntly, Mordechai had no choice but to admit shamefacedly that he had not been truthful. "I knew you wanted very much for me to go to yeshivah," he explained to Rabbi Schuster, "and I did not want to hurt your feelings." At that point, Rabbi Schuster rested his head on the Kotel as if praying. Mordechai remembers, "I looked at him and thought: He cares, he really cares about me!" With that he agreed to accompany Rabbi Schuster to Ohr Somayach, where he remained for eighteen months and left an observant Jew.[1]

Jeremy was a computer scientist, working for one of the top hi-tech companies in San Francisco and leading a life he found both depressing and unfulfilling. He bought himself a one-way ticket for Israel, with the intention of eventually heading to the Far East to find the meaning of life.

His first night was spent in a Jerusalem hostel, with a group of "low-lifes," wondering, "What am I doing in such a crazy place?" He resolved to leave Israel as quickly as possible. The next morning he was wandering around at the Damascus Gate, looking for a money changer, and headed for the Temple Mount, when an Arab boy ran up to him and told him that the Temple Mount was not his place and that he should follow him to the Kotel. Jeremy had no idea what the boy was talking about, or even what the Kotel was, and walked past the Kotel and out the Dung Gate. As he exited the Dung Gate, a passing car came to a screeching halt, and an "ultra-Orthodox Jew" poked his head through the window to offer him a ride.

"I don't know why, but I got into the car and gave him the only Jerusalem address I had — that of an apartment in the Old City. He dropped me there, and told me he would return in an hour, which he did on the dot. From there he took me to the Aish HaTorah cafeteria for lunch, and convinced me to move into the newly opened Heritage House and take some classes at Aish during the day."

---

1. Michael Kaufman, "Rav Meir Schuster — The Man Who Changed the Future of the Jewish People," *The Jewish Press*, May 10, 2014.

"Within twenty-four hours of arriving in Israel, I was in a yeshivah — and I didn't even know what a yeshivah was," recalls Jeremy with a smile. Seven months later, Jeremy moved to Monsey, where Reb Meir continued to stay in touch with him, and even to help with *shidduchim*.

But of all those who were surprised to find themselves getting into the car with Rabbi Schuster, surely none was more so than Shana K. She was so embarrassed that when someone at Ohr Somayach women's division asked her how she got there, she claimed that she had been walking by and had seen the sign and decided to find out what it was. But one of the *madrichot* quickly piped up, "Nonsense. Rabbi Schuster brought you," which left Shana even more mortified.

Prior to her arrival at Ohr Somayach women's division, it would be hard to think of a less likely candidate to become an observant Jew than Shana. Her non-Jewish father was a former high-ranking officer in the British Navy, and her Jewish mother was fleeing from being identified as Jewish. Her maternal grandfather was a successful industrialist in Germany, until the Nazis arrived at his factory one day. He jumped out the back window and escaped, but remained convinced that Orthodox Jews had caused the Holocaust by arousing Nazi hatred of Jews. Shana's mother once woke her up when she was young to watch a BBC documentary, *The Final Solution*, to show her what could happen to Jews in England as well.

Though her non-Jewish father had no objection to his children being raised Jewish, her Jewish mother was adamantly against it, and sent Shana to church Sunday school and even had her confirmed in the church on the grounds that such confirmations had saved some Jews in Germany.

Strangely, however, her mother urged her to go to a kibbutz in Israel after high school before entering the University of London. She saw that her daughter was socially awkward and had few friends, and hoped that she might fit in on a kibbutz. Meanwhile Shana's sister had become a Christian Israelite, and sent a fellow member of the sect to travel with her in Israel, primarily visiting Christian holy places. After a "Shabbos" with a Christian Israelite family in Jerusalem, Shana told her traveling partner that she wanted some time by herself.

The next morning she got on a bus, and told the bemused Israeli driver that she wanted to go where the Jews are. He told her, "They are everywhere." Finally, he directed her to the Kotel.

The sight of people apparently talking to the wall filled her with curiosity, and she climbed up to the Moslem Golden Dome to see if she could ascertain Whom they were addressing, before an Arab guard sent her away. Back at the Kotel, she did not notice the gender separation, but was struck by the mixture of old and young, since there were no old people associated with the Christian Israelite cult.

As she was standing there still wondering, "Whom are they talking to in that fashion?" Rabbi Schuster approached and asked her a question not in his usual repertoire: "Do you want to know what they are doing?" She said yes, and soon found herself in a cab on the way to the Ohr Somayach women's division, together with Rabbi Schuster. The entire ride her mother's warnings against being kidnaped by Arabs into a harem were ringing in her ears, as she made plans to bolt from the cab. Even after arriving at Ohr Somayach without incident, she was still ashamed of herself for entering the cab with a man.

When the *madrichah* on duty to receive new recruits asked her whether she believed in G-d, however, she answered, "I would have said no, but I just had the most amazing experience," referring to Rabbi Schuster's offer to answer her question about what the Jews praying at the Kotel were doing. The *madrichah* told Rabbi Dovid Abramov, the principal, "We have a precious one here. A Jewish soul who knows nothing." In a strange way that description echoed a warning her grandfather had once given her mother: "Be careful of her. She looks like a *goy*, but she has a Jewish heart. She'll give you trouble."

Even at a seminary for baalos teshuvah, Shana's ignorance of Judaism stood out. During a discussion of Yom Kippur, she was delighted to finally hear a familiar word, and blurted out happily, "I know, it's a war." On her third Shabbos, at the home of the principal Rabbi David Abramov, she expressed surprise that he was married, as she did not know rabbis could marry.

THE CARE AND CONCERN THAT YOUNG JEWS MEETING RABBI SCHUSTER for the first time felt was an expression of the manner in which he

**He Saw Only Neshamos**

viewed each Jew as a precious *neshamah*. Rebbetzin Tzipporah Heller, for decades the premier teacher in Neve Yerushalayim, describes Rabbi Schuster as unsurpassed in his ability not to judge another Jew by how they looked or what they were wearing. He saw only *neshamos*.

She gives an example. A former student called from the United States to ask whether the Hellers could house a friend of hers who was arriving the next day. Early the next morning, they received a call from the airport. The friend had arrived in Israel without shoes and with no money, and the immigration authorities wanted to send him back, suspecting that he was mentally unbalanced.

The Hellers concluded the same thing, but nevertheless drove to Ben Gurion Airport to pick up the young man. By the time they arrived at the airport, they had a plan. To ask the question "Who will take him?" was to answer it. They drove straight to the Old City to look for Reb Meir, who, as usual, soon made his appearance. They explained the situation, and Rabbi Schuster took the new arrival to the Diaspora Yeshiva on Har Zion. The Hellers later heard that he had flourished there and eventually moved on to a mainstream yeshivah.

Rebecca (Rosenzweig) Askinasi captures how oblivious Reb Meir was to external appearance. She was the manager of the women's Heritage House off and on over a period of five years, and also worked in the Information Center connected to Heritage House in the main square of the Jewish Quarter of the Old City. As a consequence, she was often in the Heritage House office when Rabbi Schuster came in to apply his sunscreen and grab something to eat.

He was a parental figure for Rebecca and spent a lot of time trying to make a *shidduch* for her, with many high-quality young men. At that stage in her life, Rebecca was struggling with weight issues. Rabbi Schuster was absolutely incapable of understanding how someone could reject a potential marriage partner because of physical appearance. He was, in her words, "too pure to understand this other currency of values."

And in that removal from anything external, writes Rebecca, "He gave me something so deep, so nourishing. I always knew that any time I would see him I'd get a jolt of pure positive energy that would uplift me."

Risa Brumer and her husband, Rabbi Jordan Brumer, were houseparents at the women's Heritage House during a very slow period after the start of the Second Intifada in late 2000. One day, she received a call from Rabbi Schuster that a young woman would be arriving that afternoon who had been sent by her rabbi in the States, and that Rabbi Schuster would pick her up the following morning to take her to a seminary. The woman arrived only long enough to put down her luggage before heading out. Risa was careful to inform her, as she always did, that curfew was at midnight and the gates would be locked.

Midnight came and went and there was still no sign of the new lodger. Mrs. Brumer grew concerned, and even though she was in the late stage of pregnancy, with two young children asleep, she set out to see whether she could locate her. She first went down to the Kotel to look for her there and then walked all the way back up the stairs to the outside square of the Old City.

Early the next morning, the new visitor to Heritage House was pounding on the door. Mrs. Brumer opened it to find a frantic young woman whose only coherent words were, "They took my watch," which she repeated as she handed Risa an official-looking form. That form turned out to be from the police department at Jerusalem's Russian compound. The watch was being held as a surety for the woman's appearance in court.

It turned out that she had attempted to go up to the Temple Mount to pray. Upon being told that she was not allowed to do so, she had insisted upon her right as a Jew to pray at Judaism's holiest site. Unable to convince her to desist in her efforts, the police had apparently arrested her and taken her to the Russian compound.

Given her abbreviated night of sleep and the stress she had been put under the previous evening, Risa was not terribly sympathetic. She told the young woman that she would have to find another place to stay, as they could not house her in the Heritage House. The young woman struck her as unbalanced, and she did not want her staying there with her family or creating an uncomfortable situation for any other guests.

Not long thereafter, Rabbi Schuster called to ascertain the whereabouts of the woman he was supposed to meet. Risa explained to him what had happened, but he could not comprehend why she had sent her away. For him, the only relevant thing was that there was a Jewish *neshamah* who had come to Israel to study Torah, and now it was incumbent on him to find her and bring her to a seminary.

Rabbi Schuster's concern for every Jewish soul repeatedly pushed him well outside his comfort zone. Initially, he did not approach women — few, if any, of whose dress would have complied with halachic standards of modesty. But he soon realized that it was impossible for him to ignore half the Jewish *neshamos* whom he encountered.[2] Here, too, he was well served by his ability to see beyond the external. That ability

---

2. As a practical matter as well, attempting to do so would have made his Leil Shabbos efforts to arrange Shabbos meals much less effective, as many of the young Jews whom he met at the Kotel came in coed groups of one sort or another.

Rabbi Schuster and Moishe Mendlowitz learning together at a Rainbow Gathering

made it possible for him to approach a woman who, as one of them wrote years later, was "not dressed in a manner that any *frum* man would normally have wanted to look in my direction."

The clearest example of his refusal to give up on any Jewish soul was the annual Rainbow Gathering, a sort of poor man's Woodstock, including drugs, young men and women in various degrees of dishabille, and only the most primitive of bathroom facilities. Yet Reb Meir sent Moishe Mendlowitz, the night manager of the Heritage House and his morning *chavrusa*, to one of the Rainbow Gatherings in a forest in Pennsylvania in the late '90s. (Chabad was also there, and provided kosher food for anyone who wanted.)

Reb Moishe was authorized to offer a ticket to Israel to any Jewish person who was willing to come and learn Torah. Remarkably, fifteen young Jews took him up on the offer, and of those between eight and ten eventually became *shomer mitzvos*, most of them after learning in Tzefat at the yeshivah of Rabbi Raphael Weingot or Rebbetzin Tova Weingot's women's seminary.

That first Rainbow Gathering was the most productive, as it attracted large numbers of young Jews from the East Coast. In subsequent years the Gatherings were in rural Western settings, and the percentage of young Jews was much smaller. One year, Rabbi Schuster himself accompanied Reb Moishe. One morning, the two of them were learning together and a young woman came over and asked whether she could learn with them. Reb Meir told her she could but first she would have to cover herself. She ran away crying.[3]

RABBI SCHUSTER'S DEEP CONCERN FOR HIS FELLOW JEWS WAS REGU-
larly expressed in acts of kindness great and small. "His kind, gentle look" is one of the standard descriptions of those relating their first encounter with him. Reuven Loewenstein, the comptroller of Heritage **A Kind** House for nearly a decade, had to repeatedly explain to **Heart** Rabbi Schuster that he could not use funds that he had collected (and which Heritage House did not need immediately) for any waif or needy person who might cross his path, without endangering Heritage House's American tax-exempt status.

Yirmi C. remembers the first two questions that Reb Meir asked him, though not the order: Are you hungry? Would you like to speak to a wise man? And forty years later, the memory of how Reb Meir immediately followed up by bringing Yirmi a sandwich is still fresh in his mind.

Reuven Eliyahu initially came to Israel together with his younger

Rabbi Schuster preparing eggs

---

3. The Rainbow Gathering experiment was dropped after a few years as not worth the investment of time because the percentage of Jewish participants was so small.

sister and her new husband, who was a recent convert. The purpose of the trip was to solidify the husband's Jewish identity. An uncle of Reuven Eliyahu's, who had become religiously observant long before the modern baal teshuvah movement began, managed to secure an apartment near Ohr Somayach for them. In addition to knocking on the apartment door each morning to wake up Reuven Eliyahu[4] to make sure he got to Ohr Somayach on time, Rabbi Schuster even prepared eggs for the group on occasion.

Nor were the kindnesses confined to those whom Rabbi Schuster was attempting to bring to yeshivah or seminary. They were part of his nature. Rabbi Moshe Pindrus, who learned together with Reb Meir in the Mirrer Yeshiva, contracted hepatitis and was unable to move from his bed shortly before his first Pesach as a married man. Fortunately, Reb Meir and his neighbor in Ezras Torah, Rabbi Yossi Abrams, came over unsolicited and did the bulk of the cleaning.

When Rabbi Mordechai Gedult, who was then teaching at Aish HaTorah, moved to the Ezras Torah neighborhood in September 1975, he did not know a single person in the neighborhood, apart from Rabbi Schuster, whom he frequently saw in Aish HaTorah. Like most new homeowners in those days in Israel, the Gedults did not have a phone. When his wife went into labor in the middle of the night, Reb Mordechai had to climb over a fence in the Tchebiner Yeshiva to reach a pay phone to summon a taxi to take his wife to Bikur Cholim Hospital, while he stayed home with their two young daughters. Not until the next afternoon was he able to make it to the hospital to see his wife and newborn son.

The following day, he ran into Rabbi Schuster and told him, "I suppose I have to make a *shalom zachar*, but I don't know anyone here." Reb Meir immediately offered to make the *shalom zachar* in his home, and did.

Even after the Lewy Body disease that eventually claimed his life had rendered him unable to do much at Heritage House, he would still come in to do anything he could to help, such as loading the laundry into the washing machine.

---

4. Reuven Eliyahu initially agreed to attend classes in order to exercise a good influence on his new brother-in-law.

THERE WAS ALMOST NO LIMIT TO THE LENGTHS RABBI SCHUSTER would go to provide a Jew with the opportunity to learn more about his

**"I Can Change Your Ticket"** or her Judaism. And money was no object. Michael Kaufman grew used to Reb Meir rushing into his home frantic because he needed money for a new airline ticket that would allow someone to extend his stay.

Lisa walked into the Heritage House Information Center and announced, "I want to learn more about Judaism." She was then 27, and near the end of an around-the-world trip that had taken her to a multitude of exotic places: Bora Bora, Tongo, and Fiji. The primary impetus for coming to Israel had been guilt feelings over miscalculating the date and not celebrating Yom Kippur in New Zealand.

But she had been struck powerfully as she emerged from the dark and dingy Arab shuk leading down to the Kotel from the Jaffa Gate and beheld the Kotel for the first time. It was suddenly and profoundly clear to her that the Kotel had something to do with her that all the beautiful places through which she had traveled did not. Thus her arrival at the Heritage House Information Center.

Lisa moved into Heritage House and began taking classes at Neve Yerushalayim. She had already spent four consecutive Shabbosos in Jerusalem when the time came for her to fly to Italy to meet her aunt for some long-planned sightseeing, and then return home.

When she went to see Rabbi Schuster to thank him for all that he had done for her, he told her that he had connections who could rearrange her round-the-world ticket in such a way as to allow her to return to

Sign for the Heritage House Drop-In Center

Israel after Italy. Lisa readily agreed that whatever time remained after Italy would be best spent studying in Jerusalem and deciding what direction she would like her life to take.

And that became even clearer after she met up with her aunt. After experiencing Shabbos in Jerusalem, she found she could not do without it on her first Shabbos in Italy. On the other hand, she did not know how to keep Shabbos on her own, and ended up spending the entire day in bed in her hotel room feigning a stomach disorder.[5]

After returning to Jerusalem, things continued to fall into place for Lisa, now Leora, and she eventually became a counselor and then manager of the Heritage House women's hostel. Only years later, when Leora was working as the assistant to the Executive Director of Heritage House, Rabbi Avraham Edelstein, did she realize that Rabbi Schuster had not rearranged her ticket; he had simply gone and purchased a new one for her.

Reb Meir told the following story to Dov Wolowitz, the major donor to the men's Heritage House. He was staying with the Wolowitzes in Lawrence, New York, and returned elated one night from a fundraising visit to Monsey. While there he had gone to visit a recently married couple, Jay and Jill,[6] and their new baby.

Reb Meir first met Jay and Jill as Jay was having tefillin put on him at the Lubavitch stand near the Kotel. When he asked them whether they were open to a Jewish experience, they answered, "Sure." He ascertained that they were staying in an Arab hostel, and told them that he would pick them up at 9:00 the next morning.

That night, however, the leader of another tour group warned them, "That's a cult — they'll make you religious. Don't go with them." Such warnings against having anything to do with Rabbi Schuster were commonly issued on kibbutzim in those days, but more often than not, they only made Rabbi Schuster more intriguing, and gave a frisson of adventure to going with him.

But Jay and Jill were genuinely unnerved. They resolved that if Rabbi Schuster had not appeared by 9:05, they would leave. He arrived a few seconds later, as they were already disappearing down the street, but he managed to overtake them and persuade Jay to accompany him to Aish HaTorah and Jill to Neve.

When he picked them up that afternoon, both said that they had

---

5. Estrin, *It Happened at Heritage House*, pp. 178–182.
6. Not their real names.

enjoyed the experience and agreed to have Rabbi Schuster pick them up the next morning. After four days, they were ready to move into the Heritage House hostels and to continue their studies. After about a month, however, Jay approached Rabbi Schuster and told him that their tickets were about to expire, and they could not be extended.

Rabbi Schuster replied, "Give me the tickets. I have some connections with travel agents. I'll see what I can do." He returned later to tell them that he had succeeded in working things out with his travel agent friend. As a consequence, Jay and Jill stayed a few more months, and became fully mitzvah observant and subsequently married.

When Reb Meir went to visit them in Monsey, Jay told Reb Meir that they had recently had a guest who knew Reb Meir's *modus operandi* well and he had informed them that Reb Meir had simply purchased new tickets for them. Jay and Jill would not let Reb Meir leave the house until they had paid for the tickets that made all their subsequent happiness possible.

In some cases, Rabbi Schuster did not even make a pretense of having "arranged" for tickets. Chananel Weiner, a relatively new student at Aish HaTorah, was talking to Rabbi Schuster one day, and he mentioned that while he was growing in yeshivah, his younger brother was waiting on tables in Colorado, with no connection to Judaism. In passing, he raised the idea of trying to go out there to meet him and bring him back to Jerusalem.

Reb Meir immediately picked up on the idea, and within moments they were scouring the internet in search of cheap tickets. In the end, Rabbi Schuster purchased both the ticket for Chananel to fly out to Colorado and one for his brother to come to Israel, and for good measure arranged overnight accommodations for Chananel in New York City during a layover.

That investment did not achieve its desired result — a longshot at best. But in another case a similar willingness to purchase a plane ticket on Rabbi Schuster's part paid huge dividends. Gary came through Heritage House to Ohr Somayach, where he was particularly impressed by a *shiur* from Rabbi Akiva Tatz. Though he had been learning at Ohr Somayach for only a couple of weeks, and his flowing blond locks still fell to his shoulders, he was excited enough about his studies that the imminent intermarriage of his brother Sam weighed very heavily on him.

One invitation to his brother to come and visit him in Israel had already been rebuffed, but Gary did not give up. He went to Rabbi Schuster and proposed offering his brother a free flight to Israel and two weeks at Ohr Somayach. As Gary had suspected would be the case, Rabbi Schuster accepted the proposal.

Sam remained in Jerusalem at his studies for a year, and eventually, he and Gary were joined in yeshivah by a third brother. Their parents followed their three sons in becoming religiously observant.[7]

---

7. Estrin, *It Happened at Heritage House*, pp. 206-7. Dena Estrin, the long-time head *madrichah* at the women's hostel, learned of this story when Sam became engaged to a former guest at Heritage House.

## Chapter Ten

# FOR EVERY NESHAMAH ONLY THE BEST

ONE OF THE CHALLENGES FOR MODERN-DAY KIRUV WORKERS is the necessity of delivering measurable results for their funders. As a consequence, they rarely have the time to accompany baalei teshuvah throughout the process of healthy integration into the religious community, and the baalei teshuvah often end up feeling that they were just numbers to inspire further funding.

Other than the help he received from the American P'eylim, Rabbi Schuster had no funder other than HaKadosh Baruch Hu, and his sole consideration with respect to any Jew who came within his range was what was best for him or her. That insistence on focusing exclusively on the individual was often a source of frustration to the institutions with which he interacted on a regular basis.

The staff at Ohr Somayach complained that he took more potential students to Aish HaTorah, and at Aish HaTorah, they complained that he brought the more talented young men to Ohr Somayach. He paid no attention to either, and continued to bring those he met to the particular institution that he thought would be the best fit, subject only to such practical considerations as how far the person in tow was likely to be willing to accompany him.

Once Yossi Kaufman, who was then the manager of Heritage House, was invited to a meeting at Ohr Somayach with the staff responsible for placing new recruits, and found himself immediately challenged as to Heritage House's criteria for directing its guests to one institution or another. He answered with a straight face: "If they have money, we take them to Aish HaTorah."

That was patent nonsense. But Yossi Kaufman meant to convey a very concrete message: Neither Rabbi Schuster nor Heritage House could be pressured to exercise anything other than their best judgment about what was optimal for the particular Jew in question. If he thought it was best for a student, or the student expressed dissatisfaction where he was, Rabbi Schuster would encourage students to transfer from Ohr Somayach to Aish HaTorah or vice versa.

There were students whom he initially brought to Rabbi Noach Weinberg at Aish HaTorah who ended up at Ohr Somayach, and others whom he brought to Rabbi Nachman Bulman at Ohr Somayach, who eventually ended up at Aish HaTorah.

Once Rabbi Schuster noticed that a college student whom he had brought to Aish HaTorah was spending all his time in the *beis medrash* engrossed in learning Gemara. At that time, Ohr Somayach placed far greater emphasis on Gemara study for new students, and Rabbi Schuster advised him that he should move to Ohr Somayach, where his thirst for Gemara would be better slaked. But the young man demurred. What he had heard about Ohr Somayach made him think that it would be too "black" for him.

Still, Rabbi Schuster did not desist. One day, he took the young man with him to the Cardo, the ancient Roman shopping district in the Jewish Quarter, and reiterated his advice that "he should go to Ohr Somayach." Eventually, Rabbi Schuster proved persuasive, and, at least as far as that particular student was concerned, correct: He returned to Los Angeles at the end of his year off from college fully committed to mitzvah observance, and lived in the dorm of Yeshiva University of Los Angeles (YULA) while completing college. He then spent two years learning in yeshivah before law school, the first year of which was at Ohr Somayach.

The fact that one of his "recruits" had not felt a particular yeshivah suited him was never the end of the issue for Rabbi Schuster. And it made no difference what institution he had originally brought him to. The juxtaposition of the contrasting experiences of Rabbi Yehuda Fierstein and Rabbi Yaakov Kleiman proves the point.

Yaakov Kleiman had been traveling for an extended period in Europe and northern Africa after graduating from the University of Pennsylvania. In Morocco, he experienced "culture shock" from being in a non-Western culture for the first time. That culture shock opened him up to the exploration of his own Jewish identity when he arrived in Israel. Within two days of his arrival in Israel, he received the tap on the shoulder at the Kotel from Rabbi Schuster, and soon found himself trotting after Rabbi Schuster to Ohr Somayach. (Rabbi Schuster was nicknamed "the strider" by Aish HaTorah students.)

Though he hit it off famously with his assigned roommate, Gedaliah Gurfein, and remains friends with him to this day, over forty-five years later, Yaakov found that Ohr Somayach did not have the kind of beginner's program he was looking for, and was more a yeshivah with a kiruv arm than a kiruv operation with a *beis medrash* attached. Learning the technical details of Shabbos observance seemed to him to be putting the cart before the horse, since he still had no idea why he should want to keep Shabbos in the first place. After a couple of days at Ohr Somayach, Yaakov left.

Shortly thereafter, however, he ran into Rabbi Schuster again, who immediately took him to Aish HaTorah, which had just opened its doors a few months earlier. The small size of the student body — then under twenty — and Old City location was exactly what he was looking for, and he found Rabbi Noach Weinberg's 48 Ways classes fascinating. He has remained associated with Aish HaTorah until today.

As a Kohen, Yaakov Kleiman became fascinated with the question of how credible it is that all Kohanim today are really descendants of a common male ancestor — Aharon HaKohen — especially as Jews from different parts of the globe look so different from one another. That question led him to the field of genetic research to determine the paths of Jewish migration over the centuries and the commonality of the Jewish gene pool. That research culminated in his well-received *DNA and Tradition: The Genetic Link to the Ancient Hebrews* (2004).

Yehuda Fierstein arrived in Israel with a backpack and his guitar. An avid cyclist, he was slated to lead a bicycle trip at the end of the summer, and then move to Corvallis, Oregon, to begin his first post-college job as a mechanical engineer with Hewlett-Packard. He began his time in Israel with a Nature Society trip to the Sinai.

At the end of the tour, he made up to meet some new friends from the trip on Friday night. But before that, he ran into Rabbi Schuster in the

Old City, who brought him to the home of Rabbi Avraham Sheinberger for the Shabbos evening meal, where he was seated at a long table with other American kids around his age.

In the middle of the meal, Yehuda decided it was time to contact his buddies from the Sinai trip, and told his host that he had to leave to make a phone call. Taken by surprise, Rabbi Sheinberger asked him whether he wanted to *bensch* first. Yehuda had no idea what he was talking about and replied, "No, I already have a chair."

Back in Jerusalem, after a tour of northern Israel, Yehuda ran into Rabbi Schuster again, who this time offered him a class on Judaism at Aish HaTorah. Yehuda did not enjoy the class, which reminded him too much of late-night bull-sessions in college on the meaning of life. He freely admits that he did not have an adequate sample set to evaluate Aish HaTorah, especially as Rabbi Noach Weinberg was then out of the country. But having as yet made no commitment to Jewish learning, the presumption was against staying, and Yehuda was off to the Dead Sea and Ein Gedi.

When he next returned to Jerusalem, he again met Rabbi Schuster, who asked, "Didn't I see you before?" Yehuda told him that he had taken him to a class at Aish, which he had not liked. Rabbi Schuster asked him why not. Yehuda's response was sufficient to provide Rabbi Schuster with an opening to bring him to Ohr Somayach and a class of Rabbi Nathan Lopes-Cardozo on abortion.

Rabbi Cardozo's philosophically-honed lecture impressed Yehuda, but it was not until he was placed in a Gemara class a few days later that he felt really set on fire. Unfortunately, by then, Yehuda was nearly out of money and had a charter flight from England back home looming. However, Rabbi Yirmiyahu Abramov, then in charge of newcomers to Ohr Somayach, had recognized Yehuda's potential and told him that Ohr Somayach would cover his flight back to Los Angeles when the time came.

It never did. Forty years later, Yehudah Fierstein is still learning full time in Jerusalem. In due course he became one of the outstanding *avreichim* in Yeshivas Mir, where he was a *chavrusa* of the late rosh yeshivah, Rav Nosson Tzvi Finkel, and also the latter's brother-in-law, Rabbi Binyamin Carlebach, and himself gave regular *chaburos*, sometimes in two tractates simultaneously. He is also the author of *Flow From the Source*, essays based on the Sfas Emes on the weekly parashah.

Had Rabbi Schuster not recognized that each institution has its own particular strengths, and no institution will appeal to every individual, neither Rabbi Kleiman nor Rabbi Fierstein would have been likely to find their way to Torah Judaism or make the contributions they have to the larger Jewish world.

## Finding the Right Match

BECAUSE REB MEIR HARBORED NO PERSONAL *NEGIOS* (INTERESTS) and had to answer to no one other than his own conscience, he was granted a unique insight when it came to guiding the young Jews with whom he came into contact. He discerned the *pintele Yid* (Jewish essence) at their core, and was able to find the right people to nurture it. Yet he himself, Rabbi Mordechai Schiller once observed, could, in most cases, no more explain his choice to take someone to one yeshivah and not another than he could explain why he ate with one hand and not the other. The decisions were intuitive.

After spending six months in Ohr Somayach, Reuven Eliyahu returned to the United States, via Paris, to sort things out. He returned half a year later, in the midst of Elul, and felt out of things: Everyone seemed to be on a spiritual high that was not yet accessible to him.

Reb Meir saw him at a Simchas Beis Hasho'evah standing apart and not participating. He took him over to Rabbi Mordechai Isbee, a Gerrer chassid and world-class *talmid chacham*[1] who taught in the Ohr Somayach *beis medrash*. Rabbi Isbee exuded an aura of *kedushah*. There were students in Ohr Somayach at the time who were afraid to attend his classes: When he closed his eyes and began rocking back and forth at the beginning of a *shiur*, they feared he would levitate the entire building off of its foundations.[2]

Reb Meir proposed a regular *chavrusashaft* with Rabbi Isbee for Reuven Eliyahu, and Rabbi Isbee agreed. They started learning *Derech Hashem*, and the entire experience of establishing a close relationship with someone of Rabbi Isbee's stature was transformative for Reuven Eliyahu. Nevertheless, at the end of the next *zeman*, Rabbi Isbee told Reuven Eliyahu that there were others in the *beis medrash* who needed him.

But Reb Meir would not hear of it. Reuven Eliyahu was a regular Shabbos guest at the Schusters' and a personal project of Reb Meir's. He

---

1. The events described took place in 1979. Subsequently, Rabbi Isbee became the Rosh Kollel of the largest Gerrer kollel.
2. The author was one of those fearful students.

told him to tell Rabbi Isbee that he had a *chazakah* on learning with him. Rabbi Isbee responded that Reuven Eliyahu should bring some friends, and they would learn once a week as a group. Even after Reuven Eliyahu moved back to the States, that learning group continued for another thirty years or more.

Rabbi Schuster once made his familiar offer of the opportunity to meet with a Jewish philosopher to a young man in his mid-20s he met at the Kotel. To which the young man responded, "I was a Phi Beta Kappa in college. There is nothing any rabbi can teach me." Nevertheless, Reb Meir persuaded him to come with him to meet Rabbi Nachman Bulman, a formidable combination of intellect and heart, thoroughly versed in the expanse of Jewish thought, as well as secular thought.

Though the young man had agreed to the meeting, he continued to display the same arrogance and dismissive attitude toward Rabbi Bulman as he had when he met Rabbi Schuster. After about ten minutes of that, Rabbi Bulman, ever a passionate man, told him, "OK, sonny, name your subject, and I will wipe the floor with you." And he proceeded to do so over the next two hours.

To the young man's credit, he was honest enough to recognize that he had been thoroughly bested on the intellectual battleground. Shortly thereafter, he entered one of the major baal teshuvah yeshivos, where he

R–L: Rav Nachman Bulman with Rav Mendel Weinbach

became the dominant figure in the *beis medrash* in the '80s.[3]

Batya (Barbara) Rosen would not have met Rabbi Meir Schuster in Jerusalem had she not agreed to accompany two non-Jewish friends on a trip to Eastern Europe. In Poland, they stayed with some relatives of one of the friends. The matriarch of the family suggested going to church at one point, and noticed when Barbara demurred. Barbara took a stick and etched a Jewish star in the dirt to explain her reluctance. The old lady looked around furtively, and motioned that she should remain silent about being Jewish.

The next day the non-Jewish friends decided to visit Auschwitz, and Barbara felt she had no choice but to join them. The impact was powerful, and she recited Kaddish at the spot.

After that experience, she decided it was time to separate from her friends and book a flight for Israel. Her first Shabbos was spent with the family of the *chazzan* of the Conservative synagogue in which she had grown up, who had become Orthodox after making aliyah. It turned out to be an intense Shabbos, with a good deal of debate. For her last Shabbos in Israel, Barbara opted for something less intense and settled in at a hostel in the Old City, where she met a medical student, with whom she made her way to the Kotel for Friday night services.

On the way, they became separated, and the next time she saw him, he was together with a tall, black-suited, bearded man, with whom he was struggling to keep up. The stranger asked her if she was interested in a "real Shabbos experience" with a family living in the Jewish Quarter. Throughout the meal, Barbara felt her ire rising, as the family concentrated the vibrant discussion almost exclusively on her companion.

She also resented the way the wife was doing all the serving, with no help from her husband. At the end of the evening she announced that she was appalled by the discrimination against women. Nevertheless, she accepted an invitation to return for the Shabbos day meal, for which the family had prepared themselves to respond to some of her criticisms.

Rabbi Schuster had intended to take Barbara to Neve Yerushalayim on Sunday morning, but when he heard about what had happened on Shabbos, he hastily arranged for her to meet with Rebbetzin Denah Weinberg instead. The Rebbetzin was a veteran at addressing the issues

---

3. Heard from Rabbi Zelig Pliskin, who heard the story directly from the "defeated" party.

Barbara had raised.[4] From Rebbetzin Weinberg, Rabbi Schuster took her to meet a landscape architect from Los Angeles, who had been studying at Neve for a year already and had become fully observant.

By then, Barbara's vacation from her government job in Washington, D.C., was over, but she left Israel promising to come back and study. A year later she did, and is still living and raising a family in Israel today.

## "Mistakes" With Christians

HOWEVER ASTUTE RABBI SCHUSTER'S CHOICES OF LEARNING VENUES for those he encountered at the Kotel and elsewhere, or his pairings with individuals to respond to specific challenges, he never made the mistake of thinking that his intelligence or expertise was the key ingredient. He knew with absolute clarity that ultimately it was Hashem guiding him. Nothing better proves the point than those instances in which he inadvertently brought non-Jews to yeshivos or to Shabbos hosts.

Perhaps Rabbi Schuster's favorite story — the one to which he almost inevitably had recourse whenever he was forced to tell a story about his work — concerned Brother Adrian, a Catholic seminarian, who came to Israel as a young man with the dream of becoming a Catholic missionary. On his visit to the Kotel, Rabbi Schuster approached him and asked him whether he would be interested in learning more about Judaism. Brother Adrian was not wearing clerical garb, and Rabbi Schuster assumed he was Jewish.

Brother Adrian reasoned that knowledge of Judaism would certainly prove useful in his missionary work, and readily agreed, without mentioning his religion. Rabbi Schuster took him to Aish HaTorah, where he remained for a number of months and progressed rapidly in his studies.

At some point, however, one of his parents became ill, and he had to return to the United States. Before doing so, he went to take leave of Rabbi Noach Weinberg. At that meeting, he told Reb Noach for the first time that he was a Christian. Reb Noach was furious at the deception, and told him that he had benefited from contributions made specifically so that Jewish young men, with little religious background, would have an opportunity to learn about their heritage. After venting his anger, however, Reb Noach told Adrian that the only possible restitution he

---

4. Feminist icon Ellen Willis devoted much space in her *Rolling Stone* feature, "Next Year in Jerusalem," to her conversations with Rebbetzin Weinberg, who impressed her greatly.

could make would be if one day he shared the knowledge he had gained at Aish HaTorah with a Jew with scant knowledge of his religion.

Eventually, Brother Adrian joined the staff of an academically superior Catholic school in Vermont. A Jewish couple — he a senior executive in a large corporation and she a school principal — living in Vermont sought the best possible academic environment for their oldest child (whom we shall call Daniel), and enrolled him in that Catholic school.

Daniel's Jewishness presented few problems for him at the school. In his last semester of high school, Daniel was only a credit short of graduation, and Brother Adrian proposed to him that in lieu of attending a class, he write a paper on a religious figure of his choice. Daniel went to the library of the temple that he and his family attended twice a year, and found himself drawn to Rabbi Akiva. When he submitted the paper, Brother Adrian looked at him quizzically and asked why he had chosen to write about a Jewish figure. At that point, Daniel did what Brother Adrian had once done to Rabbi Noach Weinberg: He revealed his religious identity.

Brother Adrian was taken aback, as he had never known that Daniel was Jewish. But he remembered the promise he had made years earlier to Rabbi Weinberg, and offered to begin learning Jewish texts with Daniel. For the remainder of the school year, the two learned both Chumash and Mishnayos together.

This particular story only came to light when Daniel took a job at Camp Magen Avraham in the Catskills several years after graduating high school. In the course of the summer, he approached the camp nurse, Rebbetzin Esther Tendler, and told her that he would like to enter the preparatory program at Ner Israel, of which her husband, the late Rabbi Yosef Tendler, was the head.

After hearing his story, Rabbi Tendler accepted Daniel on the spot, but, in the end, Daniel's parents would not allow him to attend Ner Israel. Several years later, however, Rabbi Tendler was in Israel, and ran into Daniel. Daniel's parents had allowed him to learn at Ohr Somayach, and he had become an observant Jew — well over a decade, and probably closer to two, after Rabbi Schuster's "mistake" in taking Brother Adrian to Aish HaTorah.[5]

_____

5. Yaakov Steinberg, formerly of Passaic, heard Rabbi Schuster tell the story of Brother Adrian more than once at the annual fundraiser that the Steinbergs held in their home for Rabbi Schuster. Though unable to say with certainty why Rabbi Schuster was so fond of this particular story, Steinberg notes several points that it brings out. One of those is the special

At the time Amos (then Thomas Auguste) Wittenberg first met Rabbi Schuster, he was 24 and had already been a popular Mennonite pastor in his native Holland. For several years, Amos had been preaching as a Christian, while spending ever larger blocs of time studying at Amsterdam's famous Hebrew library, Bibliotheca Rosenthaliana, and its sister institution, The Institute for Hebraic Studies. On more than one occasion, he joined the family of Dan Michman, a lecturer at the Institute, for the Shabbos evening meal, and even went with Michman to Amsterdam's Great Synagogue.

Eventually, the dual life became too much for him, and he resigned his pastoral position and came to Israel, where he stayed with Jewish friends of his parents in Jerusalem's Rechaviah neighborhood. Though powerfully drawn to the Hebrew Bible and Jewish exegesis, he had no plans to convert. During his initial time in Israel, he was at the Kotel every day, and before long it was inevitable that he encounter Rabbi Schuster.

On a Thursday afternoon, he was coming down the steps to the Kotel, and Rabbi Schuster was standing on the landing surveying the Kotel area.

"Do you want to spend Shabbat in a real Jewish atmosphere?" Rabbi Schuster asked him as he passed by.

"What happens if I say yes?"

"I'll put you up with a nice Jewish family."

"Is that a promise?"

"What do you mean? Isn't that what I just said?"

"OK, I accept, but you should know that I'm not Jewish."

Rabbi Schuster kept his part of the bargain, and set Amos up with a Dutch-speaking family in his Ezras Torah neighborhood. Of material goods, the family appeared to have few. A bare light bulb hung above the Shabbos table, which was surrounded by many children. Amos was given a folding cot to sleep on in the room with the washing machine.

But it was a wonderful Shabbos. Amos attended a Friday night *shiur* with his host, and for Minchah, they went to Ohr Somayach. After Shabbos, Amos returned to Ohr Somayach and spoke to one of the rabbis about his ambition to learn in a yeshivah. But the rabbi told him that

---

level of *siyata d'Shmaya* that always accompanied Rabbi Schuster in his work. A second point that it illustrates is what might be called the "law of conservation of spiritual energy." Any action or thought of a Jew done with purity of intention will one day find its expression in the education and ultimate redemption of another Jew, even at a remove of many generations.

was impossible as long as he had made no commitment to becoming Jewish.

Eventually, Amos arrived at Shapell's Yeshiva and had an audience with Rabbi Nosson Kamenetsky, who was then the rosh yeshivah. After a discussion of several hours' duration, Rabbi Kamenetsky told him, "Young man, I hear you talk and all I hear from you is that you want to be a Jew. Is that what you want?"

Amos responded with a question of his own: Would it be possible to learn Torah and probe it for the G-dliness within it, while retaining his own religion? Reb Nosson told him that it might theoretically be possible, but it would be very difficult. Next Amos inquired whether it made any sense to study Torah and even practice it, and still remain a non-Jew.

At that point, Reb Nosson brought the conversation to a close. "Why are you torturing yourself? Go home and make up your mind. If it is Torah you want, and you want all of it, then this is just another way of saying you want to be a Jew."

A few days later, Amos returned to tell Rabbi Kamenetsky that he wanted to be a Jew. Rabbi Kamenetsky allowed him to begin studying at Shapell's, but only the Written Torah and halachah, with a private tutor.

That was the beginning of Elul, and by Chanukah, Amos was ready for *geirus* before the *beis din* of the famed Rav Eliezer Waldenberg, universally known by the title of his halachic work, *Tzitz Eliezer*. Less than a year later, Amos married a young woman from a Dutch religious family, and for more than three decades he has made his home in London in the Golders Green community.

On his annual fundraising trips to London, Rabbi Schuster would always get together with Amos, and they would drink a toast to celebrate Amos's entry into the Jewish people.

Rabbi Schuster can be forgiven for having initially thought that Yonoson[6] was Jewish when he first met him at the Kotel. He was bearded and wearing a yarmulke on his first day in Israel in 1977 to participate in an archaeological dig. In response to Rabbi Schuster's inquiry as to whether he was Jewish, Yonoson answered honestly that he was not, but that he hoped to be one day. Rabbi Schuster, he remembers, could not have been kinder: He gave Yonoson a card so he could contact him

6. Yonoson's story is found at the website dedicated to Rabbi Schuster, www.RebMeirSchuster.org, without a last name.

if he ever wanted to spend a Shabbos with a religious family.

The next week Yonoson acted upon that offer and called Reb Meir, who assured him that he remembered him. Yonoson's first Shabbos was spent in Mattersdorf, at the home of Rabbi Yehudah Samet, the rabbi in charge of the Ohr Somayach *beis medrash* almost from the yeshivah's opening day.

Yonoson made good on his expressed intention to be Jewish one day. By the time Rabbi Schuster became ill, Yonoson was father to ten Jewish children and ten grandchildren.

The same serendipity that Rabbi Schuster experienced with his Christian "customers" was a constant feature of his activities. One day, he arrived at Ohr Somayach in a taxi with a young South African in tow.

"Where am I?" the young man blurted out. Upon hearing the South African accent of Rabbi Yirmiyahu Abramov, the young man was put somewhat at ease.

"This is a yeshivah," Rabbi Abramov explained.

At the mention of the word yeshivah, the young man's face brightened. "Oh, before I left, I visited an old aunt in Port Elizabeth, and she told me that we have a relative in Israel who teaches in a yeshivah." He did not remember offhand the relative's name, and went rummaging through his luggage for the piece of paper on which he had scribbled it.

The long-lost relative turned out to be Rav Elazar Menachem Mann Shach, the undisputed leader of the Lithuanian yeshivah world in Eretz Yisrael at the time. That afternoon, Rabbi Abramov took the young man to Ponevezh Yeshiva to meet Rav Shach. The latter was overjoyed to discover any remnant of his family, which had been almost totally wiped out in World War II.

IT NEVER OCCURRED TO RABBI SCHUSTER THAT HIS RELATIONSHIP ended when he brought someone through the portals of Aish HaTorah, Ohr Somayach, or Neve Yerushalayim. In Aish and Ohr

**Advocate**  Somayach, he was in the *beis medrash* on a daily basis, and he would go around checking on the progress of those whom he first brought in and making sure that they were satisfied. If one complained that he was not happy with his *chavrusa*, for instance, Reb Meir was quick to take the complaint to the responsible official and to demand a new *chavrusa* on his behalf.

He drove "us dilly," with his advocacy for his "catches," remembers Rabbi Yirmiyahu Abramov, who was in charge of intake at Ohr

Rabbi Schuster with Rabbi Dovid Refson, dean of Neve Yerushalayim

Somayach in its early days. "I can't" or "I'm tired" were simply unacceptable excuses as far as Rabbi Schuster was concerned, says Mrs. Gitty (Twerski) Appel, who was the chief *madrichah* in the beginners' program at Neve Yerushalayim in the 1980s. If the Neve dorms were filled, or if Reb Meir thought there was a young woman who was not yet ready for the dorms, he would bring her to Gitty Twerski and her roommate's apartment.

Rabbi Dovid Refson, the founder and dean of Neve Yerushalayim, may have helped Reb Meir get into the kollel of Machon Harry Fischel years earlier,[7] but Reb Meir showed him no mercy. If a young woman whom he had brought to Neve left, he demanded to know why. And he would accept no excuses for days on which Neve had no formal classes — Chol HaMoed, Erev Yom Kippur, summer vacation. The idea that he might bring a young woman to Neve and there would be no classes to offer her upset him greatly. When Rabbi Refson told him that he could not find anyone to teach on those days, Reb Meir was not mollified. "You'll just have to teach yourself, then," he told Rabbi Refson.

And the latter went along with Reb Meir's demands. "He was at the

---

Kotel seven days a week, every day of the year. Even on Yom Kippur he davened in the *haneitz* minyan at the Kotel so as to be free to be at the Kotel for at least part of the day. So I couldn't argue that he had no right to demand," Rabbi Refson explains. The first year that Neve instituted Chol HaMoed classes, Reb Meir brought in seven women over Chol HaMoed.

Rabbi Schuster did not rely on the institutions with which he worked to answer all the needs of those he brought in. When necessary, he created his own individualized solutions. Reb Meir first met Yoram Raanan, a graduate of the Philadelphia Academy of Arts, on a Friday night at the Kotel. To Reb Meir's standard question — "Are you Jewish?" — Yoram replied, "Are you?" That got a laugh out of Reb Meir, and he brought Yoram home with him that evening, and managed to keep him through *shalosh seudos*.

Yoram had a much better background in Jewish texts than all but a few of the young backpackers of that time — 1976 — and he agreed to go to yeshivah. After two weeks, however, he left for scuba-diving at Sharm el-Sheikh. Eventually, he returned to Jerusalem and took up residence in a hostel. And that's where Reb Meir found him a second time. Reb Meir told him that he had gone to the wrong yeshivah for him, and this time took him to Ohr Somayach, where he basically set up an

Rabbi Schuster reciting a *berachah* at the *chuppah* of Yoram and Mira Raanan

independent study major for Yoram, which included a room and studio in the Bukharian Quarter, so he could continue painting.

Over the next two years, Yoram continued painting, while maintaining a private Gemara *chavrusa* with Rabbi Beryl Gershenfeld, being opened up to Chumash by Rabbi Tzvi Abraham, a philosophy graduate of Oberlin, and eating frequently with the Schusters on Shabbos. Rabbi Schuster's efforts on Yoram's behalf proved more than justified, and over the last four decades he has become one of Israel's best-known painters for his colorful canvases, many of which are of Biblical scenes.

## Relationships Are Forever

RABBI SCHUSTER OBVIOUSLY COULD NOT MAINTAIN A RELATIONSHIP with, or even know what happened to, the tens of thousands of Jews he brought to yeshivos or seminaries over the years. Many life journeys that began with him had happy endings of which he knew nothing. Dov Wolowitz, who was his regular host in the Five Towns, was once in a restaurant with Reb Meir and a group of Dov's friends in the real estate business at Weiss's dairy restaurant on Coney Island Avenue. When the time came to pay the bill, however, the South African waiter told Mr. Wolowitz, "It's on me. Twenty years ago, I became *frum* because of that man," nodding in Reb Meir's direction. "It's the least I can do."

Yosef Nussbaum, Reb Meir's younger friend from Ner Israel, with whom he always stayed in Detroit, recounts a similar story. Nussbaum would always try to help Reb Meir in his fundraising efforts by introducing him to people. He rang the door at one home, and when the husband opened the door, he took one look at Reb Meir and bounded up the stairs, while calling his wife to come quickly, as Meir Schuster, the one who first introduced them to Torah Judaism, was in their home.

If Reb Meir could not maintain an ongoing relationship with everyone with whom he interacted, the sheer number of those with whom he remained close long after they were safely in yeshivah or even married and out in the world attests to the fact that every Jew who came within his purview was a precious soul to him, and not a notch on his gun.

The Schuster Shabbos and Yom Tov table was always packed with young men from Aish HaTorah and Ohr Somayach. Some, like Akiva Unger and Reuven Eliyahu, were weekly guests, but almost all the guests were frequent returnees. They were a diverse group, however.

Some were high-energy young men — often former athletes or runners — for whom a full day in the *beis medrash* was a challenge. They enjoyed the "action" of accompanying Rabbi Schuster on Leil Shabbos as he dropped off Jews who had gathered at the Kotel at their various Shabbos hosts, on the way back to the Schusters' home in the Ezras Torah neighborhood.

Others, like Beryl Gershenfeld and Avraham Rockmill, took to the *beis medrash* like fish to water, and have been learning and teaching Torah for nearly half a century. They were drawn to Rabbi Schuster's table not by the scintillating *divrei Torah*, though there was never a meal without a great deal of Torah discussion, but because they were inspired by a genuinely pure soul, a Jew who fit the Gemara's description of *tocho k'baro*, one whose internal being was exactly the same as that presented to the world.

The roster of Shabbos guests inevitably changed over the years as *bachurim* married and started to build their own families. But once Reb Meir had established a relationship, he did not let go of it, often over a period of years and across continents. Joe Reback is an example.

After graduating Princeton with a degree in geological engineering, Joe took a job on an oil rig in the Gulf of Mexico off the Louisiana coast. His roommate turned out to be a Pentecostal Christian, who was soon holding enthusiastic prayer gatherings in their shared room. Though Joe eventually suggested that his roommate find another place to live, the experience of the prayer meetings gnawed at him for months afterwards. He envied those whose religious practice was to "speak in tongues," their awareness of the Creator, sense of true brotherhood, and selfless commitment to their cause — all things without parallel in his Jewish experience.

He decided to search for his own spiritual identity. Though his first inclination was to seek it out in Africa, rather than alarm his family, he decided to go to Israel first. After a month of picking grapefruits on a kibbutz, Joe decided to visit Jerusalem one Friday to view the "antiquities." Before leaving the kibbutz, he was told that he should wander around in front of the Kotel toward sunset, and Rabbi Schuster would find him and set him up for a Shabbos meal, which did happen, though not quite as envisioned.

Shabbos turned out to be very rainy, and one of the other guests at his Shabbos hosts invited Joe to return with him to the Ohr Somayach dorm rather than walk all the way back to his hostel in the Old City. He ended up staying Motzaei Shabbos as well.

Joe was packed and ready to return to his kibbutz on Sunday

morning when Rabbi Schuster showed up at the yeshivah to check up on him. The latter appeared shocked that Joe intended to return to his kibbutz, despite saying that he wanted to learn more about his heritage.

But something had struck a chord with Joe. On Saturday night, someone in the dorm had been singing Moshe Yess's song "My Zaidy," the tear-jerking ending of which goes, "Who will be the Zaidy of our children? Who will be their Zaidy if not we?" Though Joe saw himself as pretty close to fully assimilated, he did have a Zaidy and Bubby, his mother's parents, who lived in Williamsburg, and whom he loved very much. His Zaidy had passed away just a few weeks prior to his trip to Israel.

And so Joe did return to Ohr Somayach, after a few more weeks of picking grapefruits on the kibbutz. Over the next twelve years, Joe would return to Ohr Somayach and other yeshivos many times, and each time, Reb Meir would greet him warmly, as Joe brought him up to date on his peregrinations. Over that period of time, Joe would travel to Africa three times, visit a monastery in Greece, and, in his words, turn over many other stones — many best left unturned — on the way.

During a rough patch in his spiritual journey, Joe was living in Los Angeles when he heard a knock on the door around midnight. It was Rabbi Schuster. "How's it going, Joe?" Rabbi Schuster asked. Despite Joe's attempts to "jolly him up a bit," Reb Meir immediately saw through the façade, "Your *neshamah* is not a laughing matter, Reb Joe. I'm worried about you. You've got to get serious. Now's the time. Promise me?"

Joe did not sleep well that night. He was haunted by a series of questions, as he reflected on the twelve years since he had first met Rabbi Schuster: "Who is this man? Why is he in my life? What have I done to merit his unending concern for me?"

THAT ENCOUNTER WITH JOE BRINGS OUT A VERY IMPORTANT ASPECT of Rabbi Meir Schuster's effectiveness: He could push and give *tocha-*

**Giving Tochachah**
*chah* (rebuke) that the recipients would have accepted from no one else in the world because they knew, as Joe wrote, "No one has cared more deeply about my *neshamah* than Rav Meir Schuster."

On one of his tours of the Ohr Somayach *beis medrash*, he saw Reuven Eliyahu wasting his time. "When are you going to sit down and start learning?" Rabbi Schuster challenged him.

"If you can beat me in arm wrestling, I'll start learning," replied Reuven Eliyahu, who no doubt assumed that he would easily prevail based on his past as a star athlete. Rabbi Schuster accepted the challenge, and they moved to a side office of the *beis medrash*, where Rabbi Schuster proceeded to shock Reuven Eliyahu by flattening his arm in a matter of seconds.

Reb Meir pushed because he cared so deeply, but that care and concern was by no means confined to his charges' learning. Akiva Unger was a regular Shabbos guest of the Schusters'. At one point, Mrs. Schuster told him that she would assume he was coming every week, unless she heard from him otherwise. Akiva was a freelance photographer for a number of international news organizations, and spent a great deal of time in the West Bank photographing demonstrations, many of them violent. When Rabbi Schuster would come into the Aish HaTorah *beis medrash*, he would automatically check Akiva's seat to see whether he was there, and worry about him if he was not. He made repeated efforts to convince Akiva to stop accepting assignments in the West Bank.

After Akiva married, he and his wife experienced fertility issues, and they began taking in foster children. Though they did eventually have a healthy son of their own, the Ungers continued to foster many children — eight in all. Most people discouraged them from doing so. But Reb

Akiva Unger with one of his subjects, former Speaker of the House Newt Gringrich

Meir was always encouraging, perhaps because it was so easy for him to comprehend the desire to give to one's fellow Jews and guide them on the right path.

Chananel Weiner is convinced that Reb Meir could discern just by looking at him that he did not daven. He had been at Aish HaTorah for a few months, and prayer, as yet, played no part of his life. Though Reb Meir did not bring Chananel into the yeshivah, they had talked from time to time in the *beis medrash*. One day, Reb Meir grabbed him and took him to the Cardo in the Old City to purchase tefillin. The negotiations over price were conducted without Chananel's participation, and when they were done, Reb Meir told Chananel that they would split the cost of the tefillin.

And ever since that induction into the tefillin-owning class of Jews, Chananel has been wearing those tefillin. "Some people need an explanation; others need a push or pull. Rabbi Schuster knew by looking at me where I needed to be, and got me there," reflects Chananel.

Reb Asher Israel, whose parents frequently hosted Reb Meir in Boro Park, is involved in kiruv in Brooklyn. He once mentioned to Reb Meir that he had met someone who credited Reb Meir with bringing him close to Judaism. Reb Meir asked for the person's number, and called him.

Reb Meir yelled at him over the phone, "If you are not learning Torah, that's not being religious. It's worthless." The next time Reb Asher met the young man, he had changed radically. When Reb Asher asked him what had happened, he explained simply, "Rabbi Schuster really gave it to me."

Inspired by Rabbi Schuster's success in giving *tochachah*, Reb Asher tried the same with someone with whom he was working. The reaction, however, was "terrible."

"You shall not hate your brother in your heart; you shall reprove your fellow, and do not bear sin because of him" (*Vayikra* 19:17). There is no greater expression of love for one's fellow Jew than to reprove him and set him on the path to growth and closeness to Hashem. But for that reproof to be effective, the love must already be established and clear to the recipient of the reproof.

With Reb Meir, it always was.

*Chapter Eleven*
# THE REAL DEAL

O NE REASON THAT RABBI SCHUSTER INSPIRED THE TRUST HE
did is that no one ever doubted that what he preached is how
he lived: *tocho k'baro.* That
quality expressed itself most clearly in
his *tefillah* (prayer). One of the apparent paradoxes of Reb Meir is how
someone so shy and often tongue-tied
when speaking to other people could
be so effusive and uninhibited when
speaking to the Ribbono shel Olam.

He was the "least inhibited person
in davening I ever saw," says Zev
(Bill) Kowitz. His prayer was physical,
filled with gesticulating, as he would
point his finger upward, imploring,
demanding, and fairly jumping up
and down. As reticent as he was about
being in the spotlight, he preferred
to daven in the front, lest he be disturbed by others turning around to
stare at him as he prayed. And when

Rabbi Schuster davening

he davened at the Kotel, he would usually try to assemble a minyan so that he could lead the *tefillos* (prayers).

Most of us, when we witness someone davening in an ecstatic fashion, cannot help thinking that there is something not quite right about the person davening that way, and sometimes suspect him of making a show of his intense fervor to impress others. No such suspicion ever attached to Rabbi Schuster. Anyone who observed him davening recognized immediately that he was simply transported "to another place," in the words of one of his annual hosts.

Just watching him pray could be a life-changing experience. Gershon Fern says, "When you saw him davening, you wanted to be part of that," i.e., part of a world where such a close relationship to Hashem is possible. "I became a different person because I saw him daven."

Yerucham Liss describes meeting a "nondescript" religious man at the Kotel who asked him if he was interested in spending a Shabbos with a religious family. Yerucham took Rabbi Schuster's number, but ended up leaving Jerusalem before Shabbos. Six months later, he was back in Jerusalem at a hotel with 150 other volunteers working in development towns around the country. When the same "nondescript" man approached him again, Yerucham took his number a second time.

But the nonstop partying, punctuated only by an occasional lecture

Gershon Fern (l.) and Baruch Mytelka (r.) with Rabbi Schuster

or tour of Jerusalem, left Yerucham with little inclination to take Rabbi Schuster up on his offer. Only when the group was moved from the luxury hotel at which they were staying and transferred to a seedy hostel did Yerucham give more serious thought to contacting Rabbi Schuster. As soon as he learned that no meals would be served at the hostel and that he would be sharing one room with numerous strangers, Yerucham found himself suddenly filled with religious fervor and called Rabbi Schuster.

Arriving late at the Kotel on Erev Shabbos, Yerucham was invited to join Rabbi Schuster's family for the meal. His initial impression of Rabbi Schuster remained intact until he saw him daven:

"Then it became suddenly obvious that he was not a typical chareidi Jew — in fact he was not a typical anything. The way he entreated, begged, and supplicated G-d drove home two compelling truths — one, that there is a G-d; two, this man knows Him well.

"There was no disconnect between Meir Schuster and Meir Schuster's beliefs — what he believed, he lived. I was also a bit disconcerted by the suspicion that I might well be one of the subjects about which he was supplicating the Al-mighty," says Yerucham.

Another young Jew described the impact of Rabbi Schuster's davening more succinctly: "It was impossible to listen to Rabbi Schuster lead a minyan at the Kotel and not look around at the end to check whether Mashiach was coming."

Rebbetzin Batsheva Berger, whose husband, Rabbi Simcha Bunim (Benny) Berger, was one of the principal lecturers at Heritage House, once found herself on a transatlantic flight with Rabbi Schuster. At some point, he rose from his seat and went to the front of the cabin to daven. Rebbetzin Berger watched transfixed by the way his whole body was shaking as he davened. "He was obviously engaged in an intense discussion with HaKadosh Baruch Hu," she remembers. And from that day on, she considered Rabbi Schuster, "my rebbi in davening."

Spencer Ross was working for Aish-St. Louis when Rabbi Schuster came into the office one day. A minyan for Minchah gathered, after which Spencer asked Rabbi Schuster how he always managed to daven with such *kavannah* (intent). Rabbi Schuster was genuinely puzzled by the question. "If the *Eibershter* is up there," he said, "how could you not have *kavannah*?"

He believed in the *Eibershter*, and he believed that one can achieve nothing in this world without His help. Prayer was one of the best ways

Rabbi Schuster looking upward as he davened

to solicit and merit that help. Thus he approached every *tefillah* with joy: He would, for instance, clap his hands in excitement before *bensching*.

While fundraising in America, he often davened at sunrise in his room. At least one host reported that his davening could be heard two floors above. He was afraid to stand above Rabbi Schuster's room when he heard him imploring, "Ribbono shel Olam! Ribbono shel Olam!" lest he share the fate of the birds burned when flying above the Tanna Rabbi Yonasan ben Uziel when he learned Torah (*Succah* 28a). Moishe Mendlowitz, who accompanied Rabbi Schuster on one fundraising trip, was sure that they would be evicted from their hotel because of the loudness of his davening.

Equally remarkable as the volume, animation, and intensity with which he davened and *bensched* was the consistency. It did not matter whether he davened in public as the *shaliach tzibbur* or alone in his room, whether it was a weekday *bensching* or the Yamim Noraim, every word of his *tefillah*, as described by Rabbi Avraham Edelstein, was said with the same intensity as the Neilah prayers on Yom Kippur, when we beseech Hashem one final time for forgiveness as the Heavenly gates of repentance close.

Rabbi Schuster spent his life encouraging young Jews to learn more about their heritage by studying Torah. When he did so, he was the **Learning** antithesis of those fathers of Jewish humor pressing their sons to learn more while failing to do so themselves.

No matter how busy or long his day, he always made sure to leave a fixed place in it for Torah study, and that time was inviolable. According to one long-time *chavrusa*, Reb Meir Rosenberg, he always learned standing up to prevent himself from falling asleep, and even that stratagem did not always prove adequate. Once he was already in the hospital, scheduled for hernia surgery the next morning, when he had Rosenberg pick him up for their *chavrusashaft* and bring him back afterward. Having been prepped for surgery the next morning was not a reason to miss study time with his *chavrusa*.

Rabbi Yirmiyahu Abramov learned together with Reb Meir for close to twenty years, and for several years, they learned both in the morning at Aish HaTorah and last thing at night over the phone. When Rabbi Abramov returned home late at night, the inevitable message was: Rabbi Schuster called over and over wanting to know when you were coming home. And no matter how late it was, he would not accept any excuses from Rabbi Abramov about being too tired to learn.

In the '70s and '80s, when throngs of young backpackers were to be found at the Kotel at almost any time of the day and every season of the year, Reb Meir had to content himself with a morning *chavrusashaft* with Michael Kaufman at the latter's home in the Old City of between forty-five and seventy-five minutes, and another one in the evening.

But as the crowds at the Kotel began to thin in the mid-'90s, Reb Meir extended his learning *seder*. He and Moishe Mendlowitz, the night manager at Heritage House, would learn for three hours in the morning, from 10:00 a.m. to 1:00 p.m., and reconvene at Heritage House in the early evening, after which Reb Meir would daven at the Kotel and then return home for a phone *chavrusashaft* with Rabbi Abramov. Reb Meir's learning with Moishe Mendlowitz was often punctuated by a good deal of shouting: At one point, it was politely suggested to them that they should learn in a side room rather than in the Aish HaTorah *beis medrash*.

Rabbi Schuster was not infrequently described by those closest to him as the "stubbornest person in the world," and that quality characterized his Gemara learning as well. As Rabbi Abramov puts it, "he brought the same tenacity and passion to his learning that he brought to everything he did." He would not go on until he was sure that he had

Rabbi Schuster and Michael Kaufman learning together.

understood the *sugya*. If he had a difficulty, he insisted on pursuing it until he had an answer.[1]

Just as in Ner Israel, Rabbi Schuster's learning *sedarim* allowed no time for any conversation apart from the topic at hand. Though Michael Kaufman was a *de facto* partner in Reb Meir's work in the Old City, and Moishe Mendlowitz and Rabbi Abramov were work colleagues, they never discussed anything unconnected to the Gemara before them. Whether the learning session was long or short, at the end "you felt you had accomplished something," says Mr. Kaufman.

THE SCHUSTERS' NEIGHBOR IN EZRAS TORAH, RABBI YOSSI ABRAMS, lists two reasons why he could never have predicted Rabbi Schuster's

**Dikduk in Halachah**

success in working with Jews far removed from religious observance. The first was his natural shyness, and the second his numerous stringencies in halachic observance. In the end, however, both served to make him more effective. His inability to speak with easy familiarity — e.g., "Hi, how are you doing?" — made it easier for those who followed him to destinations they had never heard of to trust him. And his stringencies in halachah were another aspect of how dear the life he was "selling" was to him personally.

---

1. Michael Kaufman.

One of Reb Meir's stringencies was that he insisted on being prepared for Shabbos and ready to greet the Shabbos Queen well before the onset of Shabbos. He was always careful to participate in preparing the Shabbos food. Even when he was fundraising abroad, he would always ask his hostess to let him assist in the Shabbos preparations.[2]

One time, he was staying with the Israel family in Boro Park when he received a phone call on Friday from the secretary of a major philanthropist, with whom he had been seeking a meeting for some time. Indeed meeting this particular philanthropist was one of the main purposes of that particular trip to the United States, and Reb Meir was flying back to Israel on Motzaei Shabbos.

The secretary informed him that her boss would be available to meet with him in Manhattan at 3:00 p.m. Though that meeting would have provided adequate time to return to Boro Park for Shabbos, Reb Meir was very scrupulous about being fully prepared for Shabbos long in advance in order to accept the Shabbos Queen in a state of tranquility. He had the *minhag* of accepting Shabbos early and of extending it on Saturday night.[3] As important as the meeting was to him, it was not worth departing from the habits of a lifetime.

In Rabbi Schuster's mind, the success of his efforts depended first and foremost on the purity of his intentions and the degree to which he fulfilled the rabbinic maxim "Make His Will your will" (*Pirkei Avos* 2:4). And that being the case, no contribution, no matter how large, could be worth the price of diminished *kavod Shabbos*.

---

2. Mrs. Shaindel Steinberg.

3. Mrs. Schuster discovered that *minhag* early in married life. One of the first times she made Shabbos, she asked Reb Meir to set up the *blech*, as her father had always done, and he told her that he had already accepted Shabbos.

*Chapter Twelve*

# JUST ONE SHABBOS

USIC PRODUCER DAVID NACHMAN GOLDING ("DING") recently revealed the origins of Mordechai Ben David's enduring classic, "Just One Shabbos:[1] "On one of our trips to Eretz Yisrael in the early '80s, MBD and I were amazed by Rabbi Meir Schuster. Every Friday night, he would place at least dozens, and up to hundreds, of young Jews who had never experienced a true Shabbos meal with a family in a warm, *frum* environment.... [I]t didn't take long for MBD to write the lyrics: "Western Wall on Friday night/His first time ever there/Strapped into his knapsack/With his long and curly hair....'"

Rabbi Schuster's first forays into approaching strangers at the Kotel involved offering them an authentic Shabbos experience, and those invitations remained a staple of his efforts. The sight of him leading groups of fifty or more through the Damascus Gate to nearby neighborhoods of Jerusalem was a common one.

Arranging the Shabbos meals consisted of two parts: finding those interested in experiencing a proper Shabbos meal and lining up the hosts for each Shabbos.

Joe Reback describes the experience from the point of view of those on their first adventure with Rabbi Schuster, albeit on an inclement

---

1. *Mishpacha Magazine*, December 5, 2018.

night. The same scene was repeated hundreds of times over the years:

"There is awkward silence as we trudge through the Arab quarter of the Old City and continue up toward Geulah. The rain has picked up during this time, and we are all cold and wet. A few of us in this group of strangers glance at each other, as we proceed behind the enigmatic figure leading the way, as if to say, 'Are we nuts?' But we are all young and looking for an adventure, and we have found one. As we zig and zag through the back alleys and streets of Meah Shearim, Geulah, Maalot Dafna, Sanhedria Murchevet, Reb Meir drops us off, one by one, at various homes along the way. The rabbi does not say much, if anything, during this magical mystery tour. And his answer to the question 'How much longer?' is always the same: 'Another five minutes.' But, what are our options, really? We have no idea where we are, so we keep trudging along awaiting some dramatic endpoint to this adventure."

Over the years, the number of hosts reached in the hundreds, as families' availability changed with the ages and needs of their own children or as they moved to other locales no longer within walking distance of the Kotel. On Thursday night, the regular hosts would receive a call. When they answered the phone, there was silence on the other end, usually broken only when the recipient of the call said, "Is that you, Rabbi Schuster?"[2] At that point, Rabbi Schuster would ask whether they could take guests that Shabbos and, if so, how many. Those mentioned below constitute no more than a cross-section of the different types of families and include many of those who teamed with Reb Meir over a decade or more.

One of those hosts, Michael Kaufman, was the closest thing to a partner that Rabbi Schuster had, with the possible exception of Rabbi Avraham Edelstein. He personally funded a number of the Heritage House programs. And from the time he and his wife Marcia moved into the Old City in 1980, they hosted more Leil Shabbos guests than any other family. Host families in the Old City became ever more important after the opening of Heritage House, as those staying at the hostels did not want a lengthy trek to and from their Shabbos hosts.

The Kaufmans often had thirty to forty guests for Shabbos dinner, especially during the summer months when tourism was at a peak. Michael Kaufman had devoted much thought to making the experience as effective as possible. The Friday night *divrei Torah* rarely related to

---

2. Rabbi Dovid Orlofsky has said that Rabbi Schuster was the only person who identified himself on the phone by remaining silent.

the parashah. Instead they were chosen for their impact on those possibly experiencing their first full Shabbos. Once Mr. Kaufman discovered an effective presentation, he stuck with it.

Every meal included a discussion of intermarriage. But Mr. Kaufman would not initiate the discussion; he made sure that it flowed naturally from the conversation by asking each of the guests to discuss what they considered the greatest contemporary threats to the Jewish people. Inevitably, at least one, and usually several, mentioned intermarriage. Each meal would conclude with a push for those present to become as knowledgeable about their Judaism as they were about the diverse subjects they were then studying or had studied.

The effort put into the presentation of Shabbos, the singing, the bringing of everyone into the discussion, paid off. Seth Damski, for instance, remembers that at least eight of those with whom he went to his first Shabbos meal at the Kaufmans' became fully observant. One of those, Rabbi David Begoun, was then a war correspondent for the *San Francisco Chronicle* in the Balkans. In 2008, he and his wife founded the L'Chaim Center in the Chicago suburb of Deerfield. Another guest that night now offers popular parenting classes in Lakewood.

Fittingly, the Kaufmans learned of the passing of Rabbi Schuster while in America on the way to the *chasunah* in Crown Heights of Yehudah Aber, the fourth of nine children of Rabbi Leib and Rebbetzin Gavriella Aber. Three decades earlier Rebbetzin Gavriella, then Leslie, was dropped off by Reb Meir at the Kaufmans' home overlooking the Kotel on a rainy weekday. She was then in the one-year program at Tel Aviv University and focused on learning Hebrew.

At that point in her life, Leslie had never heard of Moshe Rabbeinu or Shabbos, and she did not know that the Torah was the unique possession of the Jewish people. The decision to learn Hebrew was her first conscious decision to do something Jewish in her life. At the time she decided to spend a year in Israel, she did not even know where it was on the map, despite having enjoyed an international childhood, living in a number of foreign countries.

As she sat in the Kaufmans' living room, Leslie maintained a guarded posture, until Michael Kaufman mentioned that he was working on a book called *Feminism and Judaism*, and suggested that she take a look at a few chapters and offer her feedback. He then invited her for the Shabbos evening meal.

She would later remember, "You immediately saw my reluctance to open up, and you asked for my advice about your book on feminism. My interest was piqued. The subject of feminism appealed to me since I was into women's lib. I was sure your writing would be full of things I could poke holes in. I got a huge shock when it made so much sense. And then you invited me for dinner."[3]

That Shabbos was a life-changing experience for Leslie, starting with the blessing of the children. Over the years, Michael Kaufman writes, "many a baal teshuvah has told me that, more than anything else, it was the *berachah* (blessing) of the children, viewed from across the flames of the Shabbos candles on the table, that first prompted their return to Yiddishkeit."[4]

Certainly, it was the children who most impressed Leslie: "When I saw the family dynamics, with the kids genuinely pleasant and helpful around the Shabbos table, it affected me deeply. They were so kind and polite to everyone and respectful of their parents. I kept looking for faults and blemishes, suspecting that they were putting on an act of some sort. But no, children couldn't be such good actors for very long.... I decided then and there that I wanted to be a parent of whom my future children would be proud. I wanted a home like this!"

Rebbetzin Aber summarizes the impact of that Shabbos on her future development: "Every time I came upon a mitzvah that seemed like too much trouble, or that I hesitated to adopt, I realized I was being cruel to my future kids. Was it their fault that I was lazy? I knew that if I was going to adopt a pick-and-choose Judaism, my poor future kids wouldn't fit in as *frum* Jews.... So I pushed myself to do each new thing I learned."[5]

The three and half decades since that first Shabbos have been eventful for Rebbetzin Aber. She and her husband were Chabad *shlichim* in Sydney, Australia, for thirty years. While in Sydney, Rebbetzin Aber formed an organization, Women for Life, to encourage mikveh use in Australia. In Sydney, mikveh use has increased by 400% since the founding of Women for Life, and today most Jewish brides receive formal instruction in *taharas hamishpachah*. She also created a workbook for learning Torah with Rashi and worksheets for teachers that are in use in schools around the world.[6] Two years ago, the Abers moved to Crown Heights, where Rebbetzin Aber became the principal of the

---

3. Kaufman, *In One Era, Out the Other:* A Memoir of a 20th-21st Century Jewish Life, p. 365.
4. Ibid., p. 367.
5. Ibid., p. 369.
6. Ibid., pp. 366-67.

Rabbi Leib and Rebbetzin Gavriella Aber and family.

Chabad middle school, Machon Chana, where she continues fulfilling her deepest mission — "sharing the joy of being a *frum* Jew."[7]

Leslie was hardly the furthest away from anything Jewish at the time she first came to the Kaufmans' for Shabbos. That honor likely belongs to Marnie, who was engaged to be married to a Mormon young man, who was committed to being a Mormon missionary. He was the one who suggested, in the midst of traveling in Europe, that they should come to Israel, on the grounds that a visit to the Holy Land would provide an inspiring start to their missionary work.

Like so many other tourists, they went to the Kotel on Friday night and there met Rabbi Schuster. Marnie forthrightly told Rabbi Schuster that she was Jewish but John was a Christian. He nevertheless offered them a Shabbos meal, which they accepted after Rabbi Schuster assured John that it was free. Because it was a "slow" winter Shabbos, Michael Kaufman agreed to accept the couple after being fully briefed by Rabbi Schuster. Michael's first move was to separate the affianced couple, putting Marnie next to him and John at the other end of the table.

Marnie was enthralled by the discussion, the singing, and as the guests were getting up to leave, she told Michael how much she had

---

7. Shortly after her marriage, Rebbetzin Aber discovered from a relative that on her mother's side she is descended from Rabbi Moshe Isserles, the Rema, whose glosses on *Shulchan Aruch* are definitive halachah for Ashkenazi Jews. On her father's side she is descended from the Shelah HaKadosh.

enjoyed every moment. With nothing to lose and no time before John approached to fetch Marnie, Michael responded, "That's wonderful, Marnie. But you have to know that if you remain a Jew, you'll have this experience again and again every week of your life. And if you marry John, this will be the last time for you, as long as you live."

All the way back to where they were staying, Marnie's head was awhirl, and when they arrived, she told John that she needed to go for a walk by herself. She walked around Jerusalem all night. In the morning, she informed John that their engagement was over.

Marnie returned to Los Angeles and became involved with Aish HaTorah-LA. Eventually, she became one of the thousands of young Jews over the years for whom Dick Horowitz, Aish's principal local supporter, has sponsored a trip to Israel to learn. Two years after that fateful Shabbos, Marnie called Michael Kaufman to ask whether she could come over and thank him for saving her life. Soon thereafter, she married a student at Aish HaTorah, and together they host their own Shabbos guests.[8]

On at least one occasion, Michael Kaufman made the hand-off to Rabbi Schuster rather than the other way around. Mordechai (then

Rabbi Mordechai Zuckerman and his eight sons

---

8. Ibid, pp. 25-30.

Eduordo) Zuckerman was at the Kotel on Leil Shabbos, shortly after completing his university studies in architecture and making aliyah from his native Argentina. He was entranced by the scene in front of him when Michael Kaufman approached him and invited him for the evening meal. Just the fact that there were Jews eager to host strangers for Shabbos already made Eduordo feel good, and he was even more thrilled to discover that there were thirty or so other guests, who, like him, appeared to be experiencing their first Shabbos. Even when the hours-long meal had ended, most of the group sat in the living room continuing the discussion. At the end of the evening, Eduordo asked Mr. Kaufman, "I want this. How can I have this? What do I need to do?"

Michael connected him to Rabbi Schuster, who took him to Ohr Somayach, where an Argentinian *chavrusa* was arranged for him. He ended up remaining five years. In time, the Kaufmans hosted his *vort*. During the festivities, Mordechai turned to Michael and asked him how he could ever repay him and his family for what they had done for him. Michael answered: Be *mekarev* one Jew a year. Since then, Mordechai calls Michael Kaufman annually to tell him that he has more than fulfilled his promise.

The hosts whom Rabbi Schuster called upon were a diverse group. They ranged from recently minted baalei teshuvah to Yiddish-speaking families in Meah Shearim. The one thing they had in common was an eagerness to share their Shabbos table with complete strangers for no other reason than that they were fellow Jews. And that openness itself was part of the power of the Shabbos experience: the recognition of being part of a Jewish people that feels bound to and takes responsibility for one another.

The renowned author Sara Yoheved Rigler[9] and her musician husband Leib took two or three guests every Friday night from the mid-'80s. Her life story, which includes more than a decade in an ashram in India prior to rediscovering her Judaism, related directly to many of their Shabbos guests, especially the spiritual seekers who were themselves on their way to India. And Leib's background as a musician, singer, and songwriter ensured that the Shabbos table was filled with music.

Mrs. Chaya Weisberg has run the Heritage House women's hostel, together with her husband, Rabbi Matan Mordechai, from 2004 until

---

9. Author of, among other books, *Holy Woman: The road to greatness of Rebbetzin Chaya Sara Kramer,* published by ArtScroll/Mesorah Publications.

the present.[10] She once sent a young woman passing through Israel on her way to India, with her boyfriend, to meet Sara Yoheved Rigler. The ostensible purpose of the meeting was to discuss what to see and do while in India with someone with intimate knowledge of the country.

On the basis of that two-hour meeting, the young woman, whose prior exposure to Judaism was nearly non-existent — the Chanukah candle-lighting at the hostel was a lifetime first for her — changed her Sunday-morning plans in order to go to Neve Yerushalayim, and afterwards canceled her Sunday-night flight to India. After several weeks in the hostel, she moved into Neve, and eventually became one of the most successful *madrichot* at the women's hostel.

Besides introducing the beauty of Shabbos, ideally the Shabbos hosts would learn enough about their guests to direct them further if they were inspired to explore Judaism. One Shabbos, Mrs. Rigler discerned that one of their guests, then a student in the one-year program at Hebrew University, was both very philosophical and spiritual. She set her up to learn with her friend and neighbor in the Jewish Quarter, Sara Yehudit Schneider, who was just embarking on her path as a Torah teacher. The study partnership clicked, and that young woman became religious and married a British Breslover chassid.

In that particular case, the Riglers remained in touch throughout their Shabbos guest's religious development. But much more frequent were those instances where a woman wearing a tichel and pushing an infant in a stroller would spot Sara Yoheved in the square of the Jewish Quarter and introduce herself: "Hi, you probably don't remember me. But my first Shabbos was at your house."

In general, the hosts had minimal direct contact with Rabbi Schuster, other than the Thursday night phone call, or on those occasions when he personally dropped the guests off at the door. That was true of the Riglers as well, with one exception. But it was one that made a deep impression on Sara Yoheved.

Rabbi Schuster had decided that one of the most dedicated counselors at the Heritage House women's hostel was not well suited for the job. Sara Yoheved was angered by his decision, and organized a few other Old City residents to boycott taking any more Shabbos guests until Rabbi Schuster rehired the young woman. The next time Rabbi Schuster saw her in the Jewish Quarter, he called her over to talk. He

---

10. In 2010, the Weisbergs purchased the women's hostel from Dov Friedberg. They have continued to run it ever since under the Heritage House name.

explained to her that he had his reasons for the firing, and that his responsibility was first and foremost to the guests at Heritage House. Then he added with respect to her boycott, quietly and without rancor, "That's not the way we do things." In retrospect, Mrs. Rigler had to admit that he had been right about the unsuitability of the counselor in question. But above all, she was struck by the combination of gentleness he showed in reproving her, and his firmness in sticking to his position.

At the other end of the spectrum from the Riglers was the Hirsch family of the Batei Ungarin neighborhood, just off of Rechov Meah Shearim. Little in the Hirsch home would have reminded their guests of their own homes. The men and women sat in two separate rooms — the living room and the kitchen. Rebbetzin Hirsch could converse in English, but her husband did not speak a word of English. He communicated solely through smiles, hand signals, and Yiddish. But, insists Rebbetzin Hirsch, "they understood him."

Undoubtedly, there were first-time guests who took umbrage at the separation, though given the small size of the apartment not everyone could have fit at one table or even in the less than capacious living room.

Sensitive guests also noticed, however, how a family obviously not rich in material resources was eager to share what they had with them. Rebbetzin Hirsch's family was originally from Vienna, a cosmopolitan center for Eastern European Jewry, and her childhood Shabbos table was always filled with guests who were in Vienna for one reason or another. "Guests are a *matanah* (present) from *Shamayim* (Heaven)," according to Rebbetzin Hirsch. "That's how I was raised and that's how I raised my children."

About one thing the Hirsches' Shabbos guests could have no doubt: At the end of the Shabbos meal, they knew they had experienced something totally authentic — a Shabbos meal that would have been instantly recognizable to most of their great-grandparents. Many of the Hirsches' guests returned to them numerous times, and some have even brought their own children to bask in the atmosphere where they first experienced a Shabbos.

The Shabbos hosts varied not only in backgrounds but also in age, from young kollel couples to large families. Among the first of Rabbi Schuster's regular Shabbos hosts were Rabbi Asa Wittow and his wife Chana. Reb Asa and Rabbi Schuster were close in age, and came from similar backgrounds. They both came from non-observant families and had become religious largely on their own: Reb Meir in Milwaukee and Reb Asa in Denver.

Reb Asa also served as a vital cog in Rabbi Schuster's operations. When he was not learning in Yeshiva Torah Ore or serving as the driver for the Rosh Yeshivah, Rabbi Chaim Pinchas Scheinberg, Reb Asa earned a livelihood as a travel agent at Ideal Tours. Certain airlines like TWA and Tower Air, both now defunct, were eager for Ideal Tours' business, and Rabbi Wittow was sometimes able to convince them to rewrite existing tickets or alter them at a reduced fee for those who wished to extend their time learning in yeshivos or seminaries.[11] That was particularly important during the height of the teshuvah revolution because TWA had a cheap one-year, round-the-world ticket favored by backpackers.

Nor was changing tickets the only way in which Rabbi Wittow assisted Reb Meir. In the early days, Rabbi Schuster was frequently on the Hebrew University campus trying to interest students in the overseas programs to find time for yeshivah studies while they were in Israel. A group of students in the preparatory Hebrew-language ulpan on the Hebrew University's Givat Ram campus approached Rabbi Schuster and told him they were interested in more intensive Torah studies than were available to them on campus. None of them was fully religiously observant, but they were all curious about Torah. Rabbi Schuster's response was to set them up for a weekly Chumash/Rashi *shiur* with Reb Asa in his home. One member of that study group, Rabbi Reuven Tradburks, served for many years as a rabbi in Birmingham, Alabama, and Toronto, and is today the Israel representative of the Rabbinical Council of America.

The Wittows were among the few Shabbos hosts who always welcomed their guests for the entire Shabbos. When their children were young, they did not mind sleeping on the living room floor to clear a bedroom for guests. And when that was not possible, the Wittows found sleeping space for their guests at the home of one or more of their Mattersdorf neighbors. On at least one occasion that resulted in a humorous misunderstanding. After the Shabbos meal, the Wittows were escorting a young couple to separate dwellings, when the male asked if that was required, as they were married. (They were not yet using the same family name.) That couple ended up staying with

---

11. Rabbi Wittow was not always able to do so. And on those occasions Reb Meir purchased new tickets, and assured the holders that he had been able to arrange a new ticket through his connections to the airlines.

the Wittows for a few days, and both have been Torah educators in Jerusalem for decades.

The Greenwalds, Rabbi Zechariah and Linda, lived near the Schusters in the early years of their marriage, when Zechariah was still learning in kollel. And they took Friday night guests nearly every week. The Greenwalds were not alone in sometimes discovering the impact of those Shabbos meals only years later.

One Shabbos guest whom Rabbi Schuster personally brought to the Greenwalds' harbored aspirations to be a cantor, though he was not yet religiously observant. He obviously enjoyed that first Shabbos, as he returned two or three times more after he had begun learning at Ohr Somayach. And then the Greenwalds lost all contact with him.

Sixteen years later, Rabbi Greenwald received a call on Erev Pesach from that same young man, now married and with a number of children. He told Rabbi Greenwald that his family had recently made aliyah, and that his expectant wife might deliver imminently. He wanted to know whether they could come for the Seder. Given their evident desperation, Rabbi Greenwald felt he had little choice but to agree, despite his own large family. The family arrived two hours before the *Chag* was to begin. Not that Reb Zechariah would have had any chance of recognizing their former guest, now attired in full chassidishe dress and with a family in tow. The fact, however, that a former Shabbos guest felt able to call out of the blue sixteen years later, and with no communication in the intervening years, attests to the power of the contacts developed over a Shabbos table early in one's religious journey.

Among those who kept up connections with the largest number of Shabbos guests over the years and had the greatest impact, the Lasters, Paul and Sharon, must rank near the top of the list. Those who spent their first or early Shabbosos in the Laster home, in Jerusalem's Bukharian neighborhood, include Rabbi Yitzchak Feldman, the rav of Palo Alto's Emek HaBeracha shul for a quarter-century, author and seminary head Rabbi Jeremy Kagan, and Rabbi Yosef Edelstein of MEOR at George Washington University.[12]

Paul and Sharon combined fascinating life stories, including that of how they met, genuine warmth, lots of singing with their two sons, and

---

12. All three are graduates of either Yale or Harvard University. Paul Laster was, inter alia, confrontative, and that would have suited graduates of America's leading universities in those days, when the university's mission was still to teach students how to think, not impose an orthodoxy of what to think.

Paul Laster (back) in uniform in the Ohr Somayach *beis medrash*

a large dash of intellectual stimulation. Paul's own story made it easy to prod the guests to think hard about what it means to be Jewish. What is the significance of Israel, as the nation-state of the Jewish people? Indeed what is the Jewish people and why does its continued collective existence matter?

Paul arrived in Israel shortly after the 1967 Six Day War, having just graduated from the University of Virginia Law School. Swept up by the euphoria of those days, he remained for several years, until returning to Brandeis University for an M.A. in Jewish education. His first job in Israel was with the Jewish Agency, preparing emissaries for the Diaspora. That job forced upon him the question of what claims, if any, Israel has on Jews living around the world.

After the 1973 Yom Kippur War, which left the country demoralized, Paul returned to Israel and became an educational officer in the IDF, charged with instilling Jewish identity in combat officers. He decided on his own that the yeshivos were one logical place to look for answers, and he would bring groups of officers on a regular basis to Dvar Yerushalayim and Ohr Somayach.

He was still not religious himself: He refused to wear a yarmulke even in the *beis medrash*. But the more of those day-long meetings he participated in — seventy-eight in all — between IDF officers and former soldiers who had become baalei teshuvah and their mentors, the more it occurred to him that the latter had answers to the questions that had long plagued him. A few years later, already over 40 years old, he entered the *beis medrash* at Yeshiva Chofetz Chaim in Jerusalem's Sanhedria Murchevet neighborhood as a rank beginner, and there he remained for the next three decades.

Ron Rinat, a former naval commander, who participated in many of the discussions in the Ohr Somayach *beis medrash*, remembers, "Paul had an unbelievable power to show the IDF participants that they had not begun to think about the most fundamental issues of life in any serious fashion." It was an ability that he subsequently directed at his Shabbos guests. But it was all done with such Southern charm — the mellifluous Virginian accent he never shed, the unsurpassed raconteurial abilities with which he drew them into his story — that they barely knew what had hit them when he showed his guests that his story and his questions were theirs as well, with his on-target, prodding cross-examinations.

Yet many of those guests returned again and again — even one who remembers crying in the bathroom on his first visit from the emotional upheaval he was going through. They were drawn by both Paul and Sharon's open hospitality, clarity of vision, and capacity for active listening. And because they knew that the questioning to which they were subjected came from a place of real concern for them, not out of any desire of Paul's to prove himself smarter than they were.

Finally, mention must be made of the Machlis family. Rabbi Mordechai Machlis and his wife Henny *a"h* regularly hosted one hundred Shabbos guests in their very average-size Jerusalem apartment next door to Ohr Somayach, and sometimes up to 150, if the weather allowed spreading out of doors. Because of the Machlis unlimited generosity and hospitality, Rabbi Schuster always knew that if all else failed he had a wonderful home available to bring any of those he had not placed.[13]

The sheer generosity of the Machlis family Shabbos operation overwhelmed many a guest and left them with a completely new perspective on observant Jews. But the way that Rabbi Machlis ran the Shabbos table, at least in the view of Dena Estrin, who not infrequently brought

---

13. A fascinating full-length biography of Rebbetzin Henny Machlis, *Love With Emunah and Chicken Soup* by Sara Yoheved Rigler, has been published by ArtScroll/Mesorah Publications.

guests at Heritage House to their home, also provided a model for doing kiruv. Rabbi Machlis eschewed, in Mrs. Estrin's words, the role of "host-as-sovereign-over-the-religious-kingdom" speaking down to the uninformed plebeians. Instead he engaged in an exchange of views in fulfillment of the Sages' principle, "Who is wise? One who learns from every person" (*Pirkei Avos* 2:1). By encouraging the guests to participate fully he left them with a much more lasting impact.[14]

Reading the accounts of those who came to lives of Torah and mitzvos through Rabbi Schuster at the website established in his merit, one is struck by how many of those accounts begin with the first Leil Shabbos meal and the chord that was struck, whether by the family ambience, the festive table settings, the flickering Shabbos *licht*. No one believed in the power of that experience or did more to introduce thousands of young Jews to that power than Rabbi Meir Schuster.

---

14. Estrin, *It Happened at Heritage House*, pp. 204-5.

# *Part III*

# HERITAGE HOUSE

## Chapter Thirteen
# HERITAGE HOUSE -
# THE NEED

THE OPENING OF HERITAGE HOUSE, WITH SEPARATE HOSTEL facilities for men and women, in the summer of 1984 represented a dramatic new step in Rabbi Schuster's activities. Instead of operating solo, as he had for more than a decade, he would now be responsible for heading two institutions, not just serving as a feeder for the institutions of others. Those institutions would require staffs to reach their maximum potential, and those staffs would have to be paid. In short, Rabbi Schuster now became a fundraiser as well.

What drove him to make such a dramatic shift? For one thing, the Arab and Christian hostels, in which a large percentage of Jewish kids coming to Jerusalem stayed, had long been a source of anguish to him. But as long as the only way to prevent the backpackers from staying there was to convince them to go to a yeshivah or seminary, he was limited in what he could do to combat the problem.

For most of those with whom he came into contact, the bar — going straight to a yeshivah or seminary — was simply too high. But by offering the backpackers a hostel that was at once free and a good deal safer than the competition, he had the potential to dramatically cut into the number of Jewish young people staying in Arab or Christian hostels.

At the same time, he could provide a place in which young Jews could explore their heritage at their own pace in an environment that was at once warm and encouraging.

The idea of a hostel had long been on Rabbi Schuster's mind. In an article in *The Jewish Observer* of May-June 1980, "The Teshuvah Solicitors," Rabbi Hillel Goldberg had explored the need for Jewish hostels based on his conversations with a number of those working the Kotel and its environs, chief among them Rabbi Schuster. He wrote: "Thus, the teshuvah solicitors believe that there is a real need for, besides the yeshivos, an institution less intense than a yeshivah — a place like a hostel, a place where one can come and go, can learn periodically but not continuously, can grow at a slow pace — but where rabbis and teachers and Torah literature and classes are available at all times."

Seth Damski was one of thousands who might never have found their way to yeshivah without the intermediary step of Heritage House. With enough credits to graduate from Harvard in three years, he took a year off after his second year. Most of his Jewish friends growing up in Miami had been to Israel, but he had never been able to afford the trip. But after working as a waiter in London for several months, he had saved enough to visit Israel.

He arrived in Israel via Egypt and the Sinai, and found himself in Jerusalem late on Friday, where he learned that there would be no buses to Tel Aviv the next day. So he took a room at a hostel near the Damascus Gate.

On Friday evening, he followed the instructions in his guidebook to go to the Kotel. Standing at the divider between the Kotel Plaza and the area for prayer and watching the proceedings below, he was tapped by "an awkward-looking guy," who pointed to a group of about sixty young people around his age and asked him whether he would like to join them for a "real Shabbos meal." Shabbos sounded vaguely familiar — though he would have recognized the term Shabbat — and he took him up on that offer. He was part of a large group of twenty or so who were taken to the Jewish Quarter home of Michael and Marcia Kaufman.

Seth ended up spending most of Shabbos with the group with whom he went to the Kaufmans'. One of his companions had heard about a concert on Motzaei Shabbos featuring the Returning Light Band on Har Tzion. The musicians were dressed in chassidic garb, the musicianship top level, and the messages inspiring. Seth remembers that the concert constituted his introduction to a *mechitzah* (partition separating between men and women).

The next day, Seth had his backpack on and was headed out of the Old City for Tel Aviv when he ran into Yom Tov Glaser, one of the musicians from the previous night. A guitarist himself, Seth told Yom Tov how much he had enjoyed the concert. Yom Tov brought him to the Aish *beis medrash*, told him to just drop his backpack at the front of the *beis medrash*, and introduced him to one of the "receivers," Aaron Poston, who, like Seth, was from Miami.

Seth remained for a lecture by Rabbi Motty Berger, the "great lunch" he had been told about, and listened to some of the students who urged him to "stick around. It only gets better."

Eventually, however, Rabbi Gershon Unger, the director of the beginners' program at the time, urged him to move to Heritage House, where he remained for a couple of weeks, while going to classes at Aish. Being at Heritage House put Seth "in the system," but not completely. Even in retrospect, after decades of living as a Torah-observant Jew, he is certain that he would never have gone straight to the Aish HaTorah dorms.

He needed some "midpoint" between the hostel at the Damascus Gate and the yeshivah dorms, where he could dip his feet into the waters of Torah without fully committing. Without Heritage House, "it would not have worked," he concludes. Nor was he just in a holding pattern during that time at Heritage House. He mentions, in particular, the "fiery" parashah classes of Rabbi Avi Geller, before the *shalosh seudos* at Heritage House, as having made an impression on him. After two weeks at Heritage House, he was ready to move into the Aish HaTorah dorm for the rest of the summer, before returning to Harvard.

THE OPENING OF HERITAGE HOUSE HIGHLIGHTS TWO THINGS ABOUT Rabbi Schuster. The first is his independence. Neither Ohr Somayach

**Independent-Minded**

nor Aish HaTorah was pleased with the establishment of Heritage House. They wanted to get young men into their introductory programs much earlier, and were afraid that many whom Rabbi Schuster might have persuaded to come to yeshivah would instead content themselves with a week or two at Heritage House before resuming their travels.

Rabbi Schuster heard their complaints, but did not agree. He felt that many who could be convinced to try yeshivah or seminary were more likely to do so if they had a "midpoint," as Seth Damski put it. And he trusted in his experience, which brings us to the second point about Rabbi Schuster that was brought out by Heritage House. He was not just an automaton tapping people on the shoulder and asking them pre-scripted questions. He thought long and hard about how to best achieve his mission of combatting the pervasive ignorance of Torah among the young Jews he met. And he was an innovator, willing to change with the times and always looking for new opportunities.

Heritage House was designed to encourage those staying there to taste yeshivah or seminary to get an idea of what was being offered. The hostels closed at 9:00 a.m., an hour before most tourist sites opened, and did not provide food. That combination made the offer of free breakfasts at Aish HaTorah, Ohr Somayach, and Neve Yerushalayim attractive, and while there, why not also catch a class or two from a roster of stars: Rabbi Noach Weinberg's 48 Ways at Aish; the late Rabbi Uriel Miletsky or Rabbi Dr. Dovid Gottlieb at Ohr Somayach, or Rebbetzin Tzipporah Heller at Neve Yerushalayim. Over breakfast, the visitors also had a chance to meet and chat with students their own age.

Aish would send someone every morning to walk a group to the Aish dining room and to inform them about what classes were available that day.[1] And Ohr Somayach likewise hired a staff member, beginning in 1986, to live in the Jewish Quarter and bring travelers to Ohr Somayach each morning.[2] Meanwhile, Rabbi Schuster or other staff members were busy shuttling young women from the women's hostel to Neve Yerushalayim every morning.

Rabbi Yaakov Menken was between his second and third years at Princeton when one of the Heritage House "runners" approached him at the Central Bus Station and escorted him to Heritage House. In a remembrance of Rabbi Schuster penned just after his passing, he recalled that when someone — i.e., Rabbi Schuster — is giving you a free place to stay and asks if you'd like to try out a yeshivah, it is hard to say no: "And that's how I ended up spending a day at Ohr Somayach." In short, the free board not only made Heritage House the destination of choice for those traveling on limited budgets, it also created a presumption in favor of at least trying some of the classes being advertised in the hostels.

---

1. Avraham Lewis.
2. Chaim Salenger.

THE IDEA OF A HOSTEL RUN UNDER RELIGIOUS AUSPICES HAD occurred to others as well, as the article by Hillel Goldberg mentioned

**The Funders**

above makes clear. But only Rabbi Schuster went and found the funders to purchase suitable facilities and make it happen.

Toronto philanthropist Dov Friedberg purchased the building for the women's facility. He had learned in Ner Israel at the same time as Rabbi Schuster, though he was much younger, and the two had little contact there. The two became reacquainted in the late '70s, when Mr. Friedberg had a chance to observe Rabbi Schuster in action at the Kotel on his visits to Israel, and became a great admirer of his. In later years, he would always move Rabbi Schuster to the head of the line when there were many collectors waiting to see him, even giving him precedence over respected *roshei yeshivah*.

The 1980s was a period in which kiruv was finally at the top of the communal agenda, and Mr. Friedberg was already active in several areas, including large-scale support for a kiruv kollel in his native Chile.

One quality of Reb Meir's, in particular, attracted Mr. Friedberg to him, and caused him to become a major supporter: his *anivus* (humility). It was simply impossible to elicit the word "I" from him, Mr. Friedberg remembers, or to draw from him any enumeration of his achievements. At most, he would break into one of his beautiful smiles at the mention of someone whom he had started on the path to religious observance.

Even when it came to the proposal for a hostel, Reb Meir was too shy to even request the funding from Mr. Friedberg. He discussed the need for such an institution and what it might achieve. But it was left to Mr. Friedberg himself to propose funding it.

Mr. Friedberg actually purchased two properties for the facility. The first was a 300-year-old building that had originally served as a place to stay and *beis medrash* for travelers from Sighet in Eastern Europe.[3] He then purchased a larger house, with the thought that it might one day serve as a home for him in the Old City. But one of the neighbors complained mightily of the noise issuing from the home and threatened to take legal action. Rather than get involved in legal action that might generate a good deal of publicity, he sold the property, which left the 300-year-old guest house as the women's hostel.[4]

---

3. Mrs. Chaya Weisberg, the current manager of the Heritage House women's hostel.

4. Neither the men nor the women's hostels belonged to Heritage House. The purchasers retained title, and allowed Heritage House to operate on the premises rent-free.

Dov Wolowitz was Rabbi Schuster's primary contact for the purchase of the men's hostel. Mr. Wolowitz was one of the major backers of the kiruv movement almost from the beginning, and gave generously to both Ohr Somayach and Aish HaTorah. In addition, he was one of the major early backers of Rabbi Naftali Portnoy and Rabbi Moshe Turk when they opened the Jewish Heritage Center of Queens and Long Island in 1988. Close to two thousand Jews have become *shomer Shabbos* through the programs of the Jewish Heritage Center.

So when Mr. Wolowitz first heard about Rabbi Schuster's activities at the Kotel, he was eager to meet him. The opportunity came when he and his wife came to Israel in 1986 to visit their daughter, who was then studying in a post-high school seminary. Heritage House had already opened its doors, but the men's hostel was in a small rented apartment, and still in need of a permanent home.

Dov suggested to his wife that they go to the Kotel to find Rabbi Schuster. When he did, practically the first words from his mouth were. "I've heard a lot about what you do, and I'd like to offer you a Zevulun-Yissachar partnership." Rabbi Schuster declined on the grounds that he already had such a partnership.

Mr. Wolowitz responded by telling Reb Meir he would still like to help him and offering Reb Meir a place to stay if he should ever happen to be in the Five Towns. Both offers were ones Rabbi Schuster would soon avail himself of — likely sooner than Dov had anticipated.

Mr. Wolowitz's passion for kiruv is the key to understanding the magnitude of his commitment to Rabbi Schuster over the years. He is himself a product of the pioneers of kiruv in America, the London brothers, Rabbis Yaakov and Yechiel Yehudah London.

In the 1950s, many European-born parents, whose religious observance had lapsed considerably from what it was in Europe, still sent their children to after-school Hebrew schools. Those Hebrew school boys were the targets for the London brothers' outreach activities, for they saw clearly that the after-school Hebrew schools would prove both a weak and temporary line of defense to assimilation, as all life had been drained from the remaining religious observance at home.

To attract boys from the Hebrew schools to their high school and *beis medrash*, Heichal HaTorah, the brothers established Camp Machane Torah, in Mountaindale, New York, where the fee to attend was half that of any other camp. Although the counselors were all religiously observant, they were not allowed to speak to the campers about religious topics. That only the brothers or a few other specially trained staff members could do. Yet at the end of the summer, about half the campers wanted to go to Heichal HaTorah.

After two years at Taft High School in the Bronx, Dov took a summer job at a Bnei Akiva camp, Camp Moshava. Over the course of the summer, he became friendly with the driver who delivered supplies to the camp, Asher Tesser, who learned in Bais Medrash Govoha in Lakewood. They learned *Orchos Tzaddikim* together, and at the end of the summer, Asher convinced Dov to transfer to the London brothers' yeshivah high school, Heichal HaTorah.

From Heichal HaTorah, Dov would go on to learn for three years in Lakewood, under Rabbi Aharon Kotler, and to receive *semichah* from Rabbi Moshe Feinstein. Yet Rabbi Yechiel Yehudah London would always remain the primary Torah influence on Dov.[5] What stands out for Dov is the brothers' unbridled passion to save Jewish *neshamos*. In personality, the brothers could not have been further from Rabbi Schuster. They were firebrands, eloquent, always prepared to make a tumult to awaken Jews to the loss of Jewish souls; Rabbi Schuster was soft-spoken and quiet. What the London brothers and Rabbi Schuster shared, however, was a sense of mission that afforded them no rest.

Rabbi Yechiel London's passion never waned. Later in life, past the age when most people have retired, he devoted himself to the new Russian immigrants. On Erev Rosh Hashanah of 1989, he played the lead role in placing two hundred just-arrived Jews from the FSU in homes in Flatbush for the holiday. Thereafter he devoted himself to the new Russian immigrants, as he had once devoted himself to young American public school boys, and founded Nefesh Academy for Jewish immigrant girls.[6]

---

5. In his *hesped* for Rabbi London, Rabbi Elya Brudny of Mirrer Yeshiva devoted twenty minutes to his *gadlus baTorah*, and called him one of the *gedolei hador*.

6. Dov Wolowitz cannot speak too highly about the London brothers, who transmitted to him their passion for bringing Jews close to Hashem and His Torah. Dov loves to tell the story of accompanying Rabbi Yechiel Yehudah London on one post-camp recruiting trip to a smaller Jewish community in the Midwest. The parents of one of the campers were European Jews, and the father had a butcher shop with the ubiquitous sign of those days — *basar kasher*. The mother refused to consider sending her son to Heichal HaTorah: "He'll come back and he won't eat in our house," she said.

That night, she invited Rabbi London and Dov to dinner. Rabbi London realized that he was being tested. When the steak was served, Dov pleaded a terrible stomach upset and retreated to the bathroom. But when the mother offered her assurance that the steak was kosher, even though Rabbi London would never have relied on the level of the *hashgachah* in the normal course, he ate the steak. And the boy returned with him to Heichal HaTorah. That boy has been learning in Lakewood for over fifty years, and has thirteen children and over

Rabbi Schuster with Dov Wolowitz (l.) and his partner Eddie Chernoff

Now let us return to Dov Wolowitz's relationship with Rabbi Schuster. Not long after their initial meeting, Rabbi Schuster told Dov about his need for a larger building for the men's hostel — one which would both make the hostel more appealing to travelers and facilitate an expansion of its activities. Dov asked Rabbi Schuster how much he needed, and the latter told him $150,000. After consulting with his business and tzedakah partner Eddie Chernoff, Dov called his close friend Ruby Schron and started describing what Reb Meir did and his need for a hostel. "Okay," said Mr. Schron. "Find something, and we'll buy it for him."

---

two hundred descendants. And for good measure, both his parents moved to Lakewood and became fully observant.

Heichal HaTorah always existed on a shoestring budget: the Shabbos cholent was meatless, the Shabbat challos consisted of whatever was left over in the bakeries at closing time on Erev Shabbos, and the produce was picked up at 4:00 a.m. from the Washington Street market by Rabbi Yechiel London. Only when the brothers obtained from the city use of an abandoned convent in what is today Spanish Harlem was the yeshivah viable at all. But when a contractor offered the city $60,000 for the property, the brothers' only chance was to raise an equal sum.

One of their tactics was to send *bachurim* to collect in the upscale Fifth Avenue Synagogue. When guards were placed at the entrances to keep them out, they set up a makeshift minyan outside on the sidewalk. The rabbi of the synagogue, Rabbi Immanuel Jakobovits, later the Chief Rabbi of Britain, went to Rabbi Moshe Feinstein to complain that the brothers were creating a *chillul Hashem*. Reb Moshe suggested that the Fifth Avenue Synagogue give them a little money, and they would go away. Remarkably, the brothers succeeded in raising the $60,000 to retain the building.

Several weeks later, Rabbi Schuster called Mr. Wolowitz again to say that he had found a perfect 250-square-meter property in an ideal location on the Jewish Quarter's main thoroughfare. The only catch was that the price was $350,000, more than twice the sum he had originally quoted. Mr. Wolowitz cold-called Albert Reichmann in Toronto, the Reichmann brother most heavily involved with baalei teshuvah, to seek a loan of $200,000 to be repaid over three years. Mr. Reichmann was in conference, but did call

Dov Wolowitz affixing the mezuzah to the Heritage House men's hostel

back, even though he did not know Mr. Wolowitz.

The latter hoped Mr. Reichmann was familiar with Rabbi Schuster's work. But he wasn't. So in a rapid-fire delivery, Dov attempted to explain who Rabbi Schuster was, why he needed a hostel, and the terms of the loan he was seeking — all in approximately half a minute. Apparently he succeeded, because the next day Mr. Reichman called back and told him that he had approved the loan.

The new hostel building at 2 Ohr HaChaim, purchased by Dov Wolowitz, Eddie Chernoff, and Ruby Schron, greatly expanded the

capacity of the men's hostel. The old apartment held only twenty-five guests comfortably. The new building had beautiful Jerusalem stone on the outside, and lovely wood-covered walls and high ceilings inside. The large lounge open to the kitchen gave the appearance of an elegant old hotel, albeit one a few years past its prime, and provided space for nighttime classes for guests at the men's hostel and also from the women's hostel, as well as plenty of room to just sit around schmoozing.

*Chapter Fourteen*

# HERITAGE HOUSE - GETTING STARTED

A S MENTIONED ABOVE, THE MEN'S HOSTEL OPENED UP IN MID-to late 1984. Long before it moved into 2 Ohr HaChaim, Rabbi Schuster tapped Yaakov (Jason) Saver to run the hostel. Yaakov had long served as his eyes and ears within Aish HaTorah, to ensure that all was well with the young men Reb Meir brought to the yeshivah. He had been planning to return to the United States to finish college, after four years in various yeshivos for baalei teshuvah, when Reb Meir told him, "You can't go back. I need you for Heritage House."

Just how badly he was needed became immediately evident. On the day of the scheduled opening, Yaakov was standing in an absolutely empty apartment, with a broom and dustpan in hand, when Rabbi Schuster showed up with two backpackers in tow. Yaakov indicated to Rabbi Schuster that he'd like to have a word with him on the porch, where he proceeded to point out that there was not a stick of furniture in the apartment. He could not even offer the two backpackers a drink of water, as there were no cups of any kind to be found.

Rabbi Schuster handed him a piece of paper with a number on it, and told him to call that number and tell them what he needed. And indeed by the time the hostel reopened that evening, the furniture had arrived.

In all, the three-bedroom apartment could comfortably house well over a score of guests. The smaller bedroom contained two bunk beds, and the largest bedroom four bunk beds. (The third bedroom was the office.) In the living room were four daybeds, with pullout couches, and double beds lined the hallway. In a pinch, there were extra mattresses that could be moved out to the porch. The apartment had only one bathroom, with a toilet and a shower. Yaakov had to build a wall to separate the two.

Every guest was provided with clean sheets, a blanket, and a pillow. Just washing the linens could take almost all of Yaakov's time from the 9:00 a.m. closing of the hostel until it reopened at 5:00 p.m. He had only a tiny washing machine at his disposal, and no dryer, which meant that all the linens had to be hung out to dry.

Yet despite the somewhat spartan conditions, the men's hostel was often filled to capacity, especially in the summer. (Rabbi Schuster forbade ever turning a guest away.) Apparently, the conditions were no worse than in competing Arab and Christian hostels, and the general ambience much more attractive.

Most of the many programs that would eventually distinguish Heritage House began during those early years, including a roster of speakers. The most frequent was Rabbi Baruch Horowitz, the founder and rosh yeshivah of Dvar Yerushalayim, and someone who combined being a *talmid chacham* with broad secular knowledge.

THE FIRST FOUR YEARS OF THE HERITAGE HOUSE HOSTELS CLEARLY established what an important kiruv tool they could be. Tens of thousands of Jewish travelers passed through in those years, and almost all received either their first taste of Jewish learning or a full Shabbos experience.

**All Beginnings Are Difficult**

But it was also clear that to reach its full potential Heritage House would have to put its operations on a more professional basis. Rabbi Schuster could not serve as the chief administrator of the two hostels — something he recognized from the start. He was too much a man of action, always on the go, to ever sit at a desk.

Even when the Heritage House office moved into its own space, he never had his own room, or even a designated desk. He would drop by numerous times during the day, often for mundane tasks like applying sunscreen or to eat his daily lunch of a sandwich with tehina (with a slice of salami on Rosh Chodesh). But then he was back out again in his search for more Jewish souls.

Rabbi Zechariah Greenwald agreed to Rabbi Schuster's request that he become the executive director of Heritage House in 1989, after the men's hostel had moved to its new headquarters. He lived near the Schusters and often davened in the same minyan on Shabbos. He and his wife Linda had been hosting Shabbos guests brought by Rabbi Schuster for many years.

The job was very part time for Rabbi Greenwald. He was then in the process of establishing an alternative boys' high school, which was scheduled to open the following year, and could devote little more than an hour or two a day to Heritage House. But as the son of Ronnie Greenwald, the long-time director of Camp Sternberg and Camp Magen Avraham in the Catskills, he had grown up with a feel for the logistics of any well-functioning organization, handling large numbers of people.

He soon discovered that there were few written protocols for anything, such as receiving and screening guests to ensure that they were Jewish and did not constitute a danger to themselves or others.

Rabbi Greenwald's biggest task that year was forcing Rabbi Schuster to sit down with him and come up with a set of protocols for running the hostels, something Rabbi Schuster had no desire to do. After those meetings, he would complain that he had never before participated in such a long meeting.

The most notable deficiency identified by Rabbi Greenwald was the lack of any organized follow-up on those who passed through Heritage House and then returned home. Absent such follow-up, any impact of the time spent at Heritage House was likely to dissipate quickly.

Rabbi Greenwald urged Rabbi Schuster to hire Rabbi Yirmi Cowan, who had already been a night counselor at the men's hostel for several years, as the first director of follow-up. And he even convened a meeting of representatives of all the major baal teshuvah yeshivos and seminaries on the subject, with an eye to Rabbi Cowan facilitating follow-up for those institutions as well.

The first step to implementing an effective follow-up strategy was to make sure that there were records of who had stayed at Heritage House and for how long, what Jewish learning activities they had participated in while there, and their reactions both to Heritage House and to their various learning experiences, and contact information once they returned to their native countries. Some attempt at record-keeping had always been part of the Heritage House agenda, but now it became much more standardized.

In addition, Rabbi Cowan established contacts with kiruv workers around North America to whom guests at Heritage House could be referred. In time, Heritage House recognized that the follow-up required staff on the ground in the United States, in the same time zones as those with whom they were trying to develop contacts. But recognizing the importance of maintaining ongoing contact with those who passed through Heritage House proved to be an important first step.

RABBI GREENWALD'S INVOLVEMENT WAS INTENDED TO BE ONLY ON an interim basis from the start, and only on a very part-time basis. After

**A Full Team** his departure to run his new alternative high school, another event took place that would dramatically affect the future course of Heritage House. As any businessman would, Dov Wolowitz wanted to know how his investment was faring, and he asked Rabbi Nota Schiller, the head of Ohr Somayach, to find out for him.

Rabbi Schiller delegated the task to Rabbi Avraham Edelstein, who was then the director of outreach programs at Ohr Somayach. Rabbi Edelstein already knew Rabbi Schuster well, as he was a daily presence in Ohr Somayach, and he was also somewhat familiar with Heritage House. Every other month or so, Yaakov Saver would bring all the

Rabbi Avraham Edelstein

guests at Heritage House to Ohr Somayach for a Shabbos. That program was part of Rabbi Edelstein's bailiwick as director of outreach.

The bottom line of Rabbi Edelstein's report was that Heritage House was doing important work but was not maximizing its potential. As a courtesy to Rabbi Schuster, Rabbi Edelstein showed the report to him before sending it to Dov Wolowitz. Not surprisingly, Rabbi Schuster was not happy about the report, and told Rabbi Edelstein so. But after three or four days, he came back to Rabbi Edelstein and told him, "If you think you know how to do it better, then you become the executive director." It was to be a fateful move.

If Rabbi Schuster had been dismayed to sit in a one-hour meeting with Rabbi Greenwald, how must he have felt when his initial meeting with Rabbi Edelstein extended almost four hours? Fortunately, it was not an experience that needed to be repeated.

Rabbi Edelstein proceeded to assemble an office staff. One of his first hires was Reuven Loewenstein, a CPA, who had his own accounting practice in the United States. Mr. Loewenstein responded to an ad for a secretary. Rabbi Edelstein took one look at his résumé and pronounced him overqualified. He had been prepared for that response, and told Rabbi Edelstein that every new immigrant is overqualified for his first job in Israel. In any event, he said, there was nothing in an office that he couldn't do, and he was prepared to get started and let Rabbi Edelstein judge how to utilize his talents.

Three to four weeks later, Rabbi Schuster determined that Heritage House needed a comptroller, and that comptroller was already working in the office. In time, Mr. Loewenstein's delight in solving problems, with grit and determination, made him an invaluable linchpin for the operation.[1]

Yossi Kaufman, the long-time director of the hostels, says of Reuven Loewenstein, "If an emergency arose at 3:00 a.m. and you could make only one call, Reuven Loewenstein would be the person to call." Mr. Loewenstein, in turn, describes Rabbi Edelstein as "an administrator with the *middos* of a rosh yeshivah." Yossi Kaufman recalls a time when he completely forgot that Heritage House was hosting a group of schoolteachers that Shabbos. He approached Rabbi Edelstein with trepidation on Thursday to inform him of his mistake. Rabbi Edelstein

---

1. Rabbi Moshe Sternbuch, the rav in the shul in which Mr. Lowenstein davens, is fond of saying that if he sees Reuven on his way to shul for the *haneitz* minyan, he knows for sure that he is not late.

Rabbi Schuster receives a *kibbud* at the bris of Reuven Loewenstein's son

looked up and, without one word of reproof, said simply, "What can I do to help you?"

No discussion of the key staff of the Heritage House office would be complete without mention of Mrs. Suzanne Lieberman,[2] who made sure that the entire operation functioned smoothly. She initially interviewed with Reuven Loewenstein and then Steven Drucker, by then the manager of the men's hostel, before starting to work in 1992. Her first day on the job, she received a call at 10:00 a.m. from Rabbi Schuster, who was then on a fundraising trip in America. "Who are you? What are you doing there?" he snapped. She promptly went to Reuven Loewenstein to tell him that she was having second thoughts about the job, as it appeared that her boss was a bit crazy. He reassured her that "his bark is worse than his bite."

She was nervous about Rabbi Schuster's return the next week, but quickly found that "to know him is to love him." Everything about him was dynamic, urgent, done with energy and enthusiasm. Meanwhile, her business background heading a recruiting agency for Coca-Cola in her native England kept the office functioning on an even keel,

The foregoing descriptions and stories allude to one of the great strengths of the Heritage House administrative staff: their respect for one another and exceptional unity. The unity of the staff ultimately

---

2. See Chapter Seven, p. 96.

derived from their shared sense of purpose, and that started with the man at the top of the hierarchy: Rabbi Schuster. Pettiness of any kind was simply foreign to him. Moishe Mendlowitz, the manager of the men's hostel over the final ten years of its existence, and the person with the most day-to-day contact with Rabbi Schuster, attests that he never heard Rabbi Schuster utter a bad word about anyone.

And Rabbi Gidon Labell, three of whose siblings also became Torah-observant Jews through Rabbi Schuster, argues that it is a mistake to describe him only as quiet and introverted. His speech was also that of a *talmid chacham,* of whom our Sages say, "and I did not find any path better than silence." He was not just shy; he was also careful with his words to avoid prohibited speech.

But above all, it was the sense of mission that Rabbi Schuster imparted that made Heritage House such an exciting place in which to work. "I awakened every day with excitement," says Yossi Kaufman, "eager to get to work. I had no doubt that we were engaged in world-changing work."

IN TIME, HERITAGE HOUSE, UNDER AVRAHAM EDELSTEIN'S OVERALL direction, evolved into a smoothly functioning operation of interlocking

**A Well-Oiled Machine** gears. At the beginning of the process was recruitment. Heritage House employed three people at a time, "runners," besides Rabbi Schuster, to

Moishe Mendlowitz (l.) and Yossi Kaufman (r.) with two guests at the men's hostel:
Michael Weinraub and Daniel Bennet

find travelers for whom a free hostel would be an enticing offer. Rabbi Schuster himself frequently entered Arab and Christian hostels in search of possible clients. And so, at least on one occasion, one of the other "runners" did as well. Aliza Sofer remembers a rabbi coming into the somewhat "dodgy" Arab hostel in which she was staying, and offering her "everything" she could possibly ask for — even a bagel every day — if she would agree to come to Heritage House. She did, and credits the women's hostel with having been a major step on her path to teshuvah.[3]

In addition, Heritage House maintained the Heritage House Jewish Drop-In Center just off the square in the Jewish Quarter of the Old City. Those who entered the Drop-In Center for directions or other information or to join one of the tours of the Old City led by Shalom Weber learned at the same time about Heritage House.

Over the years, one of the three "runners" was placed at the Central Bus Station to meet backpackers arriving in Jerusalem. Mrs. Shula Wittenstein (today psychologist Dr. Shula Wittenstein) filled that role at the Central Bus Station between the births of her first and third children. She would often find herself sitting on a bench next to three Arab "runners" from competing Arab hostels.

It was still well before the days of ubiquitous cellphones. So when Shula interested someone in staying at the Heritage House, they would then cross the road via an underground tunnel to a pay phone adjacent to the bus stop for buses headed for the Kotel. From there she would call the Heritage House office and provide Rabbi Edelstein with the name and description of the prospective guest. Rabbi Edelstein (or someone else from the office, if he was not available) would then meet the guest at the other end.

Mrs. Wittenstein is the fifth of nine children of the Klatzko family of Cleveland, many of whose members have been highly successful kiruv professionals. The job for her was sort of an introduction to the family business, and she loved it, despite the sometimes inclement weather and the competition from the Arab hostels. She even had the pleasure of setting up a backpacker with the same uncommon name as herself, Klatzko, who ended up becoming religiously observant.

But Rabbi Schuster remained the primary recruiter in his own

---

3. Mrs. Sofer knows that the rabbi in question, whom she never saw again, was not Rabbi Schuster. Rabbi Schuster brought her brother to Aish HaTorah, where he ended up staying for seven years, so she was familiar with what he looked like.

inimitable style. Gedaliah Kaufman had been traveling for almost three years in Southeast Asia, and decided that he should continue his search in Israel, which he had visited previously. On the flight from India, the secular Israelis on board told him that he would be landing on Erev Shavuos, a festival of which he had never heard.

Arriving in the Jewish Quarter, he saw a sign for Discovery — "Don't just be an educated person, be an educated Jew." Following the sign, he ended up at an Aish HaTorah dorm, where one of the talmidim offered to take him to Heritage House.

At the end of three days — the festival and Shabbos — he decided to seek out the Arab hostel at which he had stayed on his prior trip to Israel. (He had previously learned Arabic in Egypt.) But on his way out the door, he ran into Rabbi Schuster, who asked him where he was going. He replied that he was going to an Arab hostel. At which point, the following dialogue ensued:

"You can't go without going to Discovery."

"Yes, I can."

Rabbi Schuster then grabbed his arm, which provoked Gedaliah to ask, "How much [for the Discovery Seminar]?

"Twenty dollars."

"Too much."

"It's on me."

Gedaliah notes that he was an experienced traveler, and would instinctively have removed his arm had anyone else grabbed it. Instead he took up Rabbi Schuster on the offer of a paid-for Discovery program, followed by two months in the Aish Essentials program, before returning to the United States for the first time in three years. But after six weeks, he was back in Jerusalem, where he spent the next nine years at Aish HaTorah, then the Mirrer Yeshiva, followed by *semichah* through Rabbi Yitzchak Berkovits' kollel. Along the way, he ran the *shalosh seudos* programs at Heritage House.

After the completion of her Birthright trip, Frieda Shapiro entered the Old City in search of a hostel that was supposedly free for all Jews. Suddenly, Rabbi Schuster appeared out of nowhere and startled her. When she replied affirmatively to his inquiry about being Jewish, he just grabbed her huge suitcase and began wheeling it to the women's hostel, as she and the friend she was with "struggled to keep up."

The next day, Rabbi Schuster showed up early in the morning to take Frieda and her friend to Neve Yerushalayim. On the way, he asked

Frieda what she was doing with her life, and she told him that she was an actress. At that point of her life — she was then only 19 — Frieda was used to people being impressed when she mentioned her chosen career.

Not Rabbi Schuster. "Why would you do that? Don't you care about your future? Don't you care about your Judaism?" he challenged her. She was, not surprisingly, "furiously indignant" at his effrontery in seemingly attacking someone whom he did not know. But she and her friend did go to Neve that day. And while working in the theater upon her return to New York the following year, those same questions kept niggling at her. The next summer she returned to the EYAHT-affiliated Jewel program, followed by Neve, and ended up as a *madrichah* at Heritage House.

Looking back, she acknowledges that the manner in which Rabbi Schuster grabbed her bag and started rolling it, not to mention his assault on her acting career, should have turned her off to Orthodox Judaism. But they did not. Once she had calmed down — which took a while — she realized that no one had ever shown such concern for her *neshamah* and the family he hoped she would build.

## Chapter Fifteen
# HERITAGE HOUSE -
# THE VIBE

**T**HE MEN AND WOMEN'S HOSTELS THEMSELVES WERE NOT structured exactly alike. The women's hostel always had a live-in couple, whereas the men's hostel did not. In part, the difference was technical: The women's hostel was a house within a communal courtyard, and the neighbors insisted on the presence of an adult couple to ensure that the noise level from the hostel not become excessive. Gila and Avraham Manolson were the first on-site couple. And besides closing the hostel in the morning and opening it at 5:00 p.m., the most formalized part of their duties was to make sure that the windows were closed in the evening so as not to disturb the neighbors.

**The Women's Hostel**

But there was a more subtle reason as well. The ability to view an observant family was usually a more important factor in the female guests' decision to explore Torah more deeply than it was for the male guests. Steven Terris, who with his wife Aliza assumed the position as the live-in couple in 1996, comments, "We won over the girls with homemade cookies and offers to let them hold our infants."

When Mrs. Shulamis Green was first hired as a senior *madrichah* at the women's hostel, she thought the job would mostly entail answering

Gila and Avraham Manolson with their young family at the women's hostel.

questions about Torah Judaism. She soon found that not to be the case at all. Instead, her task was to listen and connect to the guests, while putting aside any agenda. In a similar vein, Dena Estrin, a live-in counselor for five years, noted the irony that when the night conversation was fun and free-flowing, the guests were more likely to get into Rabbi Schuster's station wagon the next morning. When it was highly philosophical, they were more likely to head out for tourist attractions on the following day.[1] On that basis, she came to see her primary task as showing that being an Orthodox Jew is no contradiction to being warm, personable, and having wide-ranging interests, such as hiking and camping.

That task of keeping the conversation lively was made easy by the fact that so many of the guests had interesting experiences to share, such as working in a village maternity ward in West Africa. A number had just completed tours in the Peace Corps or with groups like Habitat for Humanity. Dena Estrin describes a night when the guests included a woman whose paternal great-grandfather was Ulysses S. Grant, a mother and daughter from Iran who spoke almost no Hebrew, a third woman who had been traveling for fifteen years, and yet a fourth who had an "afterlife experience" after being severely burned in an apartment fire.

Often guests arrived at the hostel after extended periods of travel, frequently on their own. The excitement of visiting new places and exploring other cultures had not infrequently given way to loneliness. Most were at some kind of crossroads in their lives — e.g., after an important relationship had ended, or following graduation from college or the completion of a graduate degree.

---

1. Estrin, *It Happened at Heritage House*, p. 143.

The warmth of Heritage House was a welcome salve for lonely travelers. Every effort was made to create a homey atmosphere. Mrs. Shulamis Green, one of the senior counselors for nearly a decade, learned from her own children how calming it was to come home at the end of the day and be greeted by the welcoming aroma of a fresh soup cooking, and she recreated that feeling at Heritage House. On the three days she opened the hostel at 5:00 p.m., she would gather a group of women to join her in selecting the ingredients at the Arab greengrocer in the shuk. Then they would repair to the hostel to prepare a huge cauldron. Often the cauldron was refreshed with the addition of new ingredients in the course of the evening.

The purchase and preparation provided a natural opportunity to introduce the young women to halachos of *maaser, Shemittah,* checking for bugs, and *berachos* for different foods. Those partaking of the soup were invited to contribute a few shekels to the kitty for the purchase of the next day's ingredients.

Popcorn and hot tea were staples of the evening discussions, and drew guests out of their rooms onto the common-area couches. "No eating; no connecting," Mrs. Green explained to Reuven Loewenstein, when seeking a popcorn allocation. He understood.[2]

Though the hostel was theoretically open to any Jew, the senior counselors who opened the premises in the evening did exercise some discretion over whom they admitted in order to preserve the positive "vibe" of the hostel. Mrs. Green, for instance, was alert for those who struck her as aggressive or having anger issues. Other times (though by no means always) those outside the target demographic of 18 to 25 were directed to the Armenian hostel across the way, with Heritage House often picking up their expenses for a night or two. Those who struck the senior counselors as seeking only to take advantage of the free board, without participating in the Heritage House activities or attending any classes, were subtly nudged out the door after the passage of time.

By far the most difficult part of the screening process arose in response to the intake question, "Were you born Jewish?" Over the years, numerous travelers found out at Heritage House that they were not Jewish, either by virtue of a non-Jewish mother or one whose

---

2. Mrs. Green soon discovered that Mr. Loewenstein turned the allocation of money into a spiritual endeavor, and came to rely on him for guidance in all ethical dilemmas. If one of the guests was going through some type of crisis and needed psychological help, he always seemed to find the money in the budget, or, equally frequently, go out and raise it himself.

A downstairs scene at the women's hostel

conversion was halachically inadequate. That discovery was often crushing. In general, if a Jew and a non-Jew were traveling together, they would both be allowed to stay, if the Jewish guest was open to exploring her Judaism. And even those with only a Jewish father were often admitted and directed to programs willing to work with that demographic. Rabbi Edelstein was often called in to deal with these situations on an individual basis.

RABBI SIMCHA BUNIM (BENNY) BERGER TAUGHT AT THE MEN'S HOSTEL at least once a week, and sometimes twice, for six years. He describes the

## The Men's Hostel

men's hostel as the perfect safe environment in which a totally unaffiliated Jew could explore Judaism in an atmosphere of warmth and unconditional acceptance. Every effort was made to keep the environment free of pressure and thereby encourage exploration.

Even the senior managers' job was primarily talking to guests. Steven Drucker was the senior manager of the men's hostel for two years in the early '90s, starting just before the 1991 Gulf War. Rabbi Schuster had known him for almost a decade at that point, ever since he and a group of six Jewish friends from Long Island had rented an apartment in the Old City. Each had traveled extensively around the world, including

Rabbi Schuster with three guests at the men's hostel

time living in Bali, exploring traditional dance and music. All six eventually became *shomer mitzvos* (religiously observant).

Initially, Rabbi Schuster was reluctant to hire him because of his lack of an extensive yeshivah background. But Steve convinced him that, to the contrary, his background made him ideal for the job: a good secular education (Columbia University), extensive travel, jazz musician. One of the points he always emphasized in his discussions with guests in the hostel was the necessity for a baal teshuvah to integrate his past into his new life as a religious Jew rather than trying to amputate his past self.

FOR ALL THAT THE HOSTELS WERE WARM AND NURTURING ENVIRONments, there was plenty of energy and intellectual ferment as well. The evening discussion at the women's hostel often started with one of the senior *madrichot* asking about any questions that might have arisen during the day's classes. The presence of Torah-knowledgeable senior *madrichot*, like Sarah Yehudit Schneider, who was at the women's hostel for over a decade, and Shulamis Green, the wife of a *maggid shiur* in Yeshivat Bircat HaTorah, was thus crucial.

**Intellectual and Emotional Ferment**

Mrs. Sarah Yehudit Schneider had not yet developed her current international following based on her teaching and writing and on-line presence (www.astillsmallvoice), but she was already learning with individuals privately. She combined a love of people with brilliance that could not be missed,[3] and offered the possibility of plumbing in depth almost any question likely to arise. "She always has interesting things to say," her fellow counselor Dena Estrin wrote of her. "Even better — she listens. An aura of compassion surrounds her like the calming scent of lavender, and her easygoing nature makes her very approachable."[4]

When Rebecca (Rosenzweig) Askinasi, who had overlapped with Sarah Yehudit at Heritage House, returned to Israel for a visit with her young son, the latter insisted that they go to meet Sarah Yehudit, offering as an explanation, "She can reach people no one else can."

Rabbi Schuster wrote the same in an approbation for one of Mrs. Schneider's many books: "Of all our staff in the women's hostel over the years, Susie has stood out as the person most capable of answering the wide range of questions that have come up. She has worked hard both to acquire the necessary knowledge and to find ways of translating this into the language of the unaffiliated."

A different sort of emotional ferment was generated by the younger counselors on both the men's and women's sides. Over half of the Heritage House counselors over the years had themselves passed through Heritage House, and an even higher percentage were fairly recent baalei teshuvah.

Rebecca (Rosenzweig) Askinasi, for instance, was the night manager at the women's hostel for four years. She was passionate about her work at Heritage House. Frequently, when she davened at the Kotel, she would beseech Hashem, "Show me how I can help You." Rebecca was excited about her own story as a baalas teshuvah and eager to share it with the women travelers. For Heritage House guests such stories made real at least the possibility of dramatic life changes.

Among the guests with whom Rebecca formed a lasting relationship was Alana Rubin, who had been a Rhodes Scholar finalist in her native Canada. While on a World Union of Jewish Students (WUJS) program in Arad, Alana had a dream about Moshe receiving the Ten Commandments. Her immediate response was to come to Jerusalem and participate in a Discovery program, while living at Heritage House.

A playwright whose works have been performed internationally, Alana Rubin captures the intensity of the Heritage House experience.

3. Shulamis Green.
4. Estrin, *It Happened at Heritage House*, p. 124.

She describes the Heritage House as the "holiest place I've ever been." And nearly thirty years after she lived in Heritage House first as a guest and later as a counselor, every single conversation remains emblazoned in her memory, along with every title in the large library that was available to guests.

RABBI SCHUSTER NEVER INTENDED THE HERITAGE HOUSE TO BE AN independent educational institution. The goal was always to bring

**Speakers** guests to one of the established yeshivos or seminaries for baalei teshuvah. But there were frequent classes available, and some of them became major events, attracting an audience even beyond the Heritage House. The lectures were usually, but not always, held in the men's hostel, which boasted a larger common room, but guests from the women's hostel were welcome.

The lectures of Gedaliah Gurfein on the weekly Torah reading often drew an overflow crowd of students from Aish HaTorah. He had the ability to make the Torah real to even those with minimal background, and to reassure them that they were connecting to something very powerful, and not just being inducted into a cult of mass conformity.[5]

Asher Wade taught once a week and led Friday tours at Yad Vashem for many years (until Yad Vashem no longer permitted independent tour guides). The Friday presentation began with a presentation on the Holocaust at Heritage House, followed by a tour at Yad Vashem, and took at least four hours. Reb Asher's compelling life story added to both the tours and the lectures, many of which delineated the differences between Judaism and Christianity. Rabbi Wade was eminently qualified to address the latter topic, as he was born and raised as a Christian. Indeed he was an ordained Methodist minister, who served as a chaplain in the U.S. Army in Germany, and married to a German woman, whose father and grandfather were both Lutheran ministers, when he first became interested in Torah.

Reb Asher can mark with precision the exact moment his entire life was upended, On November 5, 1978, the fortieth anniversary of Kristallnacht, the Sunday newspaper in Hamburg, Germany, where he was then pursuing a doctorate in philosophy, carried a photo of the old great synagogue of Hamburg, one of hundreds of Jewish houses of worship attacked by organized mobs across Germany on Kristallnacht.

---

5. Rebecca (Rosenzweig) Askinasi.

Moishe Mendlowitz, Rabbi Asher Wade, and Yossi Kaufman

Studying the photo, he realized that the site of the synagogue was now the student parking lot at his university.

That connection to the events of Kristallnacht plunged him into an inquiry as to how German academia and the German churches had responded in terms of resistance to the Nazis, and the answer in both cases was not favorable. A majority of members of the law and medical faculties at the University of Hamburg had joined the Nazi party.

He found himself plunged into a crisis by the removal of the twin pillars upon which he had built his life until then — academia and religion. That led him to a deeper inquiry into the Jews and their beliefs, which culminated with both his and his wife's conversion. He eventually received semichah.

Reb Asher's story of abandoning a faith to which he was far more deeply bound than any of his listeners were to their Judaism in order to pursue a Torah life invariably made a huge impact on listeners. His tours of Yad Vashem are remembered by all those who took part as one of the highlights of their time at Heritage House. One of the emotionally packed moments of the tour came when Reb Asher implored the group not to view the photos of Jewish women lined up for the gas chambers — women who, as he put it, would have died a thousand deaths not to be viewed in such a state.

It was not just the guests who were powerfully affected by the tour. As the night manager of the men's hostel, Moishe Mendlowitz used to go on the tour almost weekly, and it still affected him emotionally each week. He remembers one young man sobbing uncontrollably on the bus after Rabbi Wade's tour.

Rabbi Wade also did occasional counseling at Heritage House. When he became disenchanted with German academia, he abandoned his original doctorate program, and earned a doctorate in counseling instead. One young woman, who later became the senior manager of the women's hostel, told him in one meeting, "I'm not one of those people who wants to have her brain washed. I'm an artist and a dancer." He replied, "My poor child, you need to have your brain washed; they've been telling you lies your whole life." She had not been prepared for that response, and walked out sobbing.

Upon occasion, Heritage House was able to draw on the proximity of internationally renowned speakers. Rabbi Motty Berger, for instance, lived in the Old City. He spent at least half the year, from the mid-'80s through the late '90s, in North America as the lead presenter at the Discovery seminars, which played a major role in jumpstarting many kiruv organizations across North America. But when back in Jerusalem and teaching at Aish HaTorah, he would sometimes be a guest lecturer at Heritage House, where his quickness on his feet, love of free-ranging debate, and humor always made for an interesting session.

Other times, Heritage House was able to tap into rising stars before they had reached the peak of their fame. Rabbi David Aaron was one of the latter group. He was friendly with Yaakov Saver, and spoke at the men's hostel on occasion in the early days of Heritage House.

Rabbi Aaron had not yet published nine books with major mainstream publishers, such as Simon and Schuster and Random House, or been interviewed by Larry King, but the talent was already there. From his early 20s, Rabbi Aaron began teaching *Derech Hashem* and other texts in the Aish introductory program. And it was in that context that Rabbi Schuster first took note of him.

Rabbi Aaron was not a completely comfortable fit at Aish HaTorah. First, he was not a product of the yeshivah. Second, he did not teach any of the materials developed by Rabbi Noach Weinberg. Reb Noach placed a great emphasis on proofs of G-d and Torah. Rabbi Aaron had a different approach: People naturally believe in G-d. What they need to know is that Hashem believes in them.

Given these differences, it was not a complete surprise when Rabbi Aaron was laid off at one point, during one of Aish HaTorah's periodic efforts at cost-cutting. But Rabbi Schuster immediately went to Rabbi Weinberg and told him that it was a mistake to fire Rabbi Aaron, as he was one of his most effective teachers. Reb Meir's ongoing contacts with those he brought to Aish HaTorah gave him great credibility on that score, and Rabbi Aaron was soon rehired.

After about five years of teaching at Aish, Rabbi Aaron was ready to set up his own institution, Isralight, a unique program based on ten-week learning modules. Rabbi Schuster viewed the unique aspects of this program as yet another means of bringing in young people, who otherwise would never come to a yeshivah or seminary. Although Rabbi Schuster's relationship with the program was never meant to be publicized, and he severed his formal relationship with Isralight after some time, this was but one of many programs developed by Heritage House over the years.

At various points in time, Heritage House had both a Russian and a Spanish program. Rabbi Schuster even secured funding for a drop-in center in Eilat. He flew to Eilat with Michael Kaufman to surveil the scene, and while there, they put down a year's rent on a vacant store just opposite the beach, between a restaurant serving shrimp and pork and a bar from which loud rock music was emanating. The plan was to place two couples in Eilat so that the men would have built-in *chavrusos*. The families would host large groups for Shabbos. Meanwhile those who could be persuaded to attend classes would be put on planes to be met by personnel from Heritage House or the various yeshivos and seminaries.

According to Mr. Kaufman, Rabbi Schuster was like "a kid in a candy shop" the entire time they were in Eilat. Every two minutes or so, he would charge off to corral another young Jew. Between bursts of conversation, he was constantly busy writing down reminders in his little black book. When he returned to Jerusalem, Rabbi Schuster began his search for the two couples to live there.

Rabbi Edelstein was never enthusiastic about the idea of a center in Eilat. In his view, those who came to the Kotel, or even to Jerusalem, had already made a decision to engage in some kind of "Jewish activity." The same could not be said for hanging out on the beach in Eilat. For that reason, he did not think that Eilat would be worth the investment of time or manpower. Ultimately, Rabbi Edelstein's view prevailed.

AT SOME POINT EARLY IN HIS TENURE AS EXECUTIVE DIRECTOR OF

Heritage House, Rabbi Edelstein decided that he wanted to develop his own homegrown talent rather than just rely on already well-known

**Home-Grown Talent**

speakers. His first "project" was Rabbi Simcha Bunim (Benny) Berger. Why Rabbi Edelstein should have picked Berger does not require much explanation. At well over six feet tall and blond, he looked more like a "surfer dude" from his native southern California than the yeshivah rebbi he already was. He had charm, and he had Torah — the latter gained as a long-time talmid of Rabbi Moshe Shapiro. Ten years after his first foray into teaching at Heritage House, he would open his own yeshivah in Bridgeport, Connecticut.

Both Rabbi Berger and Rabbi Edelstein probably assumed that his success was guaranteed. But that proved to be far from the case. In his first try-out, Berger bombed, with both Rabbi Edelstein and Rabbi Schuster looking on. His topic was anti-Semitism, and as he admitted later, he simply had not prepared adequately. Fortunately, he was quick-witted enough that when one guest asked him a question for which he did not have a ready answer, he simply said, "Let's hear what Rabbi Edelstein has to say about that."

A number of his subsequent sessions were little better, and Rabbi Schuster was ready to call off the experiment. But not Rabbi Edelstein. He was determined to turn Benny into a Heritage House star. And he

Rabbi Simcha Bunim (Benny) Berger teaching at the men's hostel

did. Every Friday, Rabbi Berger would drive to Rabbi Edelstein's home and tell him some idea from Rabbi Moshe Shapiro that he wanted to share. And Rabbi Edelstein would help him bring the concepts down to earth, and then cull from his files relevant news items that might illustrate the point.

In the end, both Rabbi Edelstein and Rabbi Berger take great pride in the fact that they did not give up, but worked to get better. Rabbi Berger ended up teaching at Heritage House for six years, from 1992-1997, and eventually became the only twice-a-week speaker.

In the late 1990s, Heritage House started a program to prepare couples for careers in kiruv called the Heritage House Kiruv Training Program. Rabbi Berger served as the first director.[6] All the participants in the program would eventually cut their teeth at Heritage House teaching audiences not unlike those that would await them when they returned to their native countries.

Among those Rabbi Berger recruited are Rabbi Aron Yehuda Schwab, today head of the Denver Community Kollel, and his brother-in-law, Rabbi Avi Elbaz, today a rebbi at Aish HaTorah. But the list of prominent communal rabbanim and kiruv workers who used Heritage House as a forum to both work on their teaching skills and to develop their material is a long one. Rabbi Dovid Tugenhaft, the young rav of one of the most vibrant congregations in London's Hendon neighborhood, for instance,

Rabbi Dr. Dovid Gottlieb teaching at the men's hostel

6. That program eventually developed into Ner L'Elef, which was under the auspices of Heritage House, but had independent sources of funding.

Rabbi Beryl Gershenfeld teaching at the men's hostel

credits the opportunity to teach at Heritage House as crucial to his readiness for his current position.

Rabbi Berger points out that one of the most important contributions of Heritage House to those who taught there is that it forced them to work on the fundamentals of Jewish belief that are too often just assumed in yeshivos but not really studied in depth. And it also provided much-needed exposure to Jews coming from completely different backgrounds. "I could have become the rosh yeshivah in Bridgeport without Heritage House," he says. "But I would have never been able to form a relationship with the local Reform rabbi and convince him to come learn Torah with me without the experience of Heritage House."

Most of the speakers mentioned thus far were male and their venue was the men's hostel. The women's hostel, with a much smaller common area, and which itself often included a number of beds upon which guests might be sleeping, was simply less conducive to any kind of formal classes or discussions.

But there were also speakers in the women's hostel from time to time. In the early days of the women's hostel, Judith Rosenblum and Lisa Kermaier, who were then heavily involved in preparing kallahs for marriage, did a series of presentations of the laws of family purity and Jewish family life in general. The subject matter was of obvious interest to the women travelers, as the Torah perspective differs so vastly from contemporary mores in relationships. But apart from the specific subject matter of the presentations, these presentations often led to lengthy informal discussions, with the young women asking questions like, "What is it like to be a mother of so many children?" At least one of the women became a frequent Shabbos guest of the Rosenblums before marrying and settling in Israel.

Somewhat counterintuitively, the laws of family purity often resonated deeply with those who had grown up with the philosophy that human beings are just more sophisticated animals engaged in the pursuit of physical pleasure. Those laws provided a clear-cut example of the difference between Jewish wisdom and the prevailing secular zeitgeist.

Janine, a guest at Heritage House, attended a lecture nearby on family purity given by Mrs. Baila Berger, Rabbi Motty Berger's wife. From the very start, Janine could not believe what she was hearing. For years she had felt like a leper because of her view that casual relationships would somehow diminish her and make her less human. Mrs. Berger's words resonated powerfully with her and confirmed her deepest intuitions.[7]

Long before he had any formal role in Heritage House, and while still an *avreich* in Yeshiva Torah Ore, Rabbi Avraham Edelstein used to give a once-a-week class at the women's hostel. He preferred the warmth of the smaller common room at the women's hostel, though guests from the men's hostel were free to attend. The formal class and questions usually did not end until about midnight, with a hardcore group of five or six participants remaining. At that point, the remaining group would adjourn, with Rabbi Edelstein, to the central square of the Jewish Quarter, and keep going for another two or three hours of free-flowing conversation.

Rabbi Avraham Edelstein teaching a class

Those late nights often left Rabbi Edelstein at less than peak sharpness the next day in yeshivah, and he asked his rosh yeshivah, Rabbi Chaim Pinchas

---

7. Estrin, *It Happened at Heritage House,* p. 90.

Scheinberg, whether he should continue. The latter told him that he was engaged in *hatzalas nefashos* (saving souls) and was obligated to continue.

THE HUGE VOLUME LISTING THOSE WHO PASSED THROUGH THE MEN'S and women's hostels over the years makes the hostels an excellent source of lessons in kiruv. The first of those is how poor we are at pre-

**A Laboratory for Kiruv**

dicting who will be affected by the exposure to Torah. Appearance, what a person is doing or has done up to then in life, even hostility to religion in general or Judaism in particular — none of these are very useful predictive factors. A second lesson is the crucial importance of personal relationships and the potential impact of living among committed Jews, even without any initial involvement in Torah learning.[8]

Aliza's shaved head and strong feminist views certainly did not make it easy to imagine her as an Orthodox Jew when she first entered Heritage House. And the fact that she was in the middle of a PhD program in psychology did not give her much time for Jewish study before returning to the United States to resume her doctoral studies. But she enjoyed the classes she took at Neve Yerushalayim, and at the airport she found herself standing in line next to Bracha Zaret, Rabbi Schuster's former sidekick at the Kotel. Mrs. Zaret offered her a full scholarship to return to Israel to study at winter break. Aliza ended up studying at Neve and eventually doing an internship in the Neve Family Institute. Today she is an enthusiastic Orthodox Jew.

The Jewish rules of *tznius* (modesty) present a challenge for almost every secular woman who enters a baalas teshuvah seminary. But for Ortal and Donna, the challenges were economic, as well as ideological. Both were Israeli models — a career based on drawing attention to their beauty — and Ortal had already achieved a fair amount of professional success. Yet they were looking for a "Shabbat experience" at the Kotel, and a friend suggested Heritage House. After Shabbos, Heritage House connected them to learning programs in the Tel Aviv area where they lived, and over the next couple of years both became fully observant, and Ortal ended up learning at a seminary in Bnei Brak.

Amy followed her sister to Heritage House, but certainly presented one of the most unpromising profiles of any guest — a strong feminist, very leftist, and pro-Palestinian, for good measure. But she had come to

---

8. The stories in this section were provided by Mrs. Chaya Weisberg.

Israel for a Hebrew ulpan, and Chaya Weisberg's offer of five months' free board during the course of the ulpan was too good to pass up. Mrs. Weisberg was confident that five months at Heritage House would be more than enough time to break down her resistance.

For a month, Amy secluded herself in her room, but eventually she began participating in the Heritage House activities and became close to one of the *madrichot*. In time, she started going to classes, and eventually studied at a number of seminaries. Ultimately she married an Israeli baal teshuvah and so enjoyed the benefits of the ulpan as well.

Rachel extended her stay in Israel at the end of a RAJE (Russian-American Jewish Experience) trip to Israel. But she made it clear to the staff at Heritage House that she had no interest in any further Jewish learning on that trip. And besides some informal discussions about dating and Jewish marriage with Mrs. Weisberg, she kept to that resolve.

Mrs. Weisberg was pleasantly surprised, however, when she received an email from Rachel after she returned home, in which she professed a desire to one day build her marriage on a foundation of family purity. After that, Mrs. Weisberg and she had only minimal contact, until she showed up at Heritage House a few years later with her new *chassan*, and announced that they had come to spend their *"shanah rishonah"* (first year of marriage) learning in yeshivah and seminary full time.

Sarah, born and raised in Latvia, had the world at her feet when she first found her way to Heritage House. She was already an accomplished graphic artist, choreographer, and film producer at age 22. She had also been raised as a devout atheist. When she arrived at Heritage House and realized it was a religious institution, she hesitated about entering because of her immodest attire, until Mrs. Weisberg assured her it was no problem. She proved open to learning, and went to classes, first at Neve, and then for a year and a half at EYAHT. Afterward in New York, she married another Russian-speaking baal teshuvah, and both are active in kiruv programs for RAJE, in addition to their day jobs.

Dina was dating an Arab back in the United States when she first came to Heritage House, and she expressed no interest in any formal learning. But she was more than happy to discuss subjects like religious pluralism versus Truth with Mrs. Weisberg. On leaving Heritage House, she made it clear that she did not want to be "followed up" on. But she stayed in intermittent contact with Mrs. Weisberg, though their discussions were only about her art shows and the like — nothing to do with Judaism.

Four years after her first stay in Heritage House, she showed up again, and told Mrs. Weisberg that she remembered everything from their discussions years earlier. In the interim, she had become much more observant. This time she was dating a Jewish young man, who was doing a medical internship in Israel, and she was now eager to go to classes and to bring him along as well.

At first glance, there would not seem to be many opportunities for actresses in the Torah world. But Natasha, an Australian-born actress, with almost no Jewish background when she came to the women's hostel, quickly channeled her naturally spiritual and passionate nature into Torah. And today, she writes, directs, and performs in plays about becoming a baalas teshuvah all over Israel.

A friend of Yelena, a fitness trainer, had become a baal teshuvah, and he encouraged her to visit him in Israel, in the hope of interesting her in Torah studies. Though she came to Israel, she had little interest in going to classes. During her two-week stay at the women's hostel, she was not encouraged to go to classes at all, but directed to dance and yoga classes. Only toward the end of her stay did one of the *madrichot* suggest that she come along for a class or two at one of the seminaries. Though she enjoyed the classes, the impact was apparently lost when she subsequently went to work on a kibbutz. But she eventually returned to Neve Yerushalayim and became religious.

Yelena had an older sister, who was then traveling in India, whom she convinced to visit her for two weeks. The sister was virulently anti-religious, and the staff at the hostel avoided any discussions of religion with her. But, as so frequently happened, she enjoyed Shabbos and connected strongly to the religious *madrichot* and the other religious people she met. A year later, she returned to Israel to study at Shearim Seminary. Both sisters are now fully observant, and Yelena does a great deal of informal kiruv through her aerobics, fitness, and swimming classes at the Baltimore Y.

Mandy was already 37 years old by the time she walked into Heritage House. Initially, her intention was only to experience one Shabbos. And even that was a bit much for her. She was the only Shabbos meal guest the Weisbergs ever had who needed to go out for a smoke in the middle of the meal. Somewhat of a "party girl" at that stage in her life, she was surprised to discover that she actually enjoyed the "religious" hostel, the discussions with the *madrichot* and Mrs. Weisberg, and spending time with religious families. Over her summer of touring in Israel, she ended up coming to Heritage House every Shabbos, and eventually staying there during the week as well.

As she prepared to return home to London at the end of the summer, Mandy decided to actually meet the rabbi of the London shul her wealthy family supported. On a return trip to Israel and Heritage House, she met a baal teshuvah in Tzefat. They married and have three children, and continue to live in Tzefat.

Truly, as Rabbi Schuster's life work proves, we cannot know the wonders of the Jewish soul, and what will trigger its return to its Source.

*Chapter Sixteen*

# HERITAGE HOUSE AS A FORCE MULTIPLIER

R ABBI SCHUSTER'S INITIAL FORAYS INTO KIRUV BEGAN WITH placements for Shabbos meals. Even a one-time Shabbos experience often paved the way for a consideration of whether there

**Shabbos at Heritage House**

was a reason to reexamine youthful impressions of Judaism.

But the opening of the Heritage House hostels greatly augmented the potential of the Shabbos experience. For one thing, the staff at the two hostels could begin assembling lists by midweek of those who would be staying through Shabbos. That allowed time for much more thought about which Heritage House guests would be a good match for which hosts.

That was not something that could be done at the Kotel on Friday night. The number of those to be placed was simply too great for anything more than intuitive guesses based on scant information. By the mid-'80s, Rabbi Schuster could no longer handle all the Shabbos placements on his own, and he split the assignment of guests to hosts with Jeff Seidel, another full-time kiruv activist, with a primary focus at that time on the overseas students at the major Israeli universities. They began to divide the placement of those gathered at the Kotel to specific

Rabbi Schuster, Jeff Seidel and Moishe Mendlowitz

hosts on an every-other-week basis, though both would walk groups of guests to their host families.

Even with the opening of the hostels, many Shabbos guests arrived close to the onset of Shabbos and had to be placed on the old ad hoc basis at the Kotel. But still the ability to work out many placements in advance was a big advantage.

Nor were the matchmaking efforts of Heritage House counselors confined to Shabbos placements. If a guest arrived with a plane ticket for India two days hence, Jewish Quarter resident Sara Yoheved Rigler could count on a call from Heritage House. Despite her own busy career as a writer and speaker, Mrs. Rigler, who had spent over a decade in India in a Buddhist ashram, made herself available for any such cases, and had many notable successes dissuading young Jews from looking for spirituality in distant places without first exploring their own spiritual heritage.

The counselors became adept at matching guests with a passion for something — e.g., sculpture or painting — with an observant Jew in the same field. Often the shared interest fostered the development of a close connection, and even where it did not, the message that being a sculptor or painter was no contradiction to being an Orthodox Jew removed a potential obstacle to further exploration of Torah.

But the biggest change was the opportunity to offer a full Shabbos experience, not just a single meal. For instance, the woman's hostel always held a Shabbos candle-lighting and Kabbalat Shabbat service before heading down to the Kotel. The singing ushered in Shabbos in a spirit of joy. And by the time the guests and counselors reached the top of the stairs leading down to the Kotel Plaza, they were greeted by the sounds of the singing issuing from below.

While Rabbi Schuster had always returned to the Kotel on Shabbos morning to place people for Shabbos lunch, the numbers were a small fraction of those placed on Friday night. But those staying at the hostels were automatically set up for two meals.

Sometimes on Leil Shabbos, as the hostel guests returned from their Shabbos meal, there was an Ask the Rabbi session with Rabbi Avi Geller, at which guests could pursue any questions that had arisen during the meal. The hostels always had extra staff on duty for Shabbos. On the majority of Shabbosos, when Rabbi Geller was not there, the Shabbos staff members would inevitably stay up until late in the night chatting with the guests, while munching on cookies and other snacks.

The culmination of the Shabbos experience was the *shalosh seudos* at the men's hostel, which brought the male and female guests together around long tables arranged in a U shape. The *shalosh seudos* featured

Motzaei Shabbos after *shalosh seudos* at the men's hostel

Chapter Sixteen: Heritage House as a Force Multiplier ☐ 223

lots of singing, with a preference for familiar melodies with a minimum of easily repeated words. In between the singing, a speaker would share words of Torah, stories, and a succinct message designed to pierce the heart.

The most frequent *shalosh seudos* speaker was Rabbi Geller.[1] Dena Estrin, the long-time senior *madrichah* in the women's hostel, describes his mixture of Carlebach *niggunim* and words of Torah as "distinctively passionate and lively."[2] Rabbi Geller knew exactly the message he wanted to get across, and once he discovered an effective packaging for that message, drilled it home week after week.

He would begin by asking those present who could name the Seven Wonders of the Ancient World. Whether or not they could name them all, he would add an eighth — the Kotel, which had survived despite all the conquests, destruction, and rebuilding of Jerusalem. But even more remarkable still was the ninth wonder: the eternal Jewish people. But then he would add a caveat: True, the Jewish people had survived persecution and destruction. Go to Titus's arch in Rome and see the bas relief of the triumphant Roman legions carrying the Menorah and other vessels of the Temple over the words *Judea Capta* — Jerusalem has been captured. Titus certainly assumed that the loss of national sovereignty and a homeland spelled the end of the Jewish people. But it had not.

Yet only a certain group of the Jewish people remained. At the time of Chanukah, the Maccabees' first battle was not against the Seleucid Greeks, but against the Hellenizers within the Jewish people themselves. And during the Second Temple, there was an ongoing struggle between the Pharisees, who were loyal to the Oral Law, and the Sadducees who denied it. Those Hellenizers and Sadducees and later the Karaites have all disappeared from Jewish history. "Have any of you ever met a Sadducee?" Rabbi Geller would ask.

He would conclude by pointing out that Jewish pride, absent Jewish knowledge and commitment, would not sustain itself or ensure Jewish continuity. "What would you think of a soldier who throws down his gun, takes off his uniform, and disobeys orders, while insisting he is

---

1. Rabbi Geller arrived at Aish HaTorah in Elul of 1980 straight from Lakewood's Bais Medrash Govoha. He was the only attendee at Rabbi Weinberg's famous Lakewood lectures to take him up on his offer of a free ticket to Israel for any Lakewood talmid willing to come to learn and teach in Aish HaTorah.

2. Estrin, *It Happened at Heritage House,* p. 152.

Rabbi Schuster in the kitchen of the men's hostel

proud of being a soldier? His actions belie his words. Find out what you are proud of. Find out what you would be willing to die for, like so many Jews throughout the ages. Then you'll know what you're living for as well."

Rabbi Yaakov Asher Sinclair, another occasional *shalosh seudos* speaker, boasted the kind of life story sure to grab the attention of young Heritage House guests. In the early 1970s, he opened a recording studio in London that worked with some of the world's best-known bands. His Shakespearean theater training was immediately evident when he spoke.[3]

Occasionally, the *shalosh seudos* meal provided opportunities for up-and-coming talent to develop. Rabbi Chanoch (Henry) Harris got his religious start at Heritage House. And six years later, after learning at Aish HaTorah and beginning to teach there, Yossi Kaufman asked him to host *shalosh seudos* once every four to six weeks. One of those weeks, Rabbi Yitz Greenman, the founder of Aish-New York, happened to be present, and he immediately hired Harris for Aish-New York, of which he eventually became the educational director.

Rabbi Schuster was present at *shalosh seudos*, hovering on the sidelines, never participating directly. But if he was pleased with something,

---

3. Today, Rabbi Sinclair produces compelling parashah videos each week. They combine his unique vocal control with the artistic eye that has enabled him to publish two volumes combining his stunning photographs with Torah-based texts: *Seasons of the Moon* and *The Color of Heaven.*

he always let the counselor running the *shalosh seudos* know in effusive terms, and similarly if something displeased him.

Just how powerful was the Shabbos experience at Heritage House? Rabbi David Felsenthal, who with his wife, Chani, served as the dorm couple at the women's hostel in the early 1990s, attests that over an eleven-week period in the summer of 1992, nearly every young woman who stayed in the hostel for Shabbos ended up going to a seminary for a period of time. He estimates that in one summer, Heritage House sent close to one thousand guests to seminary.

In time, Heritage House added services for the Yamim Noraim and other festivals to the Shabbos experience. The first year the program was in conjunction with both Aish HaTorah and Jeff Seidel, with Rabbi Edelstein offering the explanatory commentary. In subsequent years, Rabbi Yaakov Marcus, just back in Israel from serving as the founding rav of a kiruv shul in Toronto's northern suburbs, served as the guide to the davening.[4] At different points during Rosh Hashanah and Yom Kippur, he would turn the explanatory role over to someone else and adjourn to another room to give a *shiur* on some aspect of the day to those not up to the full davening. Rabbi Edelstein had intended to split the explanatory role with Rabbi Marcus, but when he saw how superb Rabbi Marcus was, he ceded it entirely to him. He would walk to the Old City all the way from the furthest reaches of Ramot, with one or two of his children, on the first day of Rosh Hashanah and remain there for the rest of the *Chag*.

Every effort was made to secure *chazzanim* who could give the davening an upbeat, participatory feel. They included popular performers Lenny Solomon and Binny Friedman, Rabbi Chaim Perlmutter from Yeshivat HaKotel, and Rabbi Natan Greenberg, a Breslover chassid who founded the Bat Ayin Yeshiva. Rabbi Edelstein would lead the Neilah service at the conclusion of Yom Kippur. So powerful were the Heritage House services that many of the baalei teshuvah among the counselors preferred to participate in Heritage House services rather than those in their yeshivos.

---

4. When Rabbi Marcus and his family returned to Israel, Rabbi Marcus asked his rav, Rabbi Beryl Gershenfeld, where he recommended that he teach. Rabbi Gershenfeld told him that Heritage House and Isralight were the highest impact programs at that time. Besides running the Rosh Hashanah and Yom Kippur services, he taught at Heritage House every Monday night for five years. At the same time, he became a program head at Neve Yerushalayim.

HERITAGE HOUSE PROVIDED RABBI SCHUSTER WITH MUCH GREATER flexibility to cater to individual needs. For instance, the counselors at

**Another Arrow in the Quiver**

the Heritage House hostels made efforts to connect guests to members of the community with whom they shared a common passion. Just knowing that those passions did not present a barrier to a Torah life, and that their fulfillment might even be enhanced by Torah, frequently served to remove a large barrier to exploring Judaism more fully.

Dena Estrin, the senior *madrichah* at the women's hostel for five years, provides examples of such connections. Olivia showed up at Heritage House with two teenage children. After years spent raising her children and building a successful fur business with her husband in Holland, Olivia had taken up sculpting with a passion. Soon after her arrival, Dena took her to meet Carmella, a Torah-observant sculptor, whose studio was just outside the walls of the Old City. By the time Dena returned, the two were so engrossed in discussing ways to express oneself Jewishly through sculpture that they barely noticed her. For Shabbos, Dena placed Olivia and her children with the family of Rabbi Schloss, a successful painter and rebbi living in the Jewish Quarter.[5] For those athletically inclined, Dena knew she could call on her long-time friend from Neve, Lisa, a former professional tennis player, with whom they would have a common bond.

SOMETIMES, JUST HAVING THE PHYSICAL PLANT OF HERITAGE HOUSE available was the key to drawing an individual or even entire fam-

**Every Extra Room Counts**

ily close. The Ginsburg family provides a good example of the latter. Dr. Len Ginsburg, his wife Beth, and their infant daughter Daniella arrived in Tel Aviv in 1989 during the first intifada. Dr. Ginsburg had just completed a fellowship in retinal surgery at Harvard Medical School, and came to volunteer at Tel Hashomer Hospital for a year.

Shortly after arriving, the Ginsburgs were in a restaurant when they overheard a couple talking about a rabbi whom they had met at the Kotel and how the rabbi had set them up for a "wonderful Shabbat experience." The Ginsburgs knew they had to meet that rabbi. So, they went to the Kotel, and quickly met Rabbi Schuster. He invited the Ginsburgs to stay at the men's hostel that Shabbos, in the room reserved

---

5. Estrin, *It Happened at Heritage House*, pp. 157-58.

for couples, instead of the hotel where they had reservations. They could not have known then how that room, and the Heritage House in general, would change their lives forever.

That first Shabbos was filled with new friends and experiences. Rabbi Schuster set up the Ginsburgs for meals at the homes of carefully selected families in the Jewish Quarter, many of whom he had started on their path. *Shalosh seudos*, back in the large common room of the men's hostel, was filled with singing and conversation. By Havdalah, the sense of camaraderie and spirituality had captivated the Ginsburgs. Rabbi Schuster invited them back for the next Shabbos, and so the journey began.

Rabbi Schuster was an integral part of the Ginsburgs' year, and of their lives going forward. Whether it was taking Len to Aish and Ohr Somayach for classes, or driving Beth to Neve Yerushalayim, or going with Len to purchase his first pair of tefillin, he always had time. Rabbi Schuster blocked off the couple's room for the rest of the Ginsburgs' time in Israel. His only request in return was that Beth light the Shabbos candles for the men's hostel. Len recalls how moved the young men were as they watched her light. "And I was one of those moved."

Week after week, Beth and Len enjoyed a magnificent Shabbos experience and learned and grew in classes. They also watched young men and women come through the doors of the hostel, some just looking for meals and a place to stay, but leaving weeks later with *sefarim* under their arms and yarmulkes on their heads.

*Shalosh seudos* in the large common room of the men's hostel was always moving. The singing and guest lecture caused many to thirst for more. That year a young man named Michael Stern, who was then studying at Aish HaTorah, ran the *shalosh seudos*. He eventually became a rabbi, and years later he moved to Lower Merion, a Philadelphia suburb, near where the Ginsburgs live, and created a very successful kiruv program known as Rabbis Without Walls. The Sterns and Ginsburgs became very close friends, prior to Rabbi Stern's passing in his early 50s.

One Shabbos, the Ginsburgs brought with them to Heritage House a friend from Tel Hashomer, a German medical student named Thomas. Thomas's grandmother survived World War II by pretending to be Christian. A year earlier, just prior to her death, she told Thomas that his mother and he were Jews. Confused about what that meant, he came to Israel for what was to be just a one-month medical school

rotation. That first Shabbos experience was so inspirational for
Thomas, he ended up staying
at Heritage House for several
months and subsequently learning at Aish HaTorah for a year,
before returning to Germany to
complete medical school. He is a
Torah-observant Jew today.

Needlepoint given by Mrs. Schuster to Dr.
Len and Beth Ginsburg upon staying in
their suburban Philadelphia home

The Ginsburgs' relationship
with Rabbi Schuster remained
very close after they left Israel.
He stayed with them for a few days once or twice a year while fundraising in the United States. And they were the only one of Rabbi Schuster's
hosts to ever persuade Mrs. Schuster to join her husband in their home
(aided by the fact that her brother Moshe Garfinkel lived in Philadelphia).

One of those to whom Rabbi Schuster took the Ginsburgs that year
for a Shabbos meal was Rabbi Yonah Yaffe. Rabbi Yaffe was one of the
very first students at Aish HaTorah and a long-time Aish fundraiser and
teacher. He and his family befriended the Ginsburgs over the course of
their year in Israel, and Rabbi Yaffe used to stay with the Ginsburgs on
his travels to the United States.

One time, Rabbi Yaffe brought a young rosh yeshivah whom he was
helping to raise funds to the Ginsburg home for Shabbos. In the course
of that visit, Dr. Ginsburg began discussing an idea he was working on
to enable electronic health records to display on one screen everything
a doctor would need to know to make proper medical decisions. The
brother of that rosh yeshivah became the first major investor in the company that Dr. Ginsburg formed to bring his medical records company
into reality. That company has already obtained three U.S. patents and
has one pending in Israel. But for the connection to Yonah Yaffe through
Rabbi Schuster, Dr. Ginsburg is doubtful he would have ever raised the
initial capital to get the company off the ground.

Another experience of the ongoing *siyata d'Shmaya* flowing from the
connection to Rabbi Schuster changed Dr. Ginsburg's perspective on the
very essence of being a physician. Shoshana Garfinkel, a niece by marriage of Mrs. Schuster's, developed diabetes as a child, as a consequence
of which her vision deteriorated so sharply in adulthood that she could
not even see the leaves on a tree. During her first pregnancy, her vision

Rabbi Schuster escorting Dr. Ginsburg through the men's hostel

declined further to the point that when her baby was born she could not see her infant daughter's face.

Dr. Ginsburg, who was already acquainted with the family of Mrs. Schuster's brother in Philadelphia, operated on Shoshana's right eye, the better of the two, and was scheduled to operate the next week on the left eye, through which she could not even count fingers held up directly in front of her. When the bandages came off after that first surgery, however, Shoshana's sight had not only been restored in her right eye, but miraculously also in the left eye, upon which Dr. Ginsburg had not operated.

Each morning when Dr. Ginsburg recites the blessing "Blessed are You, Hashem, our G-d, King of the universe, Who gives sight to the blind," he now fully appreciates Who in fact is restoring sight. "Rabbi Shuster restored the light of Torah in the eyes of tens of thousands, and Hashem worked through him to change so many lives, including those of his niece and my family, forever," says Dr. Ginsburg.

On at least one occasion, just the availability of an extra room at Heritage House turned out to have life-changing consequences. Raphael Solomon was already 40 years old when he came to Israel from Singapore to study at Aish HaTorah in late 2008. He would have been by far the oldest student in the Aish dorms, and the idea of returning to dorm life at that stage in his life had little appeal for Raphael.

Fortunately, Moishe Mendlowitz, the manager of the men's hostel at the time, heard of his plight and offered him space in a loft above one of the common rooms. "I felt that everything was set up just for me," Raphael would later write. "With a bed in the loft, I had my privacy.... There was a computer in the living room that allowed me to keep in touch with family and the outside world. Through the Shabbat placements, I met many of the lovely residents of the Old City, many of whom are my friends today."[6]

Raphael ended up learning for two years at Aish HaTorah, something he almost assuredly would not have done but for the private room Heritage House afforded him.

SEVENTEEN-YEAR-OLD HOLLEY ABRAMS ARRIVED IN ISRAEL IN 1993, after graduating high school in Boise, Idaho, with the dream of becoming a Jew. Holley's interest in Judaism started when **From Holley to Yehudit** she was 13, and her cello teacher handed her the sheet music to Kol Nidrei. She recalls "every hair ... standing up on end," as she played, and she felt a strong need to "find

Holley as an Idaho cowgirl

6. Estrin, *It Happened at Heritage House*, p. 268.

the origins of the music." Soon she was participating in the eclectic services in the only synagogue in Idaho, and the oldest synagogue west of the Mississippi.[7]

Holley came to Israel on a six-week volunteer program, Sar-el, in which she worked in a psychiatric hospital in Hadera. In her spare time, she went from seminary to seminary hoping to find one that would take her as a gentile seeking to convert. None would, which only strengthened her resolve. She concluded that Hashem was testing her to determine how committed she was to becoming Jewish.

At the end of her program, Holley suddenly found herself without any place to stay. She turned to Rabbi Schuster, whom she had already met at the Kotel, and he told her that she could stay at Heritage House as she pursued routes to conversion. From the first time she met him, she was struck by his kindness and his shining countenance, and that permission to stay indefinitely at the women's hostel was full confirmation of her initial judgment.

Over the month or so she stayed at Heritage House, Holley met and naturally gravitated to Rabbi Asher Wade, a former Christian pastor, who both taught at Heritage House and led tours of Yad Vashem on Fridays. On Yom Kippur, Abrams went to the Kotel, where she surrendered her heart to Hashem: "I will do Your will for the rest of my life — even give up my dream of being a doctor — just help me become a Jew," she pleaded.

The very next day, Rabbi Wade told her that he had contacted Rebbetzin Tova Weingot, the head of Sha'arei Bina Seminary in Tzefat, and she was willing to accept Holley as a student. Holley jumped at the chance, and made arrangements to head for Tzefat. In the meantime, the owner of a Jerusalem music store which she had haunted in search of a cello called to tell her that he had one that he could give her. All her prayers had been answered.

In Tzefat, she studied from dawn to late at night, and a year later went through *geirus* (conversion) under the auspices of Rav Avraham Auerbach of Teveriah, a son of Rav Shlomo Zalman Auerbach. She describes how as she emerged from the mikveh, "life as a Jew felt brighter and more potent. That special feeling has never gone away."

Yet had Rabbi Schuster not allowed her to stay at Heritage House

---

7. Shraga Simmons, "The Unstoppable Yehudit Abrams," Aish.com, Aug. 21, 2018. Much of the following material is drawn from Rabbi Simmons' article. In addition, this author and his wife have hosted Yehudit Abrams for Shabbos, and I interviewed her about Rabbi Schuster.

indefinitely, she would have had no alternative to returning to the U.S. without having converted.

After her *geirus*, Yehudit took a six-month ulpan, in an effort to attain a sufficient level of Hebrew proficiency to start medical school in Israel. That she was unable to do, and she was forced to return to the United States, where she studied mechanical engineering, before studying medicine at Charles University in Prague.

That combination of engineering and medicine put her in a position to bring great benefit to women around the world. During her senior year in medical school, she applied to Singularity University, which, despite the name, is actually a technology think tank and business incubator, located on NASA's campus in Silicon Valley. She was accepted and granted a $25,000 scholarship from Google. There she interacted with famous entrepreneurs, like Larry Paige and Vint Cerg, astronauts, and Nobel laureates.

She also became friendly over that period with NASA's chief medical officer, who offered her a job at the end of the ten-week Singularity program. NASA, she says, "sets impossible standards and expects you to achieve large things." She joined a team developing medical devices to support astronaut health over extended space missions, such as manned flight to Mars. During her two years at NASA, she worked on the research and development of a "body window," a wearable ultrasound patch, which provides continuous internal imaging and medical diagnosis.

When a cousin, who had survived breast cancer, was killed in an auto accident, Yehudit began thinking about ways to use her expertise in ultrasound, gained at NASA and subsequently at a Bay Area start-up, to facilitate earlier detection of breast cancer, when the survival chances are much greater.

Yehudit, her young son, and her mother made aliyah in 2017, and she won a coveted residency at Jerusalem's Shaare Zedek hospital, which would have allowed her to finally realize her childhood dream of practicing medicine. But at the same time, she applied to MassChallenge, a prestigious, start-up accelerator for early-stage entrepreneurs developing potentially high-impact projects. Yehudit had already created a company, MonitHer, and patented an idea for a home, hand-held ultrasound device. Her design would allow much more frequent examinations than traditional mammograms, and, at the same time, reduce many of the limitations of traditional exams — false positives,

Yehudit Abram's winning presentation at the WeWork awards event

missed early-stage changes in dense tissue — by providing physicians historical images of changes in the tissue over time. Her proposal was one of those selected from among five hundred applications from forty countries.

With work space provided by MassChallenge, and contact with veteran hi-tech entrepreneurs, she was able to refine her design further in preparation for WeWork Awards. In the presence of Adam Neuman, the founder of WeWork, and an audience of 5,000, Yehudit's presentation was awarded the $360,000 first prize in the summer of 2018. Yehudit intended to use the money to develop a hardware prototype of her home monitor — the necessary prelude to raising the millions of dollars necessary to go into mass production.

As was so often the case with Rabbi Schuster, the impact of his work reverberated far beyond what even he could have anticipated. Not only are Yehudit Abrams and her son David precious souls added to the Jewish people, but she may well be on the brink of a technology that can save the lives of the millions of women around the globe — over twelve percent of the female population — who will at some point in their lives develop breast cancer.

*Chapter Seventeen*

# HERITAGE HOUSE FOLLOW-UP[1]

T ODAY, MUCH OF THE VALUE OF LARGE TECHNOLOGY COMPA-
nies lies in the vast amount of information they collect on users
of their platforms. Heritage House too compiled a good deal
of valuable information on Jewish *neshamos* passing through. Before
leaving, all guests at Heritage House filled out a card with their name,
contact information, what they had done while at Heritage House, and
how they would like to build on the experience of Israel and Heritage
House upon returning home. Sometimes, one of the counselors would
also add comments to the cards.

But all that information was only of value if there was someone to
put it to use. It quickly became clear that follow-up could not be done
effectively from Israel, and that an American follow-up operation
would be required. Mindy Lidsky was the first follow-up person hired.
She started in 1993 and continued for around ten years, until her children were sufficiently grown to require her nighttime attention.

All the follow-up personnel had themselves gone through a long
process of religious growth, and were therefore acutely aware of the

---

1. Some of the names and identifying details in this section have been changed.

challenges faced by those they connected with on the phone. Mindy Lidsky, originally from Livingstone, New Jersey, was very active in NCSY growing up. And she brought on board her friend Basya Weinrib, who was raised Conservative, before being drawn to the Bostoner Rebbe as a teenager.

When it became clear that the time differentials necessitated a third follow-up person on the West Coast, Basya suggested her friend Jody Gross, who was also born into a Conservative home, but had decided after a Shabbos in Crown Heights when she was 13 that she would be mitzvah observant, and stuck to that resolve. On a post-high school Young Judea program in Israel, Jody had actually seen Rabbi Schuster in action, as he came frequently to the program's dorms on the Hebrew University Har Hatzofim campus. During her time in Jerusalem, she was invited almost every Shabbos by Rabbi Gershon Weinberger, who worked extensively with the Young Judaea participants in those days.

The job of the follow-up coordinators effectively required cold-calling returning young people, with the goal of connecting them to families, rabbanim, or campus kiruv workers in their area, depending on their circumstances. Over the years, the follow-up personnel found that a close connection with a specific family was often the most effective, as those families could give more individual attention to the young Jew in question.

The unpleasant task of cold-calling strangers was made considerably easier by virtue of the warm feelings that those returning from Heritage House had of their stay there. When Mindy, for instance, opened the conversation, "Hi, this is Mindy from Heritage House," the stranger on the other end invariably responded effusively about Heritage House, especially if they had just returned from Israel. Many mentioned that the experience had been an "eye-opener" with respect to Torah Jews and Judaism.[2] Others spoke of the impact on them of Shabbos and how much they had enjoyed the discussions with intelligent and interesting people from around the world.[3]

Every week, the coordinators would receive a new list of Heritage House guests. Sometimes those lists were prioritized in terms of the growth potential that the Heritage House counselors or one of the senior staff had seen in particular guests. If Yossi Kaufman was particularly interested in a former guest, he would call frequently. He had

---

2. Basya Weinrib.

3. Jody Gross.

obviously read Dale Carnegie, remarks Mrs. Weinrib, and fully imbibed Carnegie's message that the best way to win someone over is to show them how important they are to you. That was indeed one of the subliminal messages behind the follow-up calls.

Rabbi Moshe Efros, who traveled the country evaluating kiruv programs for Keren Wolfson,[4] was an indispensable resource for the coordinators as they developed their lists of contacts. Heritage House also paid for them to attend several conventions of AJOP (Association of Jewish Outreach Professionals) so that they could expand their contacts and get to know personally some of the kiruv personnel in the field.

Mindy visited Heritage House in Jerusalem twice to better understand what the returning guests had experienced there. On one occasion, Rabbi Schuster even let her try to convince two backpackers in the square of the Jewish Quarter to check out the women's hostel. On that trip, she attended classes at Aish HaTorah and lectures by Rabbi Dr. Dovid Gottlieb at Ohr Somayach. She also went on Rabbi Asher Wade's Yad Vashem tour. He would stand in front of a large photograph of an elderly Jew in tallis and tefillin, and ask, "Will your children identify with this person? Will they even know what he is wearing?"

In practice, the coordinators had almost unlimited discretion. Though the lists might be prioritized, much depended on who answered the phone and who did not. In time, the coordinators began keeping records of every call and anything noteworthy that took place, but they were free to spend as much time as they wanted on any former guest. The most they were likely to hear from the home office in Jerusalem was not to become too invested in a particular case, or that such matters as conversion were not ones for which Heritage House was set up.

Such cautionary advice against getting too involved was likely to go unheeded once the coordinator was deeply involved in a particular story. Mrs. Lidsky's involvement with Jonathan, for instance, went on over a period of many years. He returned to Brandeis from Heritage House full of enthusiasm from his time in Israel, and was moving very quickly in terms of taking on religious observance.

Then one day as he and Mindy were talking, he mentioned that his mother had converted under non-Orthodox auspices. It was left to Mindy (on Rabbi Edelstein's instructions) to inform him that he was not Jewish in the eyes of the Torah. The effect was devastating. "I'm

---

4. See p. 252.

nothing. I'm a nobody," Jonathan would say. After a long period of reflection, however, he decided that he wanted to be Jewish and went through a very serious *geirus* course before committing.

But Jonathan's struggles did not end there. He was a competitive-level skier and at some point the tension between his desire to excel in skiing and Shabbos observance became too great for him. On a training trip to New Zealand, Jonathan was standing at the top of a tall mountain, with a panoramic view, and suddenly came to the realization, "I don't really want this. I want Judaism."

Eventually, Jonathan moved to Israel for several years and started a family there before moving back to America.

One night, Basya Weinrib received a call from an unhappy teenager, with a complicated back story. She had been adopted as an infant from China by a couple in which the husband was Jewish and the mother was not. At some point, the mother underwent a Conservative conversion.

Basya did not have to wait for Yossi Kaufman to tell her that Kimberly was not a case for Heritage House. But she would still talk to Kimberly from time to time, and even met her. At one point, she sent her *The Bamboo Cradle*, the true story of an American Jewish professor and his wife in China who adopted a Chinese foundling, who became in time the impetus for the family's move toward full observance. A number of years later, Basya was walking down the street in Passaic when a young woman with Oriental features whose hair was covered stopped her excitedly and told her husband standing next to her, "This is the woman who sent me the book."

Just as the gift of *The Bamboo Cradle* changed Kimberly's life, so did similar acts of *chesed* have a crucial impact on other young searching Jews. On one of the Heritage House lists, Basya spotted someone from her hometown of Fairfield, New Jersey, who was then a student at Penn State University. Penn State is located far from any significant Jewish community, and aside from Friday night dinner at the campus Hillel, there was little Jewish activity on campus, at least not for someone who had just returned from Heritage House with a determination to keep growing as a Jew. Mrs. Weinrib amassed a library of Torah books solicited from friends and shipped them to Penn State to establish a Jewish library on campus. The young man who had been the principal beneficiary of the library ended up becoming religious and moving to Passaic sometime after college.

A more straightforward and typical case involved a young woman who returned from Israel very excited and eager to go back again as soon as possible. Her problem was that she needed health insurance, and her parents could not or would not cover it. Mrs. Weinrib called Mrs. Lidsky for advice and the latter told her to fundraise the cost of the health insurance, which Mrs. Weinrib did. The young woman was deeply touched by the desire to help a fellow Jew realize her dreams. She also became religious and lives in Passaic today.

The willingness of Rabbi Schuster to spend whatever it took to bring a Jew along the path toward a full Jewish life somehow was transmitted to the Heritage House follow-up coordinators in America.

Ironically, some of the coordinators' most successful cases involved those who had never stayed at Heritage House. Some of those were searching online for Jewish learning programs and came to Heritage House, which then referred them on to the coordinators. One of the contacts who went furthest, Mindy Lidsky remembers, was a 50-year-old organic farmer in Maine. He and his wife lived without electricity or running water. He began by purchasing tefillin. He then moved on to a telephone *chavrusa*, before spending a period of time at Ohr Somayach in Monsey.

His wife did not share his enthusiasm, and he frequently drove all the way to Monsey for Shabbos. Her attitude changed, however, after a two-month visit to Israel, where they stayed in the couples room in the men's hostel.

He has been learning continuously for decades, and the farm is now in frequent use for Shabbatonim and mini-seminars.[5]

When Jody Gross thinks back over all the people she came in contact with working for Heritage House, the first who comes to mind is a professor in northern California who contacted Heritage House directly and was referred to her. He had virtually no Jewish background, but was very interested in learning more. Jody spoke with him frequently and suggested that he study for a period at Ohr Somayach in Monsey, and he took her up on that suggestion. In the same period, he also visited Israel. Eventually, he moved to Los Angeles, where the opportunities for learning were greater. Jody served as the *shadchan* for his marriage to a member of the Los Angeles community, and today they live in Israel.

---

5. Rabbi Avraham Edelstein.

Though it was not part of their job description, in many cases it was the follow-up coordinators themselves who became regular Shabbos hosts for those with whom they developed a relationship. The Lidskys frequently hosted a Rutgers student, who eventually went to Israel and married a Breslover chassid. Today her son is a regular Shabbos guest at the Lidskys'.

The clearest lesson that emerges from the cumulative experience of the coordinators is: It isn't over until it's over, and one can never know the impact of a particular experience — if not immediately, then down the line. Mindy Lidsky established a great rapport with a woman whom she had contacted, and after about six months of speaking to her on the phone invited her for Shabbos.

As soon as the woman entered the house, however, Mindy realized that the invitation was premature, and the woman was not ready for a full Shabbos. She looked totally overwhelmed by the experience, like a deer suddenly caught in the headlights of an approaching car. After Shabbos, she fled quickly, never to be heard from again.

A year later, however, Mrs. Lidsky attended a local *shiur* given by Rebbetzin Holly Pavlov from Jerusalem, and there she saw a young woman whom she could not place, but who looked vaguely familiar. Finally, her name came to Mindy, and she blurted out "Sharon." Sharon turned, and replied, "Mindy." Sharon confessed that when she had come to the Lidskys' the full Shabbos experience had been more than she could handle. But she had remained connected. She ended up attending Shearim, Rebbetzin Pavlov's seminary in Jerusalem, and building a Torah family.

The key, the coordinators found, was to build a relationship, without becoming discouraged by the inevitable ups and downs. A UCLA student returned to his native Los Angeles from Israel filled with enthusiasm for taking on more Jewish observance, despite his parents' opposition. That commitment, however, waxed and waned, as schoolwork and campus social life often gained the upper hand. After graduation, he took a job with a prestigious consulting firm.

But through all the ups and downs, he maintained constant contact with Jody Gross and continued to attend Torah classes. Ironically, it was the firm's plan to take the entire staff on vacation to Hawaii that made him realize that he was in imminent danger of being sucked in and losing his Jewish connection. Today, nearly twenty years later, he plays a pivotal role in one of the local kiruv organizations.

NOT A SINGLE PERSON CONNECTED TO HERITAGE HOUSE DOUBTS FOR a moment that the impact was huge, though it is not easily quantified.

**The Impact of Heritage House** This much is sure: Tens of thousands of young, searching Jews crossed the thresholds of the two hostels over a twenty-year period, and thousands of those ended up taking on lives of full religious observance as a consequence.

Perhaps the best testimony to the power of Heritage House comes from those who opposed its message. The popular Harvard-produced guide *Let's Go to Israel* warned against Heritage House in the 1990s, on the grounds that those running the hostels would seek to encourage religious observance. Similarly, warnings against Heritage House and Rabbi Schuster were common at kibbutz programs for volunteers and ulpanim. A new verb entered Hebrew slang, *l'shaster*, to be picked up at the Kotel or elsewhere by Rabbi Schuster.

On a visit to Monsey, after he returned to the United States in 1988, Yaakov Saver found that he recognized close to half of the students at Kol Yaakov, a yeshivah catering to baalei teshuvah, as having been at Heritage House. Every year, at one of the first meetings of the incoming students at Me'ohr, a post-high school seminary, Rabbi Zechariah Greenwald, the dean of the seminary, asks how many have a parent who stayed at Heritage House. Inevitably, at least two girls raise their hands.

But the true impact of Heritage House is not captured in aggregate numbers. It would require the life stories of all that led up to each individual's arrival at Heritage House, all that happened during his or her stay(s) at Heritage House, and his or her subsequent history. That is obviously impossible. But Dena Estrin, the live-in night counselor at the women's hostel for five years in the 1980s and early 1990s, did keep a diary of her time at Heritage House and has published vignettes from that diary about many of those she met during that period as *It Happened at Heritage House: Tales from the Legendary Jerusalem Youth Hostel*.

One thing that her dozens of stories make clear is that the impact of Heritage House cannot possibly be measured from the time of each guest's departure. Nor could one know for sure what would have a lasting impact and what not.

Sara, for instance, came to Israel on her way to Thailand, and ended up staying at Heritage House. Though impressed by much of what she learned in Jerusalem, she adhered to her original plan of going to

Thailand. Before leaving Israel, however, she decided to keep kosher on her travels. In Thailand, she found herself in a rural village surrounded by thatched huts, colorfully clad locals, and women wearing coiled braces to elongate their necks. While the rest of her traveling party was participating in a unique culinary experience, Sara whipped out her Osem soup mix.

That provoked her trekking mate to comment, "You are an even more exotic experience than these villagers!" Sara thought to herself, "This is not exotic in Jerusalem; it's quite normal." She suddenly felt her Jewishness so intently that she decided to abandon her exciting travels and return to Jerusalem and Heritage House for further immersion in the Jewish experience. She eventually became a long-time senior *madrichah* at Heritage House, prior to marrying and building a large family.

Rachel T., a medical student, stayed only two nights at Heritage House in 2006, and showed no interest in attending any classes. The only tangible thing she did while at the women's hostel was to look at a few websites for exploring Judaism with Mrs. Chaya Weisberg, the director of the hostel. But a year later, she returned to the women's hostel fully observant, having progressed from the websites to live events to Shabbos meals and classes. Between her medical internships, she spent three months at Rebbetzin Denah Weinberg's EYAHT seminary, and is today "Bais Yaakov-style *frum*," in Mrs. Weisberg's words.

Julie, from Sydney, Australia, spent only one night at the women's hostel, on a backpacking trip through Europe and Asia after graduating college. But the next morning she agreed to go to classes at Neve Yerushalayim, and enjoyed them so much that she abandoned her plan to fly to Thailand to celebrate her sister's birthday with her. Instead she stayed at Neve for two weeks before returning to Sydney and connecting to the Orthodox community there.

Mandi (Stamelman) Kauffman was already 27 years old when Yossi Kaufman offered her the position of senior live-in counselor at Heritage House. One of the conditions for taking the job was that Mandi could not date for the first six months. Rabbi Moshe Chalkowski of Neve Yerushalayim strongly advised her against accepting the offer. "Do you want to get married walking with a cane?" he asked. But Mandi felt that she could not refuse, as Heritage House had played such a major role in her own religious development.

One night, a woman who reminded Mandi of a slightly younger

version of her free-spirited self checked in to Heritage House. Like Mandi, she was a native of South Africa, filled with energy and excitement about all her adventures over the course of a long period of traveling.

Mandi did something that she had never done before, and invited the woman into her private room, where they sat talking the entire night. At the end of the night. Mandi lent the woman a book that had had a major impact on her younger self. The next day, the visitor was gone, never to be heard from again.

Despite Rabbi Chalkowski's dire predictions, Mandi did marry Rabbi Gedalia Kauffman the next year, in a match in which Heritage House played a large role. For one thing, Gedaliah ran the *shalosh seudos* at Heritage House at that time. In addition, their *shadchan* was Rabbi Shlomo Canvasser, who did counseling at night at Heritage House for three or four years, before his passing at a relatively young age. Rabbi Canvasser was a *talmid chacham* who was able to use his deeply intuitive sense of people to help them clarify their issues and see how to use them as opportunities for personal and spiritual growth. The focus of his counseling was uncovering any underlying issues and baggage a person might bring to Heritage House, in order to ensure a healthy teshuvah process.[6]

In 2005, the Kauffmans joined the team at Aish-South Africa. One day, one of the members of the community approached Mandi and invited her to a *tichel* party for her newly religious sister, who was returning to South Africa from the States to get married and did not know anyone in the religious community apart from her sister. Mandi was expecting at the time and very tired, but felt she could not decline.

As they sat around in a circle at the *tichel* party giving the kallah blessings and sharing *divrei Torah*, Mandi could not shake the feeling that she had met the kallah at some point. Only at 3:00 a.m. following the party, however, did it suddenly strike her: The kallah was the same young woman with whom she had stayed up all night talking ten years earlier at Heritage House.

The kallah subsequently told Mandi, "That night you stayed up speaking to me was actually the first time it occurred to me that maybe I could become religious." When she returned to Los Angeles, she sent back to Mandi the book that had accompanied her throughout her journey.

---

6. Rabbi Gedalia Kauffman; Rabbi Avraham Edelstein.

SUCH STORIES WERE COMMONPLACE AT THE HERITAGE HOUSE HOS-
tels — magical places where amazing things happened on a regular

**The Special Siyata D'Shmaya of Heritage House**

basis. Rabbi Meir Schuster's success was dependent from the start on open *siyata d'Shmaya*, and that *siyata d'Shmaya* was particularly manifest at Heritage House.

Indeed it attached to the woman's hostel long after Rabbi Schuster was incapacitated and incapable of overseeing Heritage House's operations any longer. In 2004, a young, recently married couple, Matan Mordechai and Chaya Weisberg, became the resident houseparents of the women's hostel. Six years later, they were informed that the hostel was being closed because of Rav Schuster's lack of ongoing involvement and the building being put up for sale by its owner.

The Weisbergs decided that they could not let that happen. On its face, their determination was more than a little quixotic. They had no substantial financial resources of their own — Matan Mordechai was then an *avreich* in the Mirrer Yeshiva — no network of potential donors, and no experience fundraising or managing a non-profit. At that point, Matan Mordechai barely knew how to use a computer. They did possess, however, great determination, and two super mentors in the world of non-profit institutions, Rabbi Dovid Refson of Neve Yerushalayim and Dovid Greenblatt of Lawrence.

Dov Friedberg, the owner of the hostel, was moved by their determination and agreed to sell them the building at a significantly reduced price and with very generous mortgage terms. Matan Mordechai became a full-time director, which forced him to leave his family and travel abroad almost every month. The Weisbergs reconfigured the hostel away from reliance on dramatically diminished traffic from backpackers toward use by groups and programs that they developed themselves, such as six-month internship programs in Jerusalem — More Israel and Way More Israel.

Though the 55-square-meter apartment on the second floor of the women's hostel was comfortable for a newlywed couple, by the time the Weisbergs had seven children all the creativity in the world — e.g., lofts built under the high ceilings, cribs placed in recessed windows — could not produce sufficient living space. All the previous resident couples had departed after one or two children (except for Gila and Avraham Manolson, the first dorm parents, who remained until the birth of their third.)

The Weisberg twins in cribs set into recessed window sills

Finally, the Weisbergs decided to convert the second-story space into more dorm rooms for their internship program, rather than relying on expensive short-term rentals, and to rent a larger apartment for their family and a large office from which their growing staff could work comfortably.

But the rental market in the Jewish Quarter is extremely tight and nothing was available. Finally, a half-underground apartment, with little light, became available. But the owner — a friend of Chaya's — decided that the apartment might not survive seven rambunctious children, including twin boys, and backed out.

At last, a real estate agent called Chaya regarding an apartment that turned out to be perfect for their needs. The rental being asked was cheaper than the semi-underground apartment and a separate office combined. One huge bedroom was big enough to hold all the children, and a third bedroom, with a separate entrance, was perfect for an office. On the first visit, Chaya was ready to sign, and she had not even opened the doors in the living room leading to a view unsurpassed in the Jewish Quarter of the Kotel and the Temple Mount.

Just one thing made no sense: Why had no other realtor shown Chaya the property in her five months of searching? And why was an apartment listed for sale at six million dollars available for such a low rent? Chaya spoke with another realtor friend, who cleared up the mystery. The owners of the apartment, then in their 80s, could no longer manage

The Weisbergs on the balcony of their new home with an unsurpassed view
of the Kotel and the Temple Mount

the treacherous steps up to the apartment. Every time a potential renter
showed up to speak to the owners, the wife bluntly told them after a
few minutes, "*Lechu mikan* — please leave." As a consequence, most
realtors had stopped showing it at all. It had been vacant for two years.

Nevertheless, the Weisbergs traveled to the Ramot neighborhood
of Jerusalem to meet the owners. The husband had served as a staff
member of Porat Yosef, Jerusalem's premier Sephardi yeshivah, and
afterwards as rosh yeshivah of his own yeshivot, Mesilot HaTorah and
HaMesilla. He had traveled the world visiting traditional, but not rigor-
ously observant, Sephardi communities and convincing parents to send
their sons to his yeshivah.

With great trepidation, the Weisbergs explained why they were
interested in the apartment, and why it so suited their needs. They
mentioned their large family, and described the work of the women's
Heritage House and their need to host large groups of Shabbos guests
on a weekly basis, as well as during the week. They waited to be told
to leave, but instead the wife told them, "*Chikinu lachem* — We've been
waiting for you. We only want to rent our apartment to a religious family involved in bringing Jewish souls closer, just as my husband and I
used our home for the entire forty years that we lived there."

The *siyata d'Shmaya* of Rabbi Schuster and Heritage House had
manifested itself once again.

*Chapter Eighteen*
# SHORASHIM

B Y THE 1990S, THE TRAFFIC AT THE KOTEL HAD BEGUN TO decline significantly. When Moishe Mendlowitz arrived in Israel in 1996, he heard frequently from Rabbi Schuster how different the situation was compared to earlier days. But it was the outbreak of the Second Intifada, just before Rosh Hashanah of 2000 (5761), that brought tourism to Israel to a virtual halt, especially of younger travelers roaming the globe.

A LESS DEDICATED PERSON MIGHT HAVE DECIDED TO REST ON HIS laurels and the nearly thirty years of phenomenal success. But that was

**No Resting on Laurels**
not Rabbi Schuster. He had a life mission, and he was not about to give it up and mope around the Kotel, just because that mission would now have to take a different form. As he had done with the creation of Heritage House, he went about building something new to match the changing circumstances.[1]

---

1. In a eulogy for Rabbi Schuster, Rabbi Dovid Refson highlighted his refusal to rest on past achievements, with reference to Rabbi Samson Raphael Hirsch's commentary (*Vayikra* 6:4) on the mitzvah of *terumas hadeshen,* the removal from the Altar of a portion of the ashes of the previous day's Daily Offering: "The start of every new day summons us to set upon our task with full and fresh devotion as though we never accomplished anything before. The memory

Rabbi Avraham Edelstein (l.) and Rabbi Yirmiyahu Abramov (r.)

One day, he came into Rabbi Avraham Edelstein's office at Heritage House and announced, "We have to do something for the Israelis." Ever the practical person, Rabbi Edelstein noted the obvious problem with that plan: "You don't speak Hebrew. I don't speak Hebrew. How are we going to work with Israelis?"

But Reb Meir was undeterred by what he regarded as no more than a detail. He insisted that there was a great need, and that they must do something. At that point, Rabbi Edelstein did what he always did in such situations: "I grabbed onto his coattails, and relied on the *siyata d'Shmaya* that always attached to him to carry us forward."

The brain trust for the new project, named Shorashim, consisted of Rabbi Yirmiyahu Abramov, who had been living in Israel since the age of 16 and who spoke a fluent Hebrew and had wide contacts in the Israeli kiruv world; Yitzchak Meir, the comptroller of Heritage House, and Rabbi Edelstein. Rabbi Schuster was counted on to continue to bring in the funding necessary to sustain the project.

The team did not know exactly what they wanted to do, or how they would do it. But one thing was clear: They had no desire to replicate any of the successful kiruv programs, such as Arachim, which were already active in the field. Their target audience would not be those only one

---

of yesterday's accomplishments must not inhibit today's performance. Thoughts of what has already been accomplished are likely to choke off all initiative for new accomplishments."

generation removed from religious observance and who harbored a warm place in their heart for the Judaism of their childhood homes, even if they were no longer fully observant.

Instead the target audience would be secular, not traditional, Israeli Jews, highly educated, with little knowledge of Judaism or any great interest in it, who presumed, without too much Jewish knowledge, that Judaism was irrelevant to their lives. These were the young Israelis who traveled to India or South America following their army service in search of "spirituality," which they were confident could not be found within Torah itself.

Among the nine centers under the aegis of Shorashim at the project's peak were those in Modiin and Haifa. Modiin is Israel's newest city built within the 1967 borders and the fastest growing. In Modiin's first municipal elections in 1998, two parties running on platforms of keeping the chareidim out of Modiin captured over half the seats on the municipal council. At the time, not a single chareidi Jew lived in Modiin.

"Red" Haifa, as it is often called, has long been Israel's only major city with public transportation on Shabbat. And in secular Haifa, the Carmel area overlooking the rest of the city, where the Shorashim center was located, is the most secular of all.

Shorashim, in short, was determined to go into the lion's den.

A CENTER IN HERZLIYA CREATED BY TWO GRADUATES OF PONEVEZH Yeshiva, Rabbi Moshe Zilberberg and Rabbi Shimon Alpha, provided

**Shorashim Finds a Model**

an early model for the Shorashim centers. Some years earlier, Aish HaTorah had opened five Discovery centers in Israel. One of the five — and the only one to remain open after Aish ceased funding the project — was in Herzliya, headed by Rabbis Zilberberg and Alpha.

Prior to opening their center, the two rabbis met weekly over the course of a year with Rabbi Noach Weinberg of Aish HaTorah. They were joined at those meetings by Reb Noach's son Rabbi Simcha Weinberg, whom they knew from Ponevezh.

At those meetings, Rabbis Alpha and Zilberberg were exposed to Reb Noach's "Toras Chaim" approach, i.e., Torah as wisdom to live by. That approach formed the mainstay of Reb Noach's 48 Ways classes, probably the most frequently listened-to recorded classes in Jewish history.

After Aish HaTorah pulled out of the Discovery centers, Rabbis Alpha and Zilberberg managed to keep their center going for three years on their own. At that point, they reached out to Rabbi Abramov for funding help. "How can we close a center that has enjoyed so much success?" they asked him.

Rabbi Abramov went to visit the center in Herzliya, and was amazed by what he saw. The magnificent center had a homey aura conducive to socializing, and a buzz of intellectual excitement. On Motzaei Shabbos, when most young secular Israelis are busy socializing, the center was packed. Rabbi Abramov recalls a group of young men from upscale Herzliya Pituach pulling up on Harley-Davidson motorcycles for a Gemara *shiur*.

The social element, combined with the sense of an "intellectual happening," which Rabbi Abramov witnessed in Herzliya would become the goal of each of the Shorashim centers. In Kfar Saba, for instance, the center created its own coffee house in a shopping area. On those nights when there was a lecture, the coffee house would close at 9:00 p.m., and the doors would open to an adjacent hall where the lecture would take place.

The early exposure to the Herzliya center demonstrated to Rabbi Abramov that it was possible to attract secular Israelis with the right mix of classes. The key was demonstrating that the Torah addresses the entire panoply of life issues that face any human being: Relationships; Self-Knowledge; Marriage: Childrearing; Free Will.

The goal of the centers was not to turn those who showed up into mitzvah-observant Jews. Nor was doing so the measure of success of the founders. Instead, they sought to share with their fellow Jews their common heritage — the Torah — and to show them a depth in Torah that they did not know existed.

About one thing Rabbi Zilberberg, for instance, was extremely strict: If a lecturer conveyed in any way a sense of superiority by virtue of his Torah observance or that he viewed his teaching primarily as an act of *chesed* in bringing knowledge to the woefully ignorant, he or she was not invited back again.

Only those who could convey delight in meeting their fellow Jews and sharing together an exploration of Torah — whatever their different levels of knowledge — were deemed suitable for teaching. And part of that delight was appreciating the magnitude of the challenges involved in adopting a religious life and rejoicing in the strength it takes for an only child, for instance, to have his mother cease talking to him for a period of time when he became *shomer Shabbos*.

The Herzliya center had also discovered that Torah classes presented with titles emphasizing something esoteric or mystical — i.e., with Kabbalah in the title — were more likely to draw audiences. Though the title might include the words *"al pi Kabbalah,"* the writings of Rav Eliyahu Eliezer Dessler were fully "spiritual" enough to satisfy the audience. "Anatomy of the Soul" might be based on the letters of Rebbe Nachman of Breslov.

Though Rabbis Zilberberg and Alpha did not make mitzvah observance the measure of their success, many did become religiously observant through their center, including many students from the Interdisciplinary Center located in Herzliya, Israel's only private university. And they were thrilled every time that happened. While there was no pressure on those who just came for the lectures and the social aspects of the center, there were other programs designed for those who were seeking to go further, including *chavrutot* for those who were interested in active Torah learning.

NOT LONG AFTER RABBI ABRAMOV'S VISIT TO THE HERZLIYA CENTER, Shorashim opened up the first center under its auspices in Jerusalem,

**The Jerusalem Center** which was headed by Rabbi Eliyahu Betzalel. That center was a major success almost from the beginning, and Rabbi Betzalel proved an inspired choice to head it. He could meet a university student for the first time, and remember to ask the same student when he next appeared at the

Rabbi Yuval Asherov lecturing at the Jerusalem center

center two or three months later how he had done on the exam for which he had been studying.

Over time, the Jerusalem center developed a very wide range of programming aimed at different population groups: e.g., university students, young professionals, young people raised in religious homes who were no longer religiously observant, and soldiers. In the same building, Rabbi Moshe Peleg established a nighttime seminary for young, working baalos teshuvah, most of whom came through Rabbi Betzalel's center.

The Jerusalem center continues in full operation today, more than a decade after Shorashim closed for lack of funding due to Rabbi Schuster's declining health. Programs are ongoing morning, afternoon, and night, with nearly eight to nine hundred Jews coming to the center a week.

The remarkable success of the Jerusalem center helped bring new funding into the project. Rabbi Edelstein interested philanthropist Zev Wolfson[2] in the concept of centers around the country. And one evening, he took Mr. Wolfson to the Jerusalem center on Rechov Shammai, in the heart of Jerusalem's downtown, where they were met by Rabbi Abramov. The crush of people on the stairs waiting to get into the evening's lecture was too great for the three men to pass. But it did not matter. The size of the crowd was all Mr. Wolfson needed to see. He turned to his companions and told them he had "seen enough." For a number of years, Keren Wolfson divided the financial support for the Shorashim centers with Rabbi Schuster.

RABBI ABRAMOV IS BY NATURE A VISIONARY, WHO REQUIRES LITTLE TO serve as the stimulus for grand plans. The model that he had witnessed

**Thinking Big**
in action in Herzliya, the phenomenal initial success of the Jerusalem branch, and the prospect of an infusion of funding from Keren Wolfson caused him to immediately start thinking of a Shorashim center in every major city in Israel.

The first thing that struck Rabbi Ariel Vilner when he initially spoke to Rabbi Abramov about opening a center in Modiin, together with Rabbi Abramov's son Uriel Chaim, was that this was an organization that thought big. The typical Israeli kiruv organization of twenty years

_____

2. Mr. Wolfson was one of the largest donors in Jewish history, in addition to arranging billions of dollars of aid for Israel via his political connections. Certainly, he was the greatest *baal tzedakah* ever with a primary focus on kiruv.

ago would have first run a few programs to determine whether there was any interest before investing in renting premises on a long-term basis. But at his first meeting with Rabbi Abramov, the latter told Rabbi Vilner to immediately find premises to rent for the project.

The goal of a center in every major Israeli city was never realized. To be successful each center required a "general," and great generals are not a dime a dozen.[3]

Shorashim centers were not like a McDonald's franchise, in which each licensee operates according to a very detailed plan that he must follow. Each center head had complete autonomy. The Shorashim central office could provide guidance and tools, but ultimately relied on the knowledge of the director of each center of the locale and his ability to structure a program around his particular strengths and interests.

Few of the centers even used the Shorashim name. That was a deliberate decision so that Shorashim would not be identified as a nationwide kiruv movement. That would have inevitably scared off precisely those whom the centers were trying to reach. Better to let each center be experienced as a local initiative of Jews reaching out to their fellow Jews, as indeed they were.

In general, everything possible was done to disarm the defensive antennae of those attending lectures or other events. Rabbi Abramov advised the Vilners in Modiin, for instance, not to list speakers on their advertisements by religious titles, such as rabbi. The venues for activities and classes were neutral sites, not shuls or the like. In Modiin, when a larger venue was needed, the community center was chosen.

The center directors were not all cut from the same cloth. Several were products of the national religious world; others were themselves baalei teshuvah or the children of an earlier generation of baalei teshuvah. And a number were products of Israel's major yeshivos.[4] Dudu Nadav, the director of the center in the north Tel Aviv suburb of Ramat Aviv, is the son of a prominent dayan; Rabbi Aryeh Mendelsohn in Rechovot is the son of the founder of the Bais Yaakov Hachadash in Jerusalem. Rabbi Moshe Peleg, a Karliner chassid, was active in Jerusalem.

One thing that they shared in common, however, is that in the course of their religious development each had been exposed to Torah presented

---

3. The description of the centers as requiring "generals" is that of Yitzchak Meir, who visited the centers more frequently than any other Heritage House employee.

4. These categories are not exclusive of one another. A child of baalei teshuvah can be the graduate of a prominent yeshivah, for instance.

in a sophisticated fashion, and was capable of doing so himself. The late Rabbi Moshe Shapiro was a role model for most of them, even if they would not necessarily have described themselves as his talmidim.

In addition, they shared a passion for connecting to their fellow Jews no matter where they were then holding religiously. Rabbi Ariel Vilner and his wife Hindy, a descendant of Rabbi Boruch Ber Leibowitz, for instance, moved to Modiin in 2000, just a year after they were married, as part of a *garin* (seed group) of Rabbi Shlomo Raanan's Ayelet HaShachar organization.[5] That was only two years after parties running on a pledge to keep all chareidim out of Modiin had captured a majority of the seats on the Modiin city council (as mentioned above).

The commitment of the center heads was particularly manifest in the efforts they made to keep their centers going even after their major funding was cut off. Rabbi Betzalel in Jerusalem was the most successful at finding comparable levels of funding. But the Modiin center under Rabbi Ariel and Hindy Vilner continues to this day. Rabbi Yissachar Kaufman[6] in Haifa, who was only 24 when he opened his center, and Rabbis Zilberberg and Alpha soldiered on for a number of years after Shorashim ceased to function. And for the same reason: When one has experienced the joy of participating in the Torah journey of hundreds of Jews, one does not give that up lightly. Rabbis Zilberberg and Kaufman subsequently went into campus kiruv through Nefesh Yehudi, and many of the other center heads are involved in other kiruv-oriented projects.

THOUGH THE CENTERS WERE AUTONOMOUS, THEY ALL BENEFITED from being under a common umbrella. At least once a month,

**Working Together**  the directors of each center gathered in the Heritage office, together with Rabbis Abramov and Edelstein, Reb Yitzchak Meir, and Rabbi Schuster, when he was in the country. Rabbi Abramov served as the chief advisor for each of the centers, and his passion transferred to the center heads. Rabbi Edelstein, who by that time had built up probably the widest web of connections among kiruv organizations worldwide, drew on his wealth of experience to provide knowledge of best organizational practices.[7]

---

5. Ayelet HaShachar is perhaps best known for placing religious families on totally secular kibbutzim and moshavim.

6. Rabbi Kaufman credits Rabbi Yirmiyahu Abramov with seeing in him *kochos* (strengths) he did not know he possessed.

7. By the time Shorashim opened, Rabbi Edelstein was primarily involved in a major project of two-year training of *avreichim* for, and placement in, outreach positions in *chutz laAretz*.

But mostly the meetings provided an opportunity for the directors to exchange ideas with one another. They discussed what had worked and what had not worked at their particular center. For instance, if Rabbi Vilner developed a successful bar and bat mitzvah program, which succeeded in involving the parents of the bar or bat mitzvah-age child in the learning, with the grand finale a trip to Jerusalem and the Kotel, other centers were likely to follow suit.

Different speakers and the types of audiences to whom they appealed was another frequent topic of conversation, and there was a good deal of overlap in speakers between the different centers. Rabbanit Yemima Mizrachi, the most popular female Torah lecturer in the world today, first taught outside of her own home in the Jerusalem center.

Efrat Zilberstein was a major draw for the Modiin center. Her parents, both of whom worked for the leading Israeli defense contractor Rafael: Dynamic Defense Company, became baalei teshuvah when she was very young. But the experience nevertheless gave her a special sensitivity to those coming from a different world. The sophistication of her presentations was a large part of her attraction. But no less important was the sight of her gently sobbing while speaking of the destruction of the Temple on Leil Tishah B'Av, and her sensitivity to each and every student. When extending invitations to her students to a Zilberstein family simchah in nearby Kiryat Sefer, for instance, each came with an individualized note.

Yuval Asherov, who lives on a moshav, Or Ganuz, near Meron, was one of those speakers who spoke frequently at multiple branches. He combines an ethereal spirituality, sharp intelligence, and a deep knowledge of Kabbalah. He was a leading Kabbalah student of Rabbi Pinchos Sheinberger, himself the principal disciple of the Baal HaSulam, Rabbi Yehuda Leib Ashlag. Asherov is also a practitioner of alternative medicine, and he uses his lectures on the subject to explicate the connections between the *neshamah* and the body in Jewish thought, and the impact of mitzvos on the *neshamah*.

Famous baalei teshuvah — athletes, leading actresses and actors, and artists — were also popular draws. Doron Sheffer, one of the greatest Israeli basketball players ever, and Aviva Mor, an internationally renowned sculptor, illustrator, painter, and art curator, were among the well-known celebrities.

Center heads also shared ideas for gaining a degree of economic self-sufficiency. One of the main sources of revenue was through the sale of books and various religious artifacts. Those models proved especially helpful when Keren Wolfson ended its funding to focus on university students and Rabbi Schuster could no longer cover his part of the budget.

The center heads viewed themselves as part of a team, each of whom had something to contribute to the others. That sense of camaraderie was reinforced by an annual Shabbaton for the center heads and their families.

FOR HIS PART, RABBI SCHUSTER ATTENDED ALL THE MONTHLY MEET-
ings of center directors, when he was in the country, and enjoyed vis-

## Rabbi Schuster's Role

iting the centers. He did not speak a great deal at the meetings, in part because of his poor spoken Hebrew, but his enthusiasm for Shorashim was evident and encouraged the directors.

Rabbi Abramov spoke frequently to the directors about Rabbi Schuster and of his impact on the worldwide kiruv movement. The stories of his *mesirus nefesh* over decades were an inspiration to those involved in Shorashim. And the knowledge that there was someone behind their efforts who would always do his maximum on their behalf and would not let go no matter what the obstacles gave them confidence and encouragement.

Though he was not actively involved in the day-to-day activities of the centers, Rabbi Schuster could frequently be seen around Kikar Shabbat in downtown Jerusalem handing out cards for the Jerusalem center. More than a few who had known him from the days when he was a perpetual motion machine at the Kotel regarded him handing out cards on the street as a comedown.

But that is surely not how Rabbi Schuster viewed the matter. His ego had never been a factor, and he was just happy that his desire to "do something for the Israelis" was being realized and that he was the engine driving the operation through his fundraising. And if he could still contribute to the effort when in the country, so much the better.

On a visit to Herzliya, Rabbi Schuster suddenly disappeared in the middle of a conversation with Reb Yitzchak Meir, just as he had done to so many others in the past. When Reb Yitzchak next saw him, he was busy trying to cajole an older couple whom he had seen at a distance to visit the center. Old habits die hard.

As always, Rabbi Schuster's greatest contribution to Shorashim was the *siyata d'Shmaya* he brought to the project, just as Rabbi

Edelstein had known would be the case at the outset. Even after Rabbi Schuster was bedbound at Misgav Ladach Hospital, Rabbi Eliyahu Betzalel used to visit him frequently. Rabbi Betzalel had no doubt that the success of his center over the span of twenty years was largely a consequence of its connection to Rabbi Schuster, and he wanted to continue to attach himself and his efforts to Rabbi Schuster in any way that he could.

Rabbi Schuster handing out cards

Though the achievements of Shorashim are less known in the English-speaking world than Rabbi Schuster's activities over more than three decades at the Kotel, they were nevertheless considerable. Over fifty thousand Jews had their first intense exposure to Torah at one of the centers, and at least three hundred marriages came about between those who met there.

More important, in Rabbi Abramov's eyes, is what the Shorashim centers demonstrated: A formula exists both for attracting secular Israeli elites to learn more about Torah and for holding their attention once they are in the door. He considered Shorashim the most exciting kiruv initiative ever launched in Israel, and the loss of its funding to be a historic tragedy. He is still convinced that his dream of a Shorashim center in every Israeli population center was — and might be again — within reach.

*Chapter Nineteen*

# FUNDRAISER

"THERE ARE TWO THINGS I WOULD NEVER HAVE SAID REB Meir Tzvi could do," comments his former neighbor in Ezras Torah, Rabbi Yossi Abrams. "The first is anything connected to kiruv, and the second is fundraising. He simply lacked the people skills for either."

Yet Rabbi Schuster did, in time, become a major fundraiser. With the opening of Heritage House, he had no choice. American P'eylim, which had supported his activities for almost a decade, was willing to support Heritage House to some degree, at least in its fledgling stage. But that would have involved Rabbi Schuster subjecting every decision and plan to the organization's board. And he would not do that.

He had no tolerance for the laborious decision-making processes of bureaucracies and boards. And no less important, he could not tolerate the limitation on his independence. Even the most creative and organizationally talented people who worked with Rabbi Schuster over the years never doubted for a moment that their role was to faithfully execute and advance his vision.

Having decided to go it alone, necessity proved the mother of invention, and Rabbi Schuster quickly developed into a successful, if unorthodox, fundraiser. For nearly a quarter-century, from the opening of the Heritage House hostels in late 1984, he almost single-handedly raised the budget for Heritage House and, after 2001, for the Shorashim drop-in centers around Israel.

In time, as ever greater numbers of young people passed through, the staff of the Heritage House grew accordingly, until the annual budget exceeded half a million dollars a year. Reb Meir was forced to leave his perch at the Kotel and his family on average four times a year. He was in England after the end of the summer school holidays, and abroad again for approximately a month, between Succos and Chanukah, in the major cities of North America outside the New York metropolitan area. The longest trip of the year, which was to the New York area, lasted from well before Purim until Erev Pesach.

"Fortunately," Michael Kaufman testifies, "Reb Meir was great at raising funds ... mostly via small donations from numerous donors.... What was the key to his success? The same qualities that enabled him to succeed in kiruv — indomitable determination and single-minded dedication...."[1]

Mr. Kaufman accompanied Rabbi Schuster on several occasions to the United States. He relates how in Los Angeles Rabbi Schuster "returned time and again to people's homes after being told the owners were out ... until he found them in. His persistence was amazing. He would not take *no* for an answer, repeatedly insisting that the person being solicited contribute. Almost always he walked out with a donation."[2]

Turned away at the gates of several fine homes in Toronto and unable to get past the reception areas in several elegant buildings, "he never allowed himself to get discouraged, continuing relentlessly forward to the next prospective donor." But at the end of the day, he succeeded in collecting a "respectable sum, mostly in the form of small to moderate donations.[3]

As in everything else he did, the secret of Rabbi Schuster's success lay in his passion. Rabbi Yirmiyahu Abramov once succeeded in gaining an appointment with an Israeli hi-tech entrepreneur to pitch the Shorashim centers. At the meeting in the entrepreneur's office, Rabbi Abramov, a world-class shmoozer capable of bringing grand visions to life, did all the talking, while Reb Meir fidgeted in his seat and looked at some papers. Meanwhile, Rabbi Abramov could tell he was making no headway.

1. Kaufman, *In One Era, Out the Other*, p. 359.
2. Ibid., p. 360.
3. Ibid.

Suddenly, Reb Meir jumped out of his seat and rushed over to the host and grabbed him. "You've got to help Klal Yisrael!" he fairly shouted. And with that outburst, he immediately fell back into his chair. The host, shaken, stammered, "OK, how much do you want?" He then wrote a very generous check.

But if Rabbi Schuster was a successful fundraiser, he was also an unorthodox one. He did not engage in small talk, and almost as soon as the check was in his hand, he was out the door and on his way to the next appointment. No effusive thanks delayed his departure. If it had been anyone else, the abrupt departure might have been deemed rude, but not with Rabbi Schuster. Likely many donors appreciated the efficiency of his visits.

At one level, Heritage House ran a traditional fundraising operation. Before every trip, for instance, Reuven Loewenstein, and his successor as comptroller at Heritage House, Yitzchak Meir, would provide Rabbi Schuster with lists of previous donors in each city he would be visiting and how much they had given in the past. In addition, a new CD and promotional brochure were prepared for donors or potential donors.

Thank-you notes were sent to donors. And large donors were the beneficiaries of extra services. Every Succos, for example, Loewenstein would arrange to have the succahs put up for a number of major donors visiting in Israel for the festival.

For four or five years, Heritage House even had a grand fundraising dinner in New York City. The first one was held at Windows of the World atop the World Trade Center, just a few years before 9/11. And those that followed were at other prestigious locations. Reuven Loewenstein would come to America a couple of weeks before the dinner to oversee details and to push ads for the dinner journal.

Sam Friedland, one of Reb Meir's hosts in Monsey, and Sam's friend Gary Torgow from Detroit decided to guarantee the expenses of the first dinner in case there was a low turnout. But they need not have worried. The dinner was a success.

But if the external forms of Heritage House fundraising conformed to familiar models, those forms all had to be shaped to the unique personality of the one who made the ultimate pitch to donors: Rabbi Schuster. For instance, a CD highlighting new Heritage House projects, such as a Russian-language program, might be created. But Rabbi Edelstein did not bother to rehearse the use of the CD or the brochures with Rabbi Schuster because he knew the latter would highlight just what he had always highlighted. The best that could be hoped for was that he would at least distribute the newly prepared material.

Or to take another example, every dinner had to have a speaker who could draw the guests and make them feel that they had something to show for the time invested in attending. It was a given that it could not be left to Rabbi Schuster to either entertain or to explain precisely what it was that he and Heritage House did. At the first dinner at Windows of the World, Rabbi Berel Wein was the featured speaker. When it came time for Rabbi Schuster to speak, however, he had already returned to his seat before anyone knew that he had arisen to speak in the first place.

The roshei yeshivah of the Philadelphia Yeshiva, Rav Elya Svei and Rav Shmuel Kamenetsky, once attended a parlor meeting for Heritage House in Philadelphia out of respect for Rabbi Schuster and his work. At some point, Reb Elya indicated to Rabbi Schuster that it was time for him to speak, but the latter demurred on the grounds that he was not a public speaker. At that point Reb Elya told him, "Just tell some stories from your work." But even that proved too much for Rabbi Schuster.

THE SUCCESS OF RABBI SCHUSTER'S FUNDRAISING DEPENDED IN large part on the extraordinary group of hosts whom he assembled over the years. He stayed with some of those hosts for a week or more annually for close to twenty years, and he felt at home with them. He could ask, "What's for dinner?" or peer into the pantry or refrigerator without hesitation.

**Hosts Abroad**

Some of the hosts actively involved themselves in his fundraising. Dov Wolowitz not only introduced him to many of his friends in real estate, but would himself do most of the speaking. Yaakov and Shaindel Steinberg made an annual parlor meeting when Rabbi Schuster stayed with them in Passaic. But if the host did not involve himself in the fundraising, Rabbi Schuster did not push him for introductions, something that endeared him to new hosts with whom he had no extensive previous relationships.[4]

Over time, his host families became among his closest friends and saw a side of him on view to very few. His characteristic intensity and drive remained fully on display when abroad as well. But his

---

4. Ira Stoll, Rabbi Schuster's host in Beverly Hills. Mr. Stoll notes that Rabbi Schuster differed from most other fundraisers who stayed in his home in this respect.

Rabbi Schuster's radiant smile

hosts also heard his laughter — real belly laughs — that made his hosts laugh almost as hard he did. Dov Wolowitz and Sam Friedland could always be counted upon to cause Rabbi Schuster to laugh heartily whenever they were together. Mrs. Miriam Chontow's first impression of Rabbi Schuster, on his initial visit to her London home, was of his "radiant smile."

A few of the hosts were old friends. Yossi Nussbaum in Detroit had been Reb Meir's younger roommate in Ner Israel. And Yonoson Israel, who hosted Rabbi Schuster in Boro Park, was both a former neighbor and *chavrusa* when Reb Meir was still in kollel.

At least two other regular hosts had experienced Rabbi Schuster in action on their journeys to Torah Judaism. Yaakov (Tom) Steinberg of Passaic (now Jerusalem) first met Rabbi Schuster while back-packing around the world on a post-college, pre-MBA tour. And Dr. Leonard Ginsburg in Philadelphia became close to Rabbi Schuster while volunteering in retinal surgery at Tel Hashomer Hospital in Israel in 1989. Over the course of that year, Dr. Ginsburg, his wife and infant daughter stayed at Heritage House for approximately forty straight weeks.

Rabbi Schuster and Yaakov (Tom) Steinberg

A number of the hosts came to Rabbi Schuster through his connections in the kiruv world. The late Reb Shlomo Adler, one of the major *askanim* of the community in Manchester, England, headed the board of the local branch of the Ohr Somayach-affiliated Jewish Learning Exchange, together with Rabbi Moshe Kupetz. He was close to Rabbi Nota Schiller, the rosh yeshivah of Ohr Somayach. Rabbi Shlomo Noach

Mandel was Rabbi Schuster's first host in Toronto. He headed the Toronto Jewish Learning Exchange, in addition to his extensive work on behalf of Mr. Albert Reichmann establishing Jewish schools in Eastern Europe. Because of his frequent travels he handed over the privilege of hosting Rabbi Schuster to his friend Nate Bleeman.

Rabbi Schuster's London host, the recently deceased Dovid Chontow, regularly learned Gemara with potential baalei teshuvah, including one who is today considered among the leading European experts in *Choshen Mishpat*, and regularly represents the Torah community before European regulatory bodies. Quite probably, Rabbi Dovid Refson of Neve Yerushalayim made the introduction for Rabbi Schuster.[5]

AND FINALLY, AT LEAST TWO OF RABBI SCHUSTER'S EARLIEST AMERI-can contacts sought him out because of their deep personal connec-

## Idealists Attract One Another

tion to kiruv: Dov Wolowitz, who headed the group that bought the building for the Heritage House men's hostel, and Mr. Pinchos Yechezkel Wagner of Monsey.[6]

The latter was already close to Rabbi Schuster even before the opening of the Heritage House hostels, and prior to Rabbi Schuster's first fundraising trips to the United States. The entire Wagner family stayed in what would become shortly thereafter the woman's hostel over Succos of 5745 (1984). Mr. Wagner dispatched two of his sons to Israel a week prior to the *Chag* to ensure that all furnishings and provisions were in place for the family to stay over the *Chag* and to entertain large numbers of guests. On the first night of Succos, Rabbi Schuster brought twenty-five potential guests and asked Reb Yechezkel how many he could take. And to the latter's delight, he continued to fill the tables the Wagners had arranged throughout Succos.

Over forty years ago, when there were far fewer major *baalei tzeda-kah* than today, Reb Yechezkel Wagner stood out. What distinguished him was not his wealth: Though a successful businessman, even in those days there were many religious Jews far wealthier than he. A rosh yeshivah from Israel who made a rule of never entering the mansions of those he was soliciting for his yeshivah lest he transgress the

---

5. Mr. Chontow's wife, Mrs. Miriam Chontow, does not know how the connection came about.

6. Sam Friedland, who succeeded Mr. Wagner as Rabbi Schuster's host in Monsey, also made the effort to develop a relationship with Rabbi Schuster on one of his trips to Israel.

proscription *lo sachmod* (do not covet) was advised that he need not worry when he came to the Wagner home at 8 Sylvan Lane in Monsey.

What set him apart was the breadth of his tzedakah, and even more so the manner in which he searched out tzedakah opportunities. That was almost certainly the way he met Rabbi Schuster. He was frequently the major initial giver to new projects and institutions for which he saw a great need, particularly in (but not limited to) the area of kiruv.

Rav Yaakov Kamenetsky was once the speaker at a parlor meeting for Passaic Yeshiva. As he arose to speak, Rav Yaakov looked around the room and was bothered by something. "*Avu iz di baal tzedekah fun Monsey? Avu iz Yechezkel Wagner?* — Where is the *baal tzedakah* from Monsey? Where is Yechezkel Wagner?" he asked. At that moment, Reb Yechezkel walked in, and Rav Yaakov said, "Now, we can begin."

Reb Yechezkel's particular emphasis of kiruv was an outgrowth of his own early life experiences. Born and raised in Palestine, until his family moved to Toronto in search of a livelihood, he never had the benefit of an intense yeshivah education. At 14, he had to leave school and stop all his formal religious training in order to assist his father in his floundering business. From that early experience, he developed an identification with all those who were deprived of a yeshivah education.

According to Rav Aryeh Schechter of Jerusalem, he was one of the first to recognize the potential for a mass-scale baal teshuvah movement in Israel. He opened a kollel named after his father for outstanding baalei teshuvah *avreichim* in Tifrach and was an early supporter of future MK Rabbi Moshe Gafni's yeshivah for young men from non-religious homes in Ofakim.

Reb Yechezkel also recognized the potential for kiruv among Israelis living in the United States. He was one of the very first sponsors of Arachim seminars directed at Israelis living in America. The lower level of his house became a dormitory over the years for hundreds of Israelis in the teshuvah process. Eventually, he opened both a yeshivah and a seminary in Monsey for young Israelis who had attended Arachim seminars.

The following story captures better than any who Reb Yechezkel Wagner was. During her seminary year in Israel, one of his granddaughters was set up with a family in the northern city of Rechasim. When her hostess heard her name, and verified that she was Reb Yechezkel's granddaughter, she was beside herself with excitement: She had been one of the products of the Arachim seminars who had lived at the Wagners' for a period of time. And it was she who told the story:

At some point, while taking inventory for his furniture business, Reb Yechezkel realized that there was major theft going on from the warehouse, and that the culprit could only be an employee. So one night he remained in his office and watched the warehouse security camera. In the middle of the night, the warehouse opened, and one of his managers — an Israeli who had attended an Arachim seminar — drove up a small truck and loaded two items into it. Reb Yechezkel remained in his office the rest of the night contemplating what to do the next morning.

The next morning he confronted the manager, who after an initial denial, broke down and confessed, citing huge debts to his family back in Israel as an excuse. Mr. Wagner told him that he would not contact the police, on two conditions. First, he had to continue to strengthen himself religiously. Second, he had to continue working for Mr. Wagner until he had repaid his debt. He then told the young man that he was giving him a raise in salary so that he could repay the debt and still send money back to his family in Israel.

It is not surprising that idealists like Reb Yechezkel Wagner were attracted to Rabbi Schuster, and he to them. The late Reb Shlomo Adler, his host in Manchester, England, serves as another example. Reb Shlomo learned in Manchester Yeshiva, and was very close to the rosh yeshivah, Rav Yehudah Zev Segal, who directed him to continue in the family tradition of *askanus* and not contemplate full-time kollel learning. He once took Rabbi Schuster to the Manchester Rosh Yeshivah for a blessing, and despite being far older than Rabbi Schuster, Rav Segal stood up when Reb Meir entered the room, so great was his respect for Rabbi Schuster's work.

Some of Reb Shlomo's public activities had very wide-ranging consequences. He persuaded British coroners to accept MRIs in place of actual autopsies in cases involving observant Jews (and also Moslems opposed to autopsies on religious grounds). After the Lockerbie terrorist bombing,

Rav Yehudah Zev Segal

in December 1988, he traveled to Lockerbie, Scotland, as part of the Manchester *chevrah kaddisha*. In all, 270 passengers and crew and eleven people on the ground were killed when the plane crashed to earth after a bomb exploded in the baggage hold.[7]

When the *chevrah kaddisha* was denied access to the bodies, Mr. Adler called his close friend Rabbi Yehudah Yona Rubinstein, whom he knew to be related through his wife to the Home Secretary for Scotland at the time, Malcolm Rifkind, and urged him to try to secure access to the bodies. Rifkind's wife initially told Rabbi Rubinstein that her husband had just returned from the crash site too shaken by what he had seen to speak. Eventually, however, Mr. Rifkind took the phone. He told Rabbi Rubinstein, based on what he had seen, that it would be impossible to identify any bodies. But he nevertheless agreed to order the *chevrah kaddisha* to be admitted.

In the end, every one of the bodies of the thirty-four Jews on board was fully intact. And even though winds had whipped through the cabin at hundreds of miles per hour as the plane plummeted to earth, not a single Jewish victim was found unclothed.

Rabbi Dr. Dovid Gottlieb, who also stayed with the Adler family on his visits to Manchester, testifies that from Reb Shlomo's 6:00 a.m. *daf yomi shiur* until he finished with communal matters past midnight, he never saw him fail to fulfill a single mitzvah. And as much as Reb Shlomo was involved in community-wide matters, he never lost sight of the needs of individual members of the community. He and his wife operated a store for less fortunate members of the community in which every item was sold at cost.

TO HOST RABBI SCHUSTER REQUIRED A BIT OF *TZIDKUS*. NOT EVERY woman would be eager to have her kitchen commandeered for days

**A Beloved Guest**

at a time to serve as his command central, as he made dozens of calls, one after another, nor would every husband give up his study for the same purpose.

Contributing to the large number of calls was the manner in which he relentlessly chased down every possible eighteen-dollar check. He would come back to Israel with hundreds of smaller checks tucked into his various pockets. But because Heritage House never relied

---

7. The closest *chevrah kaddisha* was that of Gateshead, and it was members of the Gateshead *chevrah kaddisha* who initially called on the Manchester *chevrah kaddisha* for assistance.

exclusively on large donors, it was not affected as badly as some organizations by economic crashes, such as the bursting of the dot-com bubble in 2000.

The responses to his calls, remarks Sam Friedland, came in three forms. Some would respond, "Yes, please come over." Others would cut him short: "Not now. I already told you no." And finally, there were a handful, like Sam Friedland's Monsey neighbor Steve Rosenberg, for whom it was obvious that "if Rabbi Meir Schuster calls, you come over to him." But even when someone yelled at him, says Friedland, it never got him down — nor did it necessarily deter him from trying again.

Rabbi Schuster making rapid-fire phone calls in Sam Friedland's study

He did not waste a minute. He would often be back on the phone making calls again as soon as he entered the house, without even removing his jacket. And he only returned from his efforts late at night. Once he arrived at the home where he was staying only to find the door locked and everyone asleep. He spent the night in his rented car rather than take a hotel room. Every penny raised for Heritage House was *hekdesh* (sanctified money) in his eyes, and he could not bear to waste it. Even buying a button to replace one that had come off his shirt proved too much for him, and the cars he rented, jokes Sam Friedland, were from Rent-a-Wreck.

Everything was done at breakneck speed. "You could always tell he was about to come through the door by the sound of screeching brakes as he approached the driveway," recalls Reb Yonoson Israel.[8]

---

8. Driving with Rabbi Schuster could be a terrifying experience. Rabbi Yom Tov Glaser once rode with Rabbi Schuster to Tel Aviv for the *vort* of an Aish student. When a beginning student at Aish HaTorah asked innocently, "What is so bad about intermarriage?" Rabbi Schuster, who was driving, became so animated in his response, continually turning around to look at the offending questioner, that Rabbi Glaser feared for his life. He only agreed to return to Jerusalem with Rabbi Schuster on condition that he drive.

Even if he was driving on a major thoroughfare, if he spotted someone walking with a backpack, he would brake sharply to call out to the backpacker, "Are you Jewish?" Such abrupt starts turned every ride into a harrowing adventure, according to Rabbi Avraham Edelstein.

But if he was not an unnoticed guest staying quietly in his room, each one of his hosts deemed it a privilege to have him and felt that he had a salutary effect on their families. The first thing mentioned by every host is his davening. In many homes, he had a basement room, in which he would often daven alone at sunrise, and only go to shul for *Krias HaTorah*. The sound of him "banging, stomping, screaming" could be heard two floors above.[9] One of his hostesses had to suppress her laughter when Rabbi Schuster would ask her sheepishly in the morning whether his davening had disturbed her.[10]

One time, Reb Dovid Chontow took Rabbi Schuster with him to davening at Munk's Shul in London's Golders Green neighborhood, where the prayers are decorous in the tradition of German Jewry, and ecstatic davening, like Reb Meir's, entirely foreign. Mr. Chontow was requested not to bring his guest again, but to direct him to another shul in Golders Green where the davening is less formal.

Rabbi Schuster's davening was not just a point of curiosity, it could be life-changing for his host families. Dr. Leonard Ginsburg's 10-year-old son used to sit transfixed by the way that Rabbi Schuster would look up to Heaven while *bensching*. Today, as an adult, he continues to *bensch* the same way. As soon as he arrived, says Dr. Ginsburg, the house was infused with Torah. And Dr. Ginsburg attributes the fact that all his children are yeshivah or seminary graduates and proud observant Jews today, including a daughter who is a yeshivah administrator, in large part to Rabbi Schuster's influence.

Rabbi Schuster connected with the children of his hosts, and involved himself in what was new with them. The Friedland children greatly looked forward to his stays with the family. And where there were already grandchildren, he enjoyed playing with them.

But his influence was hardly limited to the children and grandchildren of the host families. Marilyn Wolowitz's mother commented how inspiring it was to hear him *bensch* at the Shabbos table. "You could not help being changed by him," says Laurie Friedland. And her husband notes the ways he was influenced by Rabbi Schuster, including arriving at davening every morning half an hour earlier to be able to say *Korbanos* and *Pesukei d'Zimrah* with *kavannah*.

It is said that America has many *shomer Shabbos* Jews, but few Erev Shabbos Jews, as were common in Eastern Europe. Rabbi Schuster,

---

9. Reb Yonoson Israel.
10. Mrs. Marilyn Wolowitz.

Rabbi Schuster with the Friedlands' son Yonatan

however, was one of the latter. Early on Friday afternoon, he would be busy brushing his hat and polishing his shoes. And he always asked his hostess for something specific to do in preparation for Shabbos. That example too changed the appreciation of Shabbos in the homes of his host families.

While abroad, he remained entirely focused on the task at hand. He did not go shopping for himself, and Sam Friedland had to practically drag him to one of his Amazing Savings stores to pick up presents for his family. But there was one indulgence he did permit himself abroad: meals with the families of those for whom he was the catalyst for the dramatic changes in their lives. And those could be found in every city that he visited.

In Los Angeles, for instance, he had dinner every year with the family of Jim Vickman, an attorney with seven children. Every year, Jim would tell his children, "You are all here only because of Rabbi Schuster." Reb Meir would smile, and, if one looked closely, one could see tears of joy forming in his eyes as well.

Actually, it is not accurate to describe those nostalgic visits as an indulgence: They renewed his spirits by serving as potent reminders of why he drove himself so hard and left behind his family and his place at the Kotel to travel from city to city for weeks at a time.

# Part IV
# SUMMING UP

*Chapter Twenty*
# FAMILY

THE SCHUSTERS WERE A NORMAL, HAPPY FAMILY. THAT IS BEST attested to by the scores of *bachurim* at Ohr Somayach and Aish HaTorah over the years who were regular Shabbos and Yom Tov guests in the Schuster home.

Guests were a necessity for the Shabbos meals. For one thing, Rabbi Schuster was careful to always have a *mezuman* of three adult males for *bensching*. In addition, he liked to sing at the Shabbos table, but could not carry a tune. Outside assistance was required.

At his Shabbos table Reb Meir relaxed as he rarely did during the week, engaging each of the guests, sharing *divrei Torah* and discussing the parashah with his children.[1] Mrs. Schuster was "so, so normal," remembers Reuven Eliyahu, which together with the plentiful food, and Reb Meir's own elevated spirits, made the atmosphere relaxing and enjoyable. Gedaliah Zweig, in his early weeks at Aish HaTorah, made the decision to stay and learn more after spending Purim in the Schuster home.

Akiva Unger was such a regular guest that Mrs. Schuster assumed he was coming unless informed otherwise. Even after he was married, he and his wife would walk back and forth from the Old City for many

---

1. From a letter written after Rabbi Schuster's *petirah* by one of Mrs. Schuster's nephews recounting his Shabbos experiences in the home.

Akiva Unger and Rabbi Schuster at the former's *vort*

Shabbos and Succos meals, and also joined the Schusters for their Seder.

What so attracted Akiva to the Schusters' Shabbos table? "They were just the most down-to-earth people you could imagine. Plain, simple people." He adds that Mrs. Schuster's chicken soup is "out of this world — the only chicken soup for which I consistently asked for a second bowl."

Akiva was always able to make the family laugh, with his Donald Duck imitations and the like, and they enjoyed doing so.[2] But the humor was not confined to the guests. At one point, Rabbi Schuster wanted a more health-conscious diet — e.g., a ban on sugary drinks and a switch to whole wheat challah. Shortly thereafter, his son Dovid (Duvie) came in late for the meal, and had to make his own *Hamotzi*. As soon as he bit into the store-bought whole wheat challah, he started making piteous faces and declared, "There's no way that I was *yotzei* (fulfilled the mitzvah of eating bread) with this cardboard."

As previously mentioned, Rabbi Schuster had a number of *chumros*, which were not widespread, even in a completely chareidi neighborhood

---

2. Akiva was sufficiently close to Rabbi Schuster that he felt comfortable playing little pranks on him, just to get a rise out of him. In the early days of large portable phones, Rabbi Schuster used to carry three or four different ones in various pockets. One day, Akiva had the idea of calling all four numbers one right after the other, and causing Rabbi Schuster to fumble around from pocket to pocket for each one. When he finally revealed his identity, and Rabbi Schuster saw him laughing from the other end of the *beis medrash*, he ran after him to throw him out.

like Ezras Torah. In the first years of his marriage, he insisted on *kashering* all the chickens himself. And he did not want to rely on electricity from the Israel Electric Company on Shabbos and Yom Tov. That meant eating only by candlelight on Shabbos evening, and in the dark for *shalosh seudos*.

Eventually, Mrs. Schuster's brother Moshe Garfinkel, while on a visit to Israel, bought the Schusters a battery generator, and when a group of families in the neighborhood organized their own generator, the Schusters were quick to join.

The *chumros*, however, were hardly the thing that most distinguished the Schusters from other families in the neighborhood. On Leil Shabbos in the summer, it was often past 10:00 p.m. before Rabbi Schuster entered the apartment and put on his Shabbos *bekeshe*. Many neighbors were already close to *bensching* by that time.

When the children were still young, they often had to be awakened to come to the Shabbos table. And yet, there was no question of starting until Rabbi Schuster returned home, even in later years when the oldest Schuster daughter, Chani, was already visiting with her children. Only once, when Asarah B'Teves fell on a Friday, did Mrs. Schuster make Kiddush before Rabbi Schuster came home, in order to break the fast.

Nor did Rabbi Schuster have much time to relax with his wife and children on Shabbos, apart from the two main meals. Shabbos morning, he usually walked to the Old City to place Jews with families for the day meal. And after the opening of Heritage House, he always walked back again in the afternoon for *shalosh seudos* at the men's hostel.

He was so completely devoted to his mission that during the *Shabbos sheva berachos* for his daughter Chani in the Old City, he disappeared in the middle to go down to the Kotel to make sure that no Jew missed what might be his or her only opportunity to experience something of Shabbos.

Only once did he take a day off to go on an outing with the kids. Knowing that he would never agree to be away from his perch at the Kotel for Shabbos, a close friend and supporter arranged for the Schuster family to spend a few days at Kfar Eliyahu in the Galilee during the week. When they arrived, they found Rabbi Nota Schiller there with his family, which gave Rabbi Schuster a colleague in kiruv with whom to speak.

Nevertheless, within an hour of first diving into the pool, Reb Meir was fully dressed and about to head back to Jerusalem. "Enjoy yourselves, with my blessing," he told his wife and children. "But I

Rabbi Schuster with the *chassan* at his son Dovid's *chasunah*.

can't stay any longer. There's work to be done." (By the time the first grandchildren were old enough to take on outings in the late '90s, "business" at the Kotel was down considerably, and Rabbi Schuster could be persuaded to join Chol HaMoed family outings.)

He loved children in general, and his own in particular. All the families who hosted Rabbi Schuster in the States on his fundraising trips mention his great love of children, and how much time he spent speaking to the children at whatever house he was staying in for Shabbos. When he was abroad, Shabbos was indeed a day of rest. He had no responsibilities, no repeated trips to the Kotel and back, and he could relax fully with his hosts and their children, as he could not in Jerusalem.

Yet his children never doubted his great love for them. Each had a special place in his heart. From the age of 9, Duvie, the only boy, used to accompany his father on Leil Shabbos, and soon became a central player in dropping those whom Reb Meir had gathered for Shabbos meals at their various hosts'. Whenever he called the Heritage House office, his father's face broke into a huge smile.

Chani was the first of the children to be married, and already had a large family before Reb Meir became incapacitated. Her children, as well as Duvie's, were a source of great joy to him, and, according to his hosts in America, he spoke incessantly of them. Chani had five more children after Reb Meir took ill, including a boy named Meir Tzvi after his grandfather and the youngest, Shlomo Zalman, born on Rabbi Schuster's *yahrtzeit*.

Chayale, the youngest and last to marry, remained at home as long as Reb Meir was living, and she worked in the Heritage House office for well over a decade. During her time working at Heritage House, she often davened at the Kotel. Whenever her father saw her there, his face would light up and he would come over to her, unless he was involved with someone at the time.

THOUGH THE CHILDREN NEVER QUESTIONED THEIR FATHER'S LOVE for them, it is clear that without a strong, independent wife, who was willing to take on a mammoth portion of the child-raising, he could never have maintained the schedule that he did without a serious cost to his children. Looking back, the Schuster children all say that they did not feel deprived of parental attention. They credit their mother with being able to fill in whatever they were missing in time with their father.

**Mrs. Schuster's Role**

Every other year, Mrs. Schuster took the children back to the United States to visit her parents in Monsey, and in later years her father and stepmother in Florida. On one or two of those trips, she even took the children to Milwaukee to spend time with Rabbi Schuster's parents.[3] Rabbi Schuster never joined her. From the time that he first landed in Israel until the opening of Heritage House sixteen years later, he never left the country.

Mrs. Schuster devoted herself to her children, like a mother lioness protecting her cubs. Because her husband was a self-made man spiritually, she speculates, perhaps he did not fully appreciate how much children need parental support and attention. The only time she absolutely put her foot down and refused to agree to one of Reb Meir's requests was when he wanted to move to the Old City to be closer to the center of his activities. She wanted to continue to raise her children in the well-defined community of Ezras Torah, with its strong support system and religious role models.

Mrs. Schuster never complained of the extra parental load on her; indeed, she accepted it gladly. She is a very sociable woman, and always had a wide circle of friends in Ezras Torah and beyond. Her conversational abilities and regular manner were among the draws of the Schuster home for many of the frequent visitors.

Her outsized parental role, however, would no doubt have been easier if she had been able to participate more fully, even vicariously, in her husband's work.

But as she frequently said, "Meir doesn't talk." Speaking about himself or what he was doing, much less boasting of any kind, was simply foreign to him. There was no chance of his sharing even the most

---

3. Both sets of grandparents came to visit their children and grandchildren in Israel. The Garfinkels came every other year, and the Schusters for special occasions, such as Duvie's bar mitzvah.

heartwarming or funniest stories, such as the woman who only agreed to go to Neve Yerushalayim if Rabbi Schuster promised to give her his hat after the completion of her three months' commitment.

Mrs. Schuster met those guests that Rabbi Schuster brought from the Kotel, and knew the *bachurim* who returned week after week well, but she had no way of fully appreciating the scope of her husband's work or its impact. She never visited the Heritage House hostels. Her visits to the Old City and Kotel — which could have been described as her husband's office — were largely confined to the Yamim Noraim, when she and the children davened in Aish HaTorah, where Rabbi Yitzchak Shmuel Levin, a grandson of the renowned "tzaddik (righteous person) in our time" Rabbi Aryeh Levin, was the *baal tefillah.* Much of what she knows about her husband's life-work she learned only during *shivah* and in the spate of articles that appeared after his passing.

Ironically, the Schuster children all knew, even if only indirectly, more about their father's work, and took great pride in it. Duvie worked with his father from an early age, and can rattle off the names and addresses of all the regular Shabbos hosts, and Chayale worked in the Heritage House office.

Both daughters remember that when people, particularly English-speakers, would ask them their family name, and they replied Schuster, the inevitable next question was: Are you Rabbi Meir Schuster's daughter? And when they replied affirmatively, there invariably followed either a verbal or nonverbal expression of awe. Chayale attended seminary in the same building as Rebbetzin Bruria David's BJJ Seminary for English-speakers. And over the course of the year, many of the BJJ students would speak to her about her "famous" father. As a young girl, Rabbi Schuster's older daughter Chani particularly enjoyed accompanying her father as he walked through the Old City on Rosh Hashanah and was greeted effusively by person after person.

Each one of the Schuster children knew that their father was an extremely elevated person, who lived with the awareness of Hashem at every moment. And they knew that he had changed the face of the Jewish world. They wore with pride the title of Rabbi Meir Schuster's son or daughter.

## Chapter Twenty-One
# DECLINE

I N 2007, RABBI SCHUSTER WAS DIAGNOSED AS SUFFERING FROM Lewy Body dementia, a brutal degenerative disease that affects the sufferer's body, cognitive abilities, and personality. He was only 64 years old at the time, and still fully active. His son Dovid observes that the disease only struck when the Kotel Plaza had largely ceased to be a place for large-scale kiruv because the demographic that had given rise to the kiruv revolution thirty-five years earlier had largely dried up.

Lewy Body dementia has been described as something akin to being struck simultaneously with Alzheimer's and severe Parkinson's disease. There is no cure or even medications to slow the degenerative process. Even finding medications to alleviate symptoms is tricky because of the multiplicity of those symptoms and the corresponding danger of adverse interactions between the various medications required. And because of the personality changes that come with the disease it is considered even more draining on caregivers than Alzheimer's.

In the space of two years, a man who had always walked at a pace with which few could keep up and for whom walking from Ezras Torah to the Kotel three times on a Shabbos was nothing became uncertain on his feet and was reduced to short walks. Someone whose fervent davening had literally changed lives could not remain for more than a short time for the Rosh Hashanah davening.

A man whose sweetness of disposition and smile had attracted thousands and whose belly laughs sent his hosts into peals of laughter spent much of his time just staring silently at the wall. And he was often frustrated by his new limitations. Someone whose organizational abilities were crucial to his success lost much of his executive functioning ability.

By 2009, the Schusters had to leave the apartment and neighborhood in which they had lived for close to forty years for a ground-floor apartment in Mahal, just behind Ohr Somayach. And after a series of falls, it became clear that Reb Meir could no longer live at home, but needed full-time nursing care, first at Neve Simchah, a senior citizen residence, and then at Misgav Ladach's medical facility in Jerusalem's Old Katamon neighborhood, where he remained for three years, bed-bound and with round-the-clock nursing care.

**The Last Trips to America**

BUT LONG BEFORE RABBI SCHUSTER WAS ADMITTED TO MISGAV Ladach, he still undertook two fundraising trips to the United States — one in 2008 and the next in 2009. Rabbi Avraham Edelstein and Rabbi Yirmiyahu Abramov in the Heritage House office felt that as long as he could function, doing so would delay his decline and reduce his frustration. On both those trips he was accompanied and not allowed to drive himself.

On the first trip, Rabbi Schuster was first joined by Avraham Lewis, who had been a Shabbos coordinator at the Heritage House men's hostel as a *bachur* at Aish HaTorah. He knew Rabbi Schuster well and was devoted to him. While still in Ben Gurion Airport on the way out of Israel, Rabbi Schuster wandered off as Avraham was attending to some matter. The latter found Rabbi Schuster passing out cards for the Shorashim centers to Israelis he encountered in the airport.

At the end of Avraham's first tour of duty on that trip — he would return to Israel after two weeks and then go back to meet Rabbi Schuster in America two weeks later — an incident took place in Los Angeles that reveals how much of Rabbi Schuster's old fire remained. After an appointment, Rabbi Schuster and Avraham returned to the car to drive to their next meeting. He asked Rabbi Schuster, who had been visiting Los Angeles for twenty years, which way to go. The latter did not remember, but he fairly shouted, "Just go." The urgency was typical; the failure to remember the direction was not.

In Los Angeles, Reuven Goldman took over as Rabbi Schuster's shadow for the next two weeks. He too had worked many years at Heritage

House, as had his wife and sister. Rabbi Schuster even made a *sheva berachos* for Reuven and his wife Leah at Heritage House in 1989, as the first *shidduch* of Heritage House staff members.

Reb Reuven and Rabbi Schuster visited a number of other cities, in addition to Los Angeles, including Toronto, Philadelphia, and Baltimore. In Baltimore, as soon as they entered the *beis medrash* of Ner Israel, Rabbi Yissocher Frand came rushing over from the front of the *beis medrash* to wish Rabbi Schuster "*Shalom aleichem.*"

Because Rabbi Schuster had never had the greatest memory for the names of donors, it was not so difficult, in the course of the trip, to cover up if he forgot one now, or to excuse it as a function of over-tiredness. And because he had never been blessed with the "gift of gab," any difficulties in conversation could be excused as the effect of a bad day.

Donors, as well as hosts, might have wondered why for the first time Rabbi Schuster was accompanied, and why he was no longer driving. But excuses could be provided. Where Reuven Goldman noticed the biggest change was not in how Rabbi Schuster conducted himself during appointments with donors but in his ability to organize the dozens of phone calls needed to make appointments and the like. Those organizational abilities, which had always been one of Rabbi Schuster's greatest strengths, had deteriorated considerably.

Rabbi Yissocher Frand and Rabbi Schuster at a fundraiser for Heritage House for which Rabbi Frand was the featured speaker

Rabbi Schuster together with Reuven Goldman at the latter's *sheva berachos*

When Reuven accompanied Rabbi Schuster the next year, 2009, however, the situation was very different. The trip began in Brooklyn. Reuven and Rabbi Schuster went to daven Minchah at the Shomrei Shabbos *shtiebel* on 13th Avenue in Boro Park, where Rabbi Schuster had davened hundreds of times in the past and was well known to many of the regulars. When they finished, there was a heavy rainstorm, and Reuven suggested that Rabbi Schuster wait for him while he went to get the car just a short distance away.

When he returned with the car just a few moments later, however, Rabbi Schuster was nowhere to be found. Reuven frantically searched the shul, with its numerous minyanim, and called Rabbi Schuster's cellphone without response. He had no choice but to drive around the neighborhood looking for him. Finally, after a half-hour of panic, he spotted Rabbi Schuster, who, ever impatient, had decided to walk to their hosts' house, only to discover that he had no idea how to get there. He had not thought to answer the cellphone ringing in his bag either.

At the home of Sam and Laurie Friedland, who were among Rabbi Schuster's closest friends and with whom he had been staying every year for nearly two decades, it quickly became clear that Rabbi Schuster did not remember Sam's name. Fortunately, a flock of geese landed on the back lawn around the time that Rabbi Schuster arrived. Rabbi Schuster had always loved watching the geese in years past, even as his host complained of the effort required to clean up after them. When Sam blurted out a cry of despair at their return, Rabbi Schuster looked at him excitedly and cried out, "Sammy!"

After two weeks, Reuven concluded that any further efforts at fundraising were futile, and that it was not fair to Rabbi Schuster to continue. But Rabbi Schuster knew that they had come nowhere near raising the amounts he had collected on previous trips, and refused to return to Israel. After consulting with Rabbi Abramov in the Heritage House office, Reuven told Rabbi Schuster that they had to return to avoid losing the price of their return ticket, but that they would return to the United States as soon as possible to fulfill their fundraising quotas.

No sooner had they landed in Ben Gurion Airport upon their return than Rabbi Schuster was at a ticket counter to purchase a ticket back to the United States. Fortunately, his son Dovid soon arrived and coaxed his father into returning home before going back to the United States.

A little over a year later, it became clear that Rabbi Schuster needed the type of round-the-clock care that could not be provided outside of a hospital setting, and after a brief stay at Neve Simcha, he entered Misgav Ladach.

DURING THE THREE YEARS THAT RABBI SCHUSTER WAS IN MISGAV Ladach, Mrs. Schuster was there nearly every day. And Rabbi Schuster's

**The Website**

son Duvie was a constant presence at his father's side.

Rabbi Yirmiyahu Abramov, Rabbi Schuster's long-time *chavrusa* and colleague in the Heritage House, came often at the beginning. And when Mrs. Schuster arrived in the mornings, she often found Reb Avraham Feld, who had worked with Rabbi Schuster in the P'eylim office, by his bedside.

By and large, however, few apart from the senior staff in the Heritage House office and family knew of Rabbi Schuster's situation. Even those who did know found it hard to visit, as most of the time Rabbi Schuster was unresponsive, and the contrast to his former, high-energy self was too painful for them. One who did visit was the son of Reuven Eliyahu, who was then studying at Rabbi Dovid Soloveitchik's branch of Brisk. Reuven Eliyahu had maintained an ongoing relationship with the Schuster family for thirty years, and all his children knew Rabbi Schuster well. Blessed with a beautiful voice, that son would sing all of Rabbi Schuster's favorite Shabbos *zemiros*.

Among those who knew nothing of Rabbi Schuster's condition was Joe Reback, living in faraway Seattle. But when Joe's son came to Israel for a year of post-high school yeshivah learning in 2010–11, Joe made numerous efforts to contact Rabbi Schuster via Heritage House, in order to introduce his son to someone who had had an enormous influence on his life. Eventually, he reached Mrs. Chaya Weisberg, who along with her husband now headed the women's hostel, and she informed him of Rabbi Schuster's situation.

Joe's next step was to contact Rabbi Yirmiyahu Abramov, whom he had known since Reb Meir first brought him to Ohr Somayach, close to thirty years earlier. Rabbi Abramov brought him up-to-date on Rabbi Schuster's condition.

At various points in Joe's religious journey, Rabbi Schuster had seemingly chased him to the ends of the earth out of concern for his *neshamah*, and Joe was determined to do something for Rabbi Schuster.[1] He set about building a website as a tribute to the impact of Rabbi Schuster. He was determined to have the website up and running in Rabbi Schuster's lifetime in the form of a tribute and not a memorial. He felt that would provide solace to Mrs. Schuster, who had only a very partial knowledge of the scope of her husband's activities over the years.

Armed with some names from Rabbi Abramov of those who had been close to Rabbi Schuster over the years, Joe set about creating a core group to assist him. Apart from four members of the group who lived in Monsey, the members of the group did not know one another. But each one knew many others who had been tapped on the shoulder, literally or figuratively, by Rabbi Schuster, and they began reaching out to them.

Rabbi Schuster's condition was not publicly known, and the organizing group did not feel it was proper to make it known via social media. So they had to rely on individual contacts. But the circle of those involved expanded quickly, and the founders were inundated in an outpouring of love and gratitude for Rabbi Schuster in the form of stories for the website being planned. One anonymous donor was so moved by reading about Rabbi Schuster on the website that he sent in a $40,000 contribution. Another $10,000 check, which could not be traced, arrived from someone who had once seen Rabbi Schuster davening at the Kotel. The donor was quite ill at the time and wanted to use the opportunity to "grab onto the coattails of a tzaddik." He subsequently had an unanticipated recovery.

Joe took responsibility for the website, though he had to hire some professional help as well. Looking back, he credits the project

---

1. See Chapter Ten, pp. 156–157.

with having given him a certain strength he did not previously possess and having brought him out of his somewhat introverted shell. Much of that was due to the example of Reb Meir himself: "If he could do what he did, I can create this website," he thought to himself.

The website launched in March 2011, with the assumption that it would be continually evolving as new stories of the impact of Rabbi Schuster came in. Currently, there are fifty-five

Joe Reback

personal stories of the influence of Rabbi Schuster on the beneficiary's life.[2]

Joe Reback interviewed those who did not wish to write up their own stories, and Bracha Goetz turned those interviews into publishable stories. Mrs. Goetz's fellow Baltimore resident Sharon Galkin edited the stories. Mrs. Galkin had long been fascinated by Rabbi Schuster, going back to her days as a summer *madrichah* at Neve Yerushalayim in 1985, where she watched in amazement as day after day he brought unaffiliated young Jewish women, dressed for the hot, humid Mediterranean climate, to sit in on a class or to speak privately to one of the faculty members.

Eager to see more of Rabbi Schuster in action, she spent one Shabbos that summer at his hostel in the Old City and tagged along to the Shabbos hosts. Though born into an observant family in Monsey, Mrs. Galkin's personal debt to Rabbi Schuster — albeit unbeknownst to her at the time — went far beyond the inspiration of the summer of 1985. Four years earlier, Rabbi Schuster had brought her future husband Bill Galkin to yeshivah.

In the summer of 2002, the Galkin family — two parents and five children — spent a Shabbos in the Old City. After davening Minchah at the Kotel and ascending the steps from the Kotel Plaza, Sharon looked down to the Kotel Plaza and saw Rabbi Schuster, as if in a time warp, seventeen years later still walking back and forth in search of young

---

2. Those stories have provided invaluable resources for this biography.

Jews to introduce to a "wise man," as he had for her husband. She was filled with an urge to rush back to the Kotel Plaza to thank him for his role in her life, but decided he would not want that.

Many, however, did act upon the urge to thank him for having changed the entire trajectory of their lives. Twenty years after Rabbi Schuster asked Debbie whether she would like to attend some classes, Debbie, now accompanied by her daughter, was in the Old City and saw Rabbi Schuster. Nervous and embarrassed, she forced herself to go over to him and blurted out, "Rabbi Schuster, I've always wanted to thank you." He turned to her, smiled sweetly, and asked her name and where she was from. She was so choked up that she could barely answer him, before squeaking out few words.

After Rabbi Schuster's passing, an email arrived at Heritage House from a woman who wrote, "I don't think that there could have been one other person in the entire world who could have brought me back to my roots other than Rabbi Meir Schuster." She related how on a visit to Eretz Yisrael, many years after her first encounter with Rabbi Schuster near the Kotel, and subsequent taxi ride with him to Neve Yerushalayim, she had run into him again. "As soon as I saw him, I was overcome with amazement at everything that happened through him, and I burst into tears right in front of him — I just couldn't speak."

The website quickly became a meeting place for all those eager to express their thanks to Rabbi Schuster. In addition to the stories, the website included a short biography of Rabbi Schuster by Rabbi Shimon

Apisdorf, a description of the genesis of Heritage House, and various testimonials to Rabbi Schuster over the years written by Rabbi Mendel Weinbach of Ohr Somayach, Rabbi Noach Weinberg of Aish HaTorah, the Bostoner Rebbe, and many others. Perhaps the most effusive letter was that of Rabbi Michel Twerski of Milwaukee, in whose childhood home Reb Meir had become religiously observant.

The letter begins by instructing whoever is reading it not to

Rabbi Michel Twerski

allow the bearer, i.e., Rabbi Schuster, to read it: "If he would, its contents would embarrass him, and in his misplaced humility, he would refuse to show it to anyone." Rabbi Twerski goes on to explain that he has known Rabbi Schuster since he was a child and accordingly has "maintained an avid interest in his career."

Rabbi Twerski continued:

> I would not be guilty of hyperbole if I were to state at the outset that the quiet, unpretentious, and somewhat awkward individual before you right now is a walking legend ... Reb Meir has in his own deliberate, self-effacing, and deeply sincere way affected the lives and the Judaic content of tens of thousands of young Jews throughout the world.
>
> Walking the streets of Jerusalem, Reb Meir has engaged young Jews from every country in the world in a dialogue that has reminded them of their roots, confronted them with their destiny, and called them "home." Without theologizing or engaging in debate, Reb Meir has, with the unmistakable power of his profound authenticity, drawn young people not only from the oblivion of assimilation, but from the muck ... and the thousand and one manifestations of personal chaos and confusion. The schools, yeshivos, and communities of Israel and the United States abound with literally thousands of his "discoveries," and our nation collectively, as well as untold numbers of families, have been renewed and revitalized by his efforts. Frankly, I am awed by his accomplishments, and I openly confess that I envy his eternity.

The website launched March 2011, and in early April Joe Reback came to Jerusalem to visit his son Yonah and to see Rabbi Schuster at Misgav Ladach. Joe wanted to tell him in person about the website, even though most of those with whom he spoke told him that Rabbi Schuster had little or no awareness of his surroundings. But as Joe held his hand and read him a poem Bracha Goetz had written about "The Man at the Wall," tears began to flow down Rabbi Schuster's face.

**Petirah**

ON 17 ADAR I, 5774 (2014), RABBI MEIR TZVI SCHUSTER PASSED AWAY AT 12:50 p.m., and was buried on Har HaZeisim less than four hours later, prior to sunset. The speed with which the burial took place left almost no time to notify the public of his passing. That was just as he would have wanted it — without fanfare.

When Mrs. Ellen Clyman in the office of Neve Yerushalayim received

Gathering at the *kever* for the *sheloshim* of Rabbi Schuster

notice of Rabbi Schuster's passing, she immediately prepared an announcement to be sent to the entire Neve alumni list. But that message never went out, despite her attempts to send it three times and from two separate computers. Just one more sign from Heaven that the *tzaddik* did not want a large *levayah*.

Mrs. Schuster had always assumed that he would be buried on Har HaMenuchos close to his beloved oldest daughter Yocheved Faige Dina ("Shatzi"). But no suitable place could be found, and the family ultimately opted for Har HaZeisim, overlooking the Temple Mount and the Old City of Jerusalem. In retrospect, that was the obvious resting place for one widely known as The Man at the Wall.

After Rabbi Schuster's passing, the staff at Misgav Ladach told Mrs. Schuster that they assumed when he entered the facility that he would live no more than a year and a half, and yet he had lived twice as long as that.

Of the *yissurim* (afflictions) of the last seven years of Rabbi Schuster's life, one can only speculate that Hashem polished every little imperfection from such a great *tzaddik* in this world so that he could partake to the highest possible degree of the *ziv haShechinah* (Divine glory) in the World to Come and experience the closeness to Hashem that had always been his greatest desire.

## Chapter Twenty-Two

# RABBI SCHUSTER'S IMPACT ON KLAL YISRAEL

**N**O FULL ACCOUNTING OF RABBI SCHUSTER'S IMPACT IS POSsible, and is, at some level, irrelevant. His life was lived before an audience of One, and before that One all is recorded.

We will never know, for instance, how many people he interacted with over three and a half decades, though the numbers are surely staggering. In the thirteen years from his initial efforts at the Kotel to the opening of Heritage House, at which point he had to start traveling abroad for fundraising for months annually, he was active 365 days a year. Even a conservative estimate of interacting with ten people a day over that period yields close to 50,000 Jews.

Just as we cannot know the number of Jews with whom he interacted, so we cannot know how many of them went to yeshivah or seminary. Or, of those, how many became mitzvah-observant Jews. The requisite record-keeping system does not exist, and would not have affected Rabbi Schuster's approach if it had.

Numbers did not matter to him. When asked how many people he brought to yeshivos or seminaries, he rarely even tried to answer the question. He thought in terms of individual *neshamos*, not statistics.

Nor would he have claimed any of the thousands who became fully observant as "his." He knew well that no matter how important his influence in bringing someone to Torah study, he was in most cases no more than the catalyst who got the process going, and that each person whom he helped on the way to mitzvah observance was also the beneficiary of numerous other influences. Indeed his central task was to ensure that the young Jewish backpackers and others whom he picked up were introduced to those who would have the greatest influence on them.

His mission was to do everything he could to exercise a positive influence on Jewish *neshamos* irrespective of the ultimate outcome of his efforts. On those rare occasions where he managed to speak for more than a few moments in public, he would often quote the Gemara (*Shabbos* 55b) that records a discussion between the *Middas HaDin* (Attribute of Strict Justice) and HaKadosh Baruch Hu. HaKadosh Baruch Hu instructed the archangel Gavriel to place a mark on the forehead of the *tzaddikim* at the time of the destruction of the First Temple in order to protect them from punishment.

The *Middas HaDin* protested and argued that the righteous also deserved punishment: They were little better than the evildoers because "they could have rebuked and did not do so." Even when HaKadosh Baruch Hu attested, "It is revealed and known to Me that if they had attempted to rebuke the evildoers, the latter would not have accepted the rebuke," the *Middas HaDin* was not mollified: "Master of the Universe, this was known to You, but was it known to them?"

HaKadosh Baruch Hu had no answer, and that, concludes the *Gemara*, was the prelude to the destruction that followed: "Old man, young man and maiden, children and women, shall you slay, to utter destruction ... So they began with the elders ..." (*Yechezkel* 9:6-7).

From that Gemara, Rabbi Schuster derived the responsibility incumbent upon each Jew to do everything in his or her power to give *tochachah* to his or her fellow Jews — literally, to prove to them — and bring them closer to Torah and the One Who gave it. That responsibility is not diminished one iota by the fact that those efforts might appear to have failed.

No matter how much Rabbi Schuster did in this regard, it was never enough in his eyes. The day after Yom Kippur one year, he told an astonished Rabbi Avraham Edelstein that they had to redouble their efforts. All his thoughts of teshuvah the previous day had centered on the fact that he had to do more to bring back young Jews to their heritage.

Even if we had precise statistics on the number of young Jews Reb

Meir brought to yeshivah or seminary, even of the number who eventually became mitzvah observant, we would still not know the full measure of his impact. Many who experienced their first Shabbos under Reb Meir's auspices, or whom he brought to Heritage House for a few days, or who attended a Discovery Seminar at his suggestion, or who even spent a week or two in yeshivah, did not become fully *shomer mitzvos*.

But that does not mean that those efforts were for naught. Some, perhaps many, of those in that category nevertheless thought about their Jewish identity differently after being compelled for the first time to consider what it means to be Jewish. As a consequence, they might not have intermarried or they might have provided their children with a religious education, which they otherwise would not have. Even if they only gained a more favorable opinion of religious Jews, Rabbi Schuster once said, his efforts would have been worthwhile.

STILL, ALL THE METHODOLOGICAL QUESTIONS OF HOW IMPACT IS measured aside, it is beyond cavil that few figures over the last half-

**The Bottom Line**

century have had a comparable impact on the shape of the Jewish world to that of Rabbi Meir Tzvi Schuster. Rabbi Mendel Weinbach, the Rosh Yeshivah of Yeshivas Ohr Somayach from its inception, stated the matter succinctly: "If not for Meir Schuster, the baal teshuvah institutions as we know them today would not exist."[1] His partner, Rabbi Nota Schiller, estimates that minimally one-half of those who entered Ohr Somayach over the years did so through Rabbi Schuster.[2]

According to Rabbi Dovid Refson, at least one-third of the 35,000 women who have attended Neve Yerushalayim were first brought in by Rabbi Schuster. And that estimate is almost surely conservative. Mrs. Ellen Clyman, a senior administrator at Neve today, recalls that in her five years at Neve from 1981 to 1986, virtually every new student came to Neve together with Rabbi Schuster.

Ben Karen, like Rabbi Schuster a native of Milwaukee, tells a story that provides some sense of the endless stream of young Jews Rabbi Schuster brought to Aish HaTorah and other institutions in the late '70s. Ben was newly married and learning in the Aish kollel when he received a message from a close childhood friend, Mark Stepner, whom he had

---

1. Nissel, Rabbi Menachem, "Meir Schuster: Chance Encounters of a Different Kind," *Yated Ne'eman*, April 14, 1989.
2. Dov Wolowitz.

not heard from in years. The two had both played French horn in the Milwaukee Youth Symphony Orchestra, conducted by Mark's father.

Mark was then teaching English in Teheran, as the demonstrations against the Shah were gaining momentum, and he wrote that he wanted to spend a couple of weeks with the Karans in Jerusalem. Mark had a Jewish background and was intellectual, so Ben was eager to get him to Rabbi Noach Weinberg's 48 Ways class. But it was only as Mark was about to return to Teheran that he finally agreed to go.

The class was interrupted time after time by Rabbi Schuster bringing in another individual or group from the Kotel. Karan estimates that there were at least five interruptions in the space of an hour. And each time a new group came in, Rabbi Weinberg would start over. Ben could see that his friend Mark was about to bolt, when Reb Meir brought in yet another young man, with very long blond hair covering his face. The young man announced, "Rabbi, I'm sorry to interrupt your class. But I was shlepped from the Kotel. Please accept my apologies."

Then he swept his hair from over his eyes, and behold, it was Ricky Aaron, a master flutist in the same Milwaukee Youth Symphony, and a good friend from the same Milwaukee neighborhood as Ben and Mark. The three old friends spontaneously jumped up and started hugging one another.

Ricky had been on a kibbutz when he suddenly had the feeling that he had been in Israel too long without going to the Kotel. And there he was approached by an "unassuming Orthodox man," who also turned out to be from Milwaukee, who asked him whether he wanted to "meet a wise man." And thus had Rabbi Schuster brought about an impromptu Milwaukee reunion in the midst of Reb Noach's 48 Ways class.

EVEN IF WE KNEW THE PRECISE NUMBER OF THOSE WHOM RABBI Schuster started on the path to full mitzvah observance, we would still

## Through the Generations and Across Families

not have the full measure of his impact. On the one hand, one would have to multiply that number by all that person's descendants. By the time of Rabbi Schuster's *petirah*, for instance, Reuven Dembs, one of the early students whom Rabbi Schuster brought to Shema Yisrael, already had forty-seven grandchildren.

Sometimes the ramifications of his input were not felt just vertically through the generations, but horizontally across an entire family. Ariel, a young Argentinian Jew, met Reb Meir in the unlikeliest of locales, Eilat,

Dembs family *simchah*

where the heat often reaches 100 degrees, and which is known as a party town. Jews in fedoras and black suits are not sighted every day in Eilat. But Rabbi Schuster was then contemplating establishing a branch in Eilat.

Reb Meir asked Ariel whether he had plans to visit Jerusalem, and gave him his card. A few weeks later, Ariel was in Jerusalem and called Rabbi Schuster, who directed him to the Heritage House and set him up for a Shabbos. The husband of the host couple was Brazilian, and the conversation flowed. Over the course of Shabbos, many of Ariel's misconceptions about Torah Judaism were debunked. He subsequently enrolled in a Jerusalem yeshivah with a Spanish-speaking program.

Fearing a radical break with his life up until then, Ariel took time off from his yeshivah studies and went to a kibbutz near Jerusalem to think about what he had learned. After two months, he returned to yeshivah, and at that point his parents dispatched a younger sister from Argentina to talk some sense into her brother. That plan did not go well, and she ended up studying in the women's division of the Spanish-speaking program.

Ariel's parents realized they would have to rescue their children themselves. But speaking to their children's rabbis in Jerusalem, they understood what had attracted their children to Torah. Upon returning to Buenos Aires, they began studying regularly with a young local rabbi. Observing the revolution that was taking place in his family, Ariel's older brother also came to visit his siblings in Israel, and started intensive Jewish learning after returning home.

Yoel Labell came from an "observant" Reform family in Andover, Massachusetts — meaning his father attended Friday evening services after dinner. He came to Israel after college to observe the communal

Yoel and Gidon Labell in their younger days

and socialist aspects of kibbutz living firsthand. Once in Israel, like most young Jews in the early '80s, he eventually made his way to the Kotel. And there Rabbi Schuster tapped him on the shoulder and asked him, "Would you like to see a yeshivah?" Yoel had already embarked on a career as a journalist, and thought to himself, "This will make a great story." And for good measure, he was eager to show the yeshivah heads where they had erred in their religious path. The latter, however, he found difficult to do: The arguments to which he was exposed in Aish HaTorah were far more logically persuasive than he had anticipated.

Still, Yoel went to a kibbutz for five disappointing months. While

Rabbi Gidon Labell teaching a Gemara class at Aish HaTorah

A Labell family gathering

there, he was visited by his younger brother Gidon, who was still in high school. Together they spent the Seder in the Old City at the home of Yaakov Kleiman. After that Pesach experience, Yoel began learning at Aish HaTorah, where Gidon again visited, while in college, on the supposition that Yoel was on to something. Gidon never returned to college. He has remained at Aish for well over three decades, as a student and rabbi, and is considered one of the most noteworthy *talmidei chachamim* produced by Aish.

In time, Yoel's religious journey also convinced two of his three sisters to come and check out Torah Judaism, and both are themselves matriarchs of Torah families today. A recent family photo shows a four-generation Jewish family.

On at least one occasion, Rabbi Schuster served as a sort of *shadchan* as well. Seth and Nili[3] dated off and on throughout university, and he was a bulwark of support for her when she was undergoing often debilitating cancer treatments early in her college career.

She, however, came from a far more traditional family than he did, and after being declared cancer-free, her gratitude to Hashem for the gift of life, for which she had so fervently prayed, put her firmly on the path to religious observance.

After graduating college, Seth went traveling in Europe. But frustrated by incessant rain, he decided to visit a friend on a kibbutz in sunny Israel. As if in answer to Nili's prayers, on a visit to Jerusalem,

---

3. Not their real names.

he received the proverbial tap on the shoulder from Rabbi Schuster just outside the Damascus Gate, and agreed to go to a *Pirkei Avos* class at Aish. At Aish, Seth, who was a pre-veterinary major in college, was pleasantly surprised not just to find that Torah was highly relevant, but that those teaching at Aish were thoroughly rational.

After three weeks at Aish, Seth returned to the college town where Nili was still completing her B.A. (delayed by the three semesters she had to take off because of her cancer treatments) and connected to the Young Israel on campus. A year later, he and Nili decided independently to go to Israel to learn Torah.

Nili assumed that now that they were on the same path, a proposal would soon follow. But Seth decided he should devote himself to "catching up" before committing to the responsibilities of marriage. His rabbis brought things to a head, however, by telling him that he could not object to Nili starting *shidduchim* if he was still not ready to get married. As soon as she did, however, and Seth realized that he could not count on her still being available when he was ready to get married, a proposal was forthcoming.

Reb Meir's tap on the shoulder did not lead directly to the *chuppah*, but Seth and Nili have always viewed it as an indispensable step toward their establishment of a Torah home, and attached great symbolic importance to Rabbi Schuster's recital of one of the *sheva berachos* at their oldest child's *chasunah*.

In time, Nili's brother and sister-in-law also became Torah-observant, providing Rabbi Schuster with sixteen "grandchildren," all from that initial tap on Seth's shoulder. Nili and Seth have lived in Israel for thirty-five years, where she is an editor, doula, cancer support counselor, and *shadchanit*, and he has primarily learned and taught Torah since receiving *semichah* from Rabbi Yitzchak Berkovits.

## Chapter Twenty-Three
# HIGH-IMPACT "CATCHES"

N UMBERS ALONE CANNOT DO JUSTICE TO RABBI SCHUSTER'S influence on the Jewish world. Many of those whom he first brought to yeshivah or seminary have themselves become high-impact individuals, whether in kiruv, as rabbanim and principals, or as authors of important and widely read *sefarim*, and even as philanthropists.

OVER THE PAST DECADE LORI PALATNIK'S[1] JEWISH WOMEN'S Renaissance Project (JWRP) has had as great an impact as any other **Educators** kiruv program. Like Aish HaTorah's Discovery Program of the 1990s, JWRP provides kiruv professionals across the world a program that is at once attractive to a wide range of participants and potentially life-changing — a packed trip to Israel, together with other Jewish mothers. "Transformative" and "life-changing" are the two most frequently used terms by the 17,000 participants, as of 2018, in the trips.[2]

Lori Palatnik speaking about
Rabbi Schuster

---

1. See Chapter Seven.
2. See Rosenblum, Yonoson, *Rav Noach Weinberg: Torah Revolutionary*, Mosaica Press, 2020, pp. 450–455.

Not surprisingly, kiruv has been the most fertile field for those whose first introduction to Torah life was through Rabbi Schuster. Rabbi Nachum Braverman,[3] together with Irwin Katsof, built Aish-LA, one of the first and the largest of the Aish HaTorah branches. Since 1981, Aish-LA has been able to tap into the fabulous Jewish wealth of Los Angeles to the tune of over one hundred million dollars to support a host of worldwide projects, as well as the local kiruv activities, including a shul and a large pool of kiruv professionals targeting every Jewish population demographic in the Los Angeles area.[4]

Rabbi Aryeh Markman has been the executive director of Aish-LA since 1994, a mere decade after he first met Rabbi Schuster while taking a six-week break from his job leading international tours. Approaching the Kotel, Aryeh was apprehensive, not sure whether he "really wanted to meet G-d or not." Crossing the Kotel Plaza in his hiking boots, T-shirt, and Levi jeans, Markman realized later, he must have looked to Rabbi Schuster like a "forty-pound salmon swimming upstream."

Reb Meir came up to him immediately and asked whether he had a place to stay. Though Aryeh said he was taken care of, Reb Meir insisted on having his son Duvie take Aryeh to see Heritage House. As soon as the latter walked in, he felt like he was back in college in his Jewish fraternity house. From Heritage House it was a quick jump to Aish HaTorah.

Aish HaTorah's first major branch was Toronto. Shalom Schwartz,[5] another one of Reb Meir's catches, headed the five-person rabbinic team that opened the branch. The impact of Aish-Toronto on the city was immense. In its early years, the branch reached a large number of the outstanding young people in the non-Orthodox, but Jewishly active, segment of the community. At one point, Torontonians constituted over one-third of all those in the Aish HaTorah *beis medrash* in Jerusalem.

Toronto, via Aish-Toronto, has also proven a fecund source of funding for Aish HaTorah's worldwide operations. The Dan-Hytman family alone has contributed over fifty million dollars to two magnificent Aish HaTorah buildings overlooking the Kotel and Temple Mount in Jerusalem, to Project Inspire and to the Toronto Jewish community, which includes two shuls today.

Rabbi Schuster found Ze'ev Kraines on a Hebrew University program

---

3. See Chapter Six, page 85.
4. *Rav Noach Weinberg: Torah Revolutionary*, op cit., p. 305.
5. See Chapter Eight, pp. 107–110.

Ze'ev Kraines dancing at a friend's *chasunah* in Ohr Somayach days

after his freshman year at Cornell University and brought him to Shema Yisrael. Over his too-brief life, Rabbi Kraines covered more bases than perhaps any of those first brought to yeshivah by Rabbi Schuster: assistant congregational rabbi in Charleston, South Carolina; school principal in Mexico City; mashgiach in the Ohr Somayach kollel in the Glenhazel neighborhood of Johannesburg; principal of Johannesburg's Sha'arei Torah primary school for fourteen years, and founding principal of the Mesivta Sha'arei Torah high school, in which capacity he developed school curricula made freely available to other schools across South Africa; rabbinical advisor to numerous Orthodox youth groups; and member of the Executive Board of the South African Rabbinical Association, where his was often the most sought-after opinion.[6]

In addition, Rabbi Kraines and his wife Nechama were the first full-time rabbinic couple of the Ohr Somayach-Sandton shul, in a neighborhood of a Johannesburg suburb in which there had not previously been a shul. They guided the shul for over twenty-seven years, until just prior to Rabbi Kraines's recent passing.

Ze'ev and Nechama's *vort* took place at the historic Churva Synagogue in the Jewish Quarter of the Old City. After the *vort*, they naturally made their way to the Kotel. There they saw Rabbi Schuster patrolling the

---

6. Chief Rabbi Warren Goldstein.

Kotel precincts as always, and immediately said to one another that just seeing Rabbi Schuster, who had played such a large role in their lives, was a good omen for their future life together. And so it turned out to be for them and their twelve children and all those they influenced to come closer to Hashem over four and a half decades.

Few Torah educators have had as much an impact as Rabbi Shlomo Goldberg over the past twenty-five years, as principal of Yeshiva Aharon Yaakov/Ohr Eliyahu, a Los Angeles primary school and junior high school, with well over four hundred students in its boys' and girls' divisions.[7] He has been recognized with the Distinguished Educator Award (2003) of the Miliken Family Foundation and as an Outstanding Educator (2005) by Torah Umesorah, for which he serves as a senior lecturer to day school principals, teachers, and parents.

His writings on education appear regularly in a wide variety of Torah publications, and his book *On His Path: Principles in Chinuch from the Weekly Parashah* (2017) is now in its second printing.

The purpose of a middle school, according to Rabbi Goldberg, is to create a person, i.e., to provide the foundations for the child's future spiritual, intellectual, interpersonal, and physical life, and to instill in each child a belief in his or her power to change and grow. Consonant

Rabbi Goldberg speaking about Rabbi Schuster for a Project Inspire tribute

with the heavy *mussar* emphasis of Yeshivas Chofetz Chaim, in which Rabbi Goldberg learned for many years, after starting at Aish HaTorah, he tells the students, "I don't know if your high school dean will appreciate what you gained here, but your spouse and children definitely will."

As principal, Rabbi Goldberg seeks to repay a debt to mentors, including Rabbi Schuster, who "opened the door to a world of Jewish tradition ... [and who] recognized my inner potential and ... shared generously of their

---

7. See Chapter Seven, pp. 98–99. Rabbi Goldberg also served as a rabbi in Santa Fe, New Mexico, and Venice, California.

time, energy, insight and knowledge to recognize who I am and what I could be ...."

Helping Jewish children reach their potential is his life goal. *Chinuch*, he emphasizes, quoting Rabbi Yaakov Kamenetsky, is the only mitzvah whose form changes with time. The commandment "And you shall teach them and guard them *to perform* them" (*Devarim* 5:1) means that the mitzvos must be taught in such a way that the recipient will be eager to perform them, and the means of doing so necessarily changes from generation to generation.

THE LANDSCAPE OF TORAH LITERATURE OVER THE LAST TWO DECADES would have been vastly different without the contributions of authors

**Authors** whom Rabbi Schuster first brought to yeshivah. That is particularly true of works on Torah themes aimed at as broad as possible a Jewish audience. Shimon Apisdorf was in the semester program at Haifa University in 1978 when he decided to spend a weekend in Jerusalem to see if he could get any of his questions answered.

His first meeting with Rabbi Schuster at the Kotel did not go well when Rabbi Schuster told him that the two non-Jewish friends he had come to the Kotel with could not come with him for a Shabbos meal. Still, contact was made, and Shimon did take up Rabbi Schuster on his invitation to come to one of Rabbi Noach Weinberg's 48 Ways classes on Sunday morn-

ing. For the rest of the semester, he returned every three or four weeks to Aish for Shabbos, and when the semester was over he returned to Aish for six weeks.

While Shimon was at University of Haifa, Rabbi Schuster wrote to him frequently, and during those six weeks at Aish HaTorah, checked on him constantly. Following college graduation, Shimon returned to Aish, and became a regular guest at the Schusters' for Shabbos, often sleeping on the pullout cot in the living room.

Shimon Apisdorf as a young college student

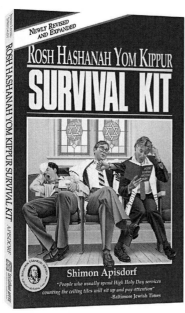

The cover of the Rosh Hashanah
Yom Kippur Survival Guide

To date his eleven books have sold over a quarter of a million copies, more books than many Jewish publishing houses have sold in their history. *The Rosh Hashanah Yom Kippur Survival Kit* alone has sold over 120,000 copies and has been purchased in bulk by kiruv organizations around the world, including Chabad and NCSY. Passover and Chanukah Survival Kits followed.

Joining the Survival Kits, as short, entertaining, and witty introductions to major Torah themes, are the volumes in Rabbi Apisdorf's Nutshell series, designed for "the intellectually curious but chronically short on time." Among the volumes in the Nutshell series are treatments of G-d, Israel, the Holidays, and Pesach. *Chanukah: Eight Nights of Light, Eight Gifts for the Soul* and *The One-Hour Purim Primer* fit a similar model of compact and entertaining reference books that kiruv professionals can feel comfortable distributing widely to those with whom they are working.

Gila Manolson[8] has focused her attention on subjects on everyone's mind but which many Torah educators do not feel comfortable discussing: the fraught relations between men and women in the modern world; the basis of the Torah's proscription of all premarital physical contact; *tznius* as more than modest dress, but as one's self-image as a spiritual being; and the discovery of individuality.

The importance of her subject matter can be deduced from the fact that her many books have been translated into six languages, and she has traveled the globe teaching and lecturing.

Jeremy Kagan took time off from his undergraduate studies at Yale in 1979 to come to Israel to explore his Judaism. Having grown up in Hawaii, with no appreciable Jewish community, his knowledge of Judaism was quite limited. But he knew enough to be curious about it,

---

8. See Chapter Eight, p. 109.

listing Judaism in his college application as one of the numerous topics he hoped to explore at Yale.

At Yale, he was first exposed to the existence of Torah and Orthodox Judaism by an Orthodox roommate. He also came to the conclusion early on that "it's nice to be nice" was not an adequate basis to ground morality. That was enough to convince him that during his six months in Israel, one day at least should be spent at a yeshivah seeing what that was about.

Jeremy came to Israel committed to a four-month Hebrew-language program on a kibbutz. He visited Jerusalem repeatedly, uncannily running into Rabbi Schuster each time at different locations around the city. The first time they spoke, he told Rabbi Schuster that he intended to go to yeshivah for a day. At each subsequent meeting, Reb Meir recognized him and always had the same question: "Jeremy, when are you going to yeshivah?"

When his kibbutz program finished, Jeremy tried a number of other programs to learn something about his Jewishness, none of which proved satisfactory. With two weeks left in Israel, he returned to Jerusalem to make good on his decision to spend time in a yeshivah and his promise to Reb Meir. His Yale roommate was in Jerusalem for the year and took him to visit a number of yeshivos before he settled on Ohr Somayach, which would surely have been Rabbi Schuster's choice.

Rabbi Kagan considers himself an example of a large group of those whom Rabbi Schuster did not physically escort to yeshivah, but who were influenced by their numerous interactions with him and, no doubt, by his prayers on their behalf.

He stayed for two weeks at Ohr Somayach on that first visit, but was back a year later for nearly a year and a half, despite requiring only three credits to graduate Yale. He eventually went back to Yale to complete his degree in philosophy, and then returned to learn full time in earnest for many years. Today, Rabbi Kagan is dean of a prominent post-high school seminary for young women, primarily from the United States and England.

He is also the author over the past decade of a trilogy of profound English-language works of Torah thought, one of which was awarded the National Book Award for Modern Jewish Thought, probably the first time the award has been conferred upon a work by someone whose Jewish learning has been exclusively in traditional yeshivos.

Rabbi Kagan's books are not written to be read and absorbed quickly, and they will not be runaway best-sellers like Rabbi Apisdorf's works. But he has made accessible to modern readers, who are not necessarily versed in modern Jewish thought or capable of plumbing the depths of the sources themselves, such thinkers as the Maharal of Prague, the Vilna Gaon, Rav Tzadok of Lublin, and, in our day, Rabbi Moshe Shapiro.

Pinchas (Paul) Winston was on a brief detour from his European travels when Rabbi Schuster met him at the Kotel and asked him, "Are you Jewish?" Pinchas accepted his offer of a Friday night meal, thinking it would be fun to tell his family and friends back home, "Hey, I had a Shabbat meal with a real live Orthodox family."

That meal with a young baal teshuvah couple in Ma'alot Dafna, just above Ohr Somayach, made a sufficient impression that Pinchas spent a few days in Ohr Somayach before returning to his European adventures. Back home in Toronto, he became one of the first students of Aish-Toronto, for which he and his wife would work not so many years later.

A long-time resident of the Jerusalem suburb of Telshe-Stone, Rabbi Winston has published dozens of *sefarim*.

Bracha Goetz is the author of dozens of children's books, and one adult memoir of her struggles with eating disorders while an undergraduate at Harvard and during her first year in medical school. Those struggles, in what appeared to be a storybook life, opened her up to the exploration of Torah. A summer stint in Hadassah Hospital's oncology ward, visiting dying patients, while on a "secret mission to learn the

purpose of living," made a meeting with Reb Meir almost inevitable. And that meeting occurred within days of her arrival in Israel after her first year in medical school. Soon she began studying at Ohr Somayach Women's Division.

Little more than a year later, on Zos Chanukah, she was at the Kotel with the young man she was dating, Larry (Aryeh) Goetz.[9] He explained to her that the potential for dedication to the Jewish people is at its height on the last night of

Rabbi Schuster reciting one of the *sheva berachos* after *bensching* at the *chasunah* of Aryeh and Bracha Goetz

9. See pp. 309–310.

Chanukah, and asked her, on that night so filled with potential, if she would agree to continue her life journey together with him.

At that moment, they both saw Rabbi Schuster "looking for more lost *neshamos*," the very epitome of the dedication to the Jewish People that they hoped to make central to their future life together.

The creative impact of Rabbi Schuster's "finds" is not confined to the written word, but extends to the world of film as well. Before David (Dave) Lenik came to Israel in 1983, his boyhood friend Neil offered him the following advice: "If you go to Jerusalem, you're going to go to the Kotel. And if you go to the Kotel, it might happen that someone will come up to you and ask if you want to take a class. Take the class, you might like it."

David did not have to wait, however, until he reached the Kotel. Walking down the steps through the Arab shuk, just inside the Jaffa Gate, and headed in the general direction of the Kotel on a Shabbos afternoon, he had a feeling that someone was "stalking him." He turned around slowly and caught sight of a tall man in a black coat, hat and glasses eyeing him from a distance. A few hundred feet later, he turned around again, this time more quickly, and saw the same stranger, who had in the interim narrowed the gap. David confronted him directly: "Listen, I don't know what you are about, but if you want to be helpful, show me where the entrance to the Kotel plaza is."

About ten minutes later, Dave was staring at the Kotel, with a cardboard kippah perched on his head, when he sensed once again that he was in Rabbi Schuster's sights. With his friend Neil's words in the recesses of his mind, David asked him what he wanted, to which Rabbi Schuster "mumbled" something about "learning about Judaism and taking a class." Having already resolved to take his friend's advice, Dave followed Rabbi Schuster to the Aish *beis medrash*, despite being "underwhelmed by his marginal attempt at chitchat."

Once inside the nearly empty Aish *beis medrash*. Reb Meir called over a student and told him that Dave had some questions about Judaism, and then he was gone before Dave even had a chance to say goodbye.

At the time he came to Israel, Dave was completing a screenplay, and after learning at Aish for several years, he returned to the United States to pursue a career in filmmaking, doing both commercial work and a series of documentaries for Torah Umesorah, Zechor Yemos Olam, on positive, inspiring stories of Holocaust survivors.

Most recently, he collaborated with another veteran documentary

David Lenik with an actor
playing Rav Meir Shapiro

maker, Reb Menachem Daum, on a film on the life of Rav Meir Shapiro of Lublin, initiator of the *daf hayomi* and founder of Yeshivas Chachmei Lublin, *Only with Joy*.[10] Beginning in the '90s, Daum began recording interviews with surviving talmidim of Chachmei Lublin. David's contribution was to find a way to turn those interviews and still photographs into a sustained narrative using both historical re-enactments and animation.

Lenik is currently producing a version of *Only with Joy* for school-age children, under the auspices of Torah Umesorah. In addition, he is working on a feature-length film developed with the specific intent of changing the general public's perceptions of the chareidi/chassidic community.

A NUMBER OF THOSE WHOM RABBI SCHUSTER BROUGHT INTO THE Torah world went on to great success in their professional and financial endeavors, success that would redound to the benefit of both Heritage

**Philanthropy** House and the larger Jewish world. Among those none looms larger than Dr. Richard Roberts of Lakewood, who is today one of the largest supporters of Lakewood's multitude of religious institutions, as well as a major donor to Republican political candidates.

Dr. Roberts was always proud of being Jewish growing up in the Philadelphia suburbs, even though he had scant Jewish education and had never met a religious Jew. Even fasting on Yom Kippur was not a given in his family. When he did so as a teenager, one of his aunts told him around 4:00 p.m., "OK, you proved your point. Now you can eat."

After completing medical school at the University of Pennsylvania in 1983, Roberts and a friend decided to travel around the world for a year.

---

10. The title is taken from Rabbi Meir Shapiro's last words to his talmidim, as they danced around his deathbed at his request, singing one of the many *niggunim* he composed in his lifetime, *Becha botchu avoseinu*. Noticing some of the talmidim sobbing, with his last strength he wrote two words: "*Nohr b'simchah* — Only with joy!"

Rich Roberts on his post-medical school travels

They ran into Rabbi Schuster, who in their eyes "looked like he came from Mars," in the Arab section of the Old City. He asked them what they were doing the following evening, which was Shevii shel Pesach. "Probably going to a movie," they replied. But when he suggested that they spend the *Chag* with a religious Jewish family, they were game for what they viewed as likely to be "an interesting cultural experience."

It turned out to be far more than that. Their host was Rabbi Pinchas Kasnett, one of the early students at Shema Yisrael, and the conversation that night was, in Dr. Roberts' words, "the most intellectually honest discussion that I had ever had." The two medical students ended up staying for a few days. By the time he left the Kasnetts, Roberts was wearing a kippah and had decided to eat only kosher food.

After completing his medical training and also obtaining a Ph.D. in biophysics, Roberts took over the family pharmaceutical business, URL Pharma, which was then floundering. In 2012, he sold it to a large Japanese pharmaceutical company.

On Rabbi Schuster's next to last fundraising trip to the States, he and Avraham Lewis went to visit Dr. Roberts in Lakewood. To Avraham, the meeting, which took place on the front doorstep of Dr. Roberts's home, appeared entirely perfunctory. As usual, Rabbi Schuster barely glanced at the check Dr. Roberts had written to Heritage House, if at all. Only when they got back in the car did Avraham discover to his amazement that the check was for $150,000 — just a small token of Dr. Roberts's *hakaras hatov* (gratitude) for having been set up with the Kasnett family a quarter-century earlier.

That check led to the only call Mrs. Schuster ever remembers receiving from her husband rejoicing in a large donation.

RABBI SCHUSTER'S INNER LIFE REMAINED PRECISELY THAT — INNER. One could gain some hints from watching him daven or observing the manner in which he drove himself, but rarely did he share his deep-

**Emulation as Praise**

est thoughts. Every once in a while, however, those thoughts came rushing to the surface and burst forth.

Sam Friedland was one of his hosts in Monsey for close to twenty years, and one of the handful of people with whom Reb Meir felt most comfortable. One Shabbos morning, they were walking to shul when Sam commented, "I don't even know what we are doing here." Reb Meir stopped and became uncharacteristically animated. He stuck his finger forcefully into Friedland's breastbone and responded, "You want to know what we are doing here? You want to know what we are doing here? I'll tell you. We are here to bring light into the world, and not, *chas v'shalom*, darkness."

He was a spreader of light and inspired others to seek to spread light

Sam Friedland tells his favorite Rabbi Meir Schuster story
on the Project Inspire documentary

into the world. His example made clear that it could be done. But also that doing so requires commitment and dedication. That inspiration too is part of his impact.

Different people caught different rays of light, as refracted by Reb Meir, but few missed them altogether. Larry (Aryeh) Goetz came to Israel the year after graduating college for a six-month ulpan studying Hebrew, and six months volunteering as the town planner of the southern city of Ofakim. The latter job provided him with the opportunity to put his bachelor's degree in town planning to use.

Near the end of his time in Israel, he visited Jerusalem and made the obligatory pilgrimage to the Kotel. At the Kotel, he followed the custom of leaving a note in the crevices of the Wall. His note read something to the effect of "I need Your help figuring out the next step in my life."

As he came out of the prayer area, Reb Meir was there to suggest a class in Judaism. And having nothing else planned for the day, Aryeh accepted, and soon he and Reb Meir were on a Number 1 bus to Ohr Somayach. Aryeh went to one class, had lunch with a group of students, and was on his way back to Ofakim. For Aryeh it was his first exposure to Orthodox rabbis, indeed to Orthodox Jews of any sort, and he marked off the experience as a positive one.

A few weeks later, as Aryeh was completing his stint in Ofakim, someone mentioned to him that he should visit Aish HaTorah before leaving Israel. Because his experience at Ohr Somayach had been a positive one, he had no reticence about taking up that suggestion. He ended up staying at Aish HaTorah, marrying, and becoming one of the first members of the Aish HaTorah kollel. All in all, he and his wife Bracha remained in Israel for nine years before moving to Baltimore.

In Aryeh Goetz's view, Reb Meir Schuster was a sort of Johnny Appleseed planting seeds everywhere he could. Aryeh's visit to Ohr Somayach had been one such seed, and though it did not lead directly to his decision to go to yeshivah or become religious, it had opened up the possibility of his doing so.

Out of gratitude to Reb Meir, he resolved to be a minor Johnny Appleseed in Baltimore over the years, inviting Jews he met in his work as a social worker, or just by "serendipity," for a Shabbos in the Goetz home. At a recent memorial for Rabbi Schuster, he described one such encounter at the local Whole Foods store. On entering the store, he spotted a young man who looked very much like some of those he had seen in photographs of Reb Meir at the Kotel, and decided to initiate a

Rabbi Aryeh Goetz

conversation. The young man's nose ring threw him off for a moment, but did not ultimately deter him any more than the attire of those whom he met at the Kotel had deterred Reb Meir.

After ascertaining that Michael was an employee at Whole Foods whose job it was to prepare pizzas, Aryeh asked him whether he was Jewish. Michael replied that he had grown up in a Jewish suburb in New Jersey, which he proceeded to demonstrate by reciting a *berachah*. He was not raised Jewish, but in the course of research on a family tree, it turned out that he was of German Jewish descent, and his parents had hidden that fact from him, with unfortunate consequences. The woman he wanted to marry refused him on the grounds that he was not Jewish, and by the time he found out that he was, she had already married someone else. Subsequently, Michael married a non-Jewish woman and had one young child. When Aryeh inquired how he felt about learning that he was in fact Jewish, Michael told him that he was still digesting his new identity and working things out.

Aryeh told Michael that he was a rabbi and that if he had any Jewish questions he could always call him. He also took Michael's contact information. At the end of the conversation, Michael shocked Aryeh by asking him, "Rabbi, do you mind if I give you a hug?" which he did, right across from the frozen fish section of Whole Foods.

A seed had been planted, though whether it will give forth fruit remains to be seen.

Reb Raziel S. is another Jew who views his life work as in many respects giving back what he received from Rabbi Schuster. He first met Rabbi Schuster at the Central Bus Station, while in Israel on a college independent study project writing poetry. Not long into the conversation, Reb Meir invited Raziel for Shabbos. Raziel thought he was one of those special Jerusalem souls, lonely and looking for company. He was pleasantly surprised upon reaching the Schuster home to find that he was a married man with a family.

Something clicked for Raziel that Shabbos and in a *shiur* from a dynamic *talmid chacham* to which Rabbi Schuster brought him on Motzaei Shabbos. "It was hard to say no to him; he was so excited and enthusiastic [about the *shiur*]," Raziel remembers.

Though Raziel did summon up the ability to resist Reb Meir's entreaties to stay in yeshivah, within a day or two of returning to the kibbutz where he was staying, he came back to the yeshivah. When Reb Meir found him in the *beis medrash*, he had an indescribable "look of glee on his face," and made it clear to Raziel that if he had any special needs he would be there to make sure that they were fulfilled. As long as Raziel stayed in yeshivah, he knew that Reb Meir was continually checking up on him, and that knowledge eased his adjustment to yeshivah greatly.

After returning to the States and learning for several more years, Raziel became a *melamed* in a school, in which many of the boys suffer from emotional and learning difficulties. He has tried to pattern himself on Reb Meir and the way he gave him the greatest gift of all, "a real, authentic connection to the Ribbono shel Olam."

He sums up his career so far: "Because of what Reb Meir did for me and the way he touched my life, hundreds of boys have become deeper, prouder Jews, when it looked like the winds of society would turn them the other way." Just another example, in Raziel's opinion, of how Reb Meir's desire to give to other Jews changed the very flow of Jewish history.

It is the purpose of this biography of Rabbi Meir Schuster to inspire others to bring their own ray of light to the world, just as he did.

*Chapter Twenty-Four*
# EPILOGUE

## Rabbi Meir Tzvi Schuster's Message of Hope for Each of Us

I N THE INTRODUCTION TO THIS BIOGRAPHY, WE NOTED THAT THE story of Rabbi Meir Tzvi Schuster's life challenges us in ways that biographies of many great Torah figures do not. In the case of the latter, it is often too easy for us to treat their lives as without implications for our own. We do not ask ourselves why we have not achieved their greatness in Torah, for the answer would seem to be all too readily apparent: They were born with great abilities that we do not possess, and in many cases, came from an illustrious line of Torah scholars.

But no one ever contemplated the extraordinary impact of Rabbi Meir Tzvi Schuster and consoled himself that he had not had the same impact on the world because he was not born with the same extraordinary talents that facilitated Reb Meir's success in kiruv. More often, the response to Rabbi Schuster's story was: If Meir Schuster can do kiruv, then I certainly can too.

Most of those who assumed that they could do as well or better than Rabbi Schuster in inspiring young men and women to learn more about their Judaism found out to their shock that it was not so easy, and that his success did not prove that anybody could do it.

But when we analyze the phenomenal success of Rabbi Schuster over the course of close to four decades, the message is one of hope that is applicable to each and every one of us. What we often perceive as limitations on our ability to positively affect the world are almost always overestimated. And what we perceive as prerequisites to success are frequently unnecessary.

Rabbi Dovid Refson, the founder and dean of Neve Yerushalayim, the flagship seminary for baalos teshuvah, is fond of quoting a saying of his late father: "There is no limit to what one can achieve, as long as he is willing to give others the credit." Rabbi Meir Schuster's life suggests an even more empowering parallel: There is no limit to what one can achieve as long as he knows that the ultimate credit belongs to Hashem.

To talmidim who told Rabbi Noach Weinberg, the legendary founder of Aish HaTorah, that his demands were too much for them and incapable of being achieved, Reb Noach always had the same answer: If Hashem were helping you, could you do it? The inescapable answer could only be yes. And when Reb Noach sought a concrete example to prove his point, he had to look no farther than Rabbi Meir Schuster.

That Rabbi Meir Schuster benefited from incredible *siyata d'Shmaya* is incontestable. Rabbi Sender Chachamovits, the founder of Binyan Olam, a yeshivah for Spanish-speaking baalei teshuvah, once proposed to Rabbi Avraham Edelstein, the director of Heritage House, the idea of opening up an additional Heritage House hostel for Spanish-speakers. The fundraising responsibility would be completely upon him, as would the running of the hostel. If so, Rabbi Edelstein inquired, why did he want the hostel to be under the Heritage House umbrella? Just one reason, replied Rabbi Chachamovits: to be included in the *siyata d'Shmaya* of everything connected to Rabbi Schuster.

That *siyata d'Shmaya* was first and foremost manifest in the *chein* (favor) he found in the eyes of those to whom he spoke. In the Torah, *chein* is always described as a Divinely given trait.

And so it was in Rabbi Schuster's case, for he certainly had little of those qualities that the world associates with *chein*, except perhaps for a radiant smile. He was totally lacking any aptitude for easy speech or a talent for conversation. As such, he could not intellectually dazzle any of the young backpackers he met (in the rare cases where intellectual dazzle was what they were seeking). As with Moshe Rabbeinu, whom the Torah describes as being "heavy of speech," no one would ever be able to claim that they were beguiled by the glibness of Reb Meir's speech, for words did not flow trippingly from his tongue.

And yet he did find *chein* in the eyes of tens of thousands of complete strangers over the years, who followed a man dressed unlike any other they had ever met to places and institutions of which they had never heard.

For individual after individual, he just happened to be there at precisely the right minute — whether tapping them on the shoulder just after they had stood in front of the Kotel and asked Hashem to show them a sign, or happening along precisely when someone was at a crossroads deciding what to do next. That too was *siyata d'Shmaya*.

So was his ability to determine which yeshivah or seminary would be right for which young person or know what Torah figure would make the best initial impression on a particular young person to open him or her to the possibility of making a radical change in his or her life.

But identifying the source of Reb Meir's success as *siyata d'Shmaya* is only the first step in the contemplation of his life message. The next step is to ascertain the source of that *siyata d'Shmaya*. Why is one person the recipient of so much overt *siyata d'Shmaya* and another much less?

In answering that question, Reb Meir constitutes something close to the ideal laboratory test case. The first key is to recognize oneself as the beneficiary of *siyata d'Shmaya*. Without recognizing the Source of one's success, one cannot give thanks to Hashem for it. And without *hakaras hatov*, one cuts off the flow of that *siyata d'Shmaya*.

Reb Meir never succumbed to the temptation to view his success as a tribute to him. The language of "I did this" was totally foreign to him. He did not speak of his achievements because he did not view them as his. He was a "master of self-effacement."[1] The most he ever permitted himself was a smile of joy when he heard of someone who had grown in his or her connection to Torah and mitzvos under his auspices. The smile was for the result and for the fact that he was privileged to play a role in the realization of that result, not because he felt he had brought it about.

He saw himself exclusively in one role: *eved Hashem* (a servant of G-d). He had no *zich*, no sense of self, other than as Hashem's loyal foot soldier. Chazal say that one who says something "in the name of the one who said it" brings *Geulah* (Redemption) to the world. The proof is Esther, who had recorded in the Royal Books of Persia that Mordechai had uncovered and revealed a plot on the life of Achashverosh. She

---

1. Hillel Goldberg, "The Teshuvah Solicitors," *Jewish Observer*, May–June 1980, p. 10.

thereby set in motion the reprieve from Haman's decree of destruction on every Jew.

To say something in the name of another, without taking the slightest credit for oneself, as Esther did, demonstrates an absence of ego and self-interest. And only such a person, the Maharal explains, is capable of bringing the Redemption.

Reb Meir's lack of ego is evident in at least two ways. First, it was impossible to insult him. What would have been humiliation for anyone else simply rolled off his back because he was never the issue. The author of these words first met Reb Meir in the summer of 1976. I was then studying Hebrew at Ulpan Etzion, in Jerusalem's Baka neighborhood, on a sabbatical year between completing law school and commencing practice.

He appeared one day during the lunch break, as the twenty-something young men and women in the ulpan sat around on the grass soaking up the sun's rays and chatting with one another. None, it is safe to say, had any desire to be interrupted in either activity by a gangly religious figure dressed in black. A number of insults and snide remarks were directed toward him, probably mostly by the young men eager to impress their female friends. I pray that I was not one of them, though it is hard to be confident on that score, but for sure I remained silent and did not protest the cruel treatment of a fellow Jew.

Two things stick out in my memory from that day. The first is how undeterred he was by the disparaging remarks directed at him. And the second is that, despite those disparaging remarks, he still left that day with one of my fellow students — a fellow Chicago native — in tow. Twenty or more years later, I came across the name of that student again. He had become the rav of a religious moshav. And within three years of that encounter, my new wife and I were privileged to start receiving Friday night guests on a regular basis from Rabbi Schuster.[2]

Reb Meir's immunity to insult hints at another one of his strengths: He may not have had an ego, but he did not lack for self-confidence. He did not doubt that his efforts would be blessed with *siyata d'Shmaya* and bear fruit. And he did not doubt that he was making a contribution

---

2. My mother remembers receiving a call from Rabbi Schuster on a Thursday night prior to the birth of our first son the following evening. In response to his inquiry as to whether we could take Shabbos guests, my mother replied that my wife was almost certain to give birth within the next twenty-four hours. Undeterred, Rabbi Schuster wondered whether my mother would be interested in taking Shabbos guests in our stead.

to improving Hashem's world.[3] Rabbi Dr. Yaakov Greenwald in his *sefer With Truth and With Love,* based on his correspondence with the Steipler Gaon, defines the essence of self-confidence from a Torah perspective: "To the extent that he believes everything is from Hashem and that Hashem wants him to succeed and has granted him the power to succeed, to that extent he will have the confidence to do what he believes Hashem wants him to do." He could have been describing Reb Meir.

Besides his immunity to insult, the other mark of Reb Meir's genuine *anivus* was his complete lack of interest in the far more glamorous task of being the one to make the final "sale" on Torah observance. He knew that there were others better grounded philosophically than he to answer the questions and challenges of those being exposed to the Torah worldview for the first time. He offered Jewish young people access to "a wise man," a "Jewish philosopher," but he never tried to be that wise man himself.

He believed with every fiber of his being that, as he put it, "Torah sells itself." He had no greater goal than to make the introduction of a Jewish *neshamah* to Torah. He had no trouble accepting his role as a conduit for bringing young Jews to yeshivos and seminaries, where others might have chafed at the lack of intellectual stimulation or the absence of glory in his role. But such considerations played no role with him. His only desire was to be a faithful *eved Hashem,* and for that role any vital task that no one else could or would do as well was sufficient. The temptation to transform Heritage House, for instance, into a full-time learning institution, rather than serve as a transit point to the other well-established institutions, never occurred to him.[4]

His lack of ego was something that the dozens of young Jews with whom he came into contact daily intuited. Though many — likely a considerable majority — rejected his overtures, none ever resented him, for they understood that what motivated him was their good and not his own ego. His standard questions — Can I interest you in staying in a Jewish hostel? Do you want to learn more about your Jewishness? Would you like to attend a class on Judaism? — had nothing to do with him. His hostel did not charge — indeed he had to spend months abroad every year to keep it going; he would not be the one giving the class.

---

3. Reb Dovid Romand.

4. I am grateful for this insight to Dov Wolowitz, who purchased the property that housed the Heritage House hostel for men for Rabbi Schuster.

Rabbi Schuster telling an interviewer, "Kiruv is the most important thing in the world"

Mrs. Schuster's first cousin Aaron Gibber, who learned with Reb Meir in Ner Israel, put it well in his *hesped*. "He did not see how they were dressed, or where they came from, or where they were going. All he saw was the *neshamah* of a fellow Jew."

"This is not about me, one could almost hear him say to thousands he approached, this is about you. Your *neshamah*. Your special *neshamah* that is calling out. You don't hear it. But I do. And I care." And they followed him because he cared.

Recognition that the fruits of his efforts would be determined by Hashem, and Hashem alone, was not a passive doctrine for Reb Meir. Just the opposite. After first ensuring that one's goals and purposes are fully aligned with Hashem's goals for the Jewish people, and through them the whole world, the next thing needed to gain Hashem's help is to demonstrate how important those goals are to one. As he once told Avraham Zuroff of *Mishpacha Magazine*, the only secret of successful kiruv is: "You have to want it very much. You must be sincere and persevere." The Master is ever eager to assist His loyal servants to fulfill His purposes.

Mrs. Bracha Zaret, together with her husband Rabbi Tuvia Zaret, has directed the leading American campus kiruv program, Jewish

Awareness Movement (JAM), at UCLA and other southern California campuses for more than three decades. She began her career in kiruv as a protégé of Rabbi Schuster, patrolling the women's side of the Kotel, even as he patrolled the men's side.

She was once seated at an AJOP (Association for Jewish Outreach Professionals) conference with a communal rabbi, who is himself a baal teshuvah. He was lamenting how difficult it was to get people interested in Torah. Mrs. Zaret answered simply, "It's not so hard. You just have to care enough." She could have been speaking for her mentor.

Everything that he did proclaimed his devotion to his mission: the passionate, physical nature of his davening, the urgency that he attached to everything that he did; the lengths to which he would go for a single Jewish soul — driving to distant kibbutzim and back to contact someone whom he had met in Jerusalem, paying for new plane tickets to extend the stay of those who were on limited tickets and expressed an interest in learning more; never taking a day off to relax or to spend time with family; and hounding the institutions to which he brought young Jews to eschew vacations and make sure there were always classes available for newcomers whom he delivered to the institutions.

Dov Wolowitz, who purchased the building for the Heritage House for men, once expressed to Rabbi Shlomo Freifeld, one of the pioneers of American kiruv, his amazement at the success of Rabbi Schuster despite his total lack of charisma. Rabbi Freifeld gave a bang on the table and told him, "Charisma never made a single person religious. Showing that you care is what draws people. Nothing is more important than that."

Rabbi Schuster's great success lay in his ability to instantly convey that caring to complete strangers, on the one hand, and to his ultimate boss, Hashem, on the other. The two, of course, were intertwined. He sought to return Hashem's lost children to Him, and what he offered those children was the possibility of connection to Hashem.

"He loved Hashem and he loved Jews. And he was willing to devote every fiber of his being to bringing Hashem and His children together," is how one of the thousands he picked up at the Kotel expressed it.

Rav Moshe Shapiro, the leading *baal machshavah* of our generation, used to say, "We did not come into the world just to move the furniture from one corner of the room to the other." Each of us is born with a designated role to play in partnering with Hashem to bring the world to its ultimate destiny.

Rabbi Meir Tzvi Schuster's life teaches us how much one man can do for the good. And more, he demonstrates that the magnitude of each of our contributions is not determined at birth and is not primarily a function of natural endowments. No one who knew Rabbi Meir Schuster in his early years ever dreamed that he would become one of the central players in shaping the future of the Jewish people through his critical role in the baal teshuvah movement.

But he was. He took the repeated message of his rebbi, Rabbi Dovid Kronglas, to heart — the message that each of us has a necessary role to play in G-d's plan. And to the degree that we take our mission seriously, and fashion ourselves into conduits of Hashem's blessing to the world, this is how much our impact will be felt.

Those rare individuals who succeed in negating themselves out of devotion to Hashem will, in the end, prove the most effective conduits of His blessing and have an impact out of all proportion to their natural gifts, be they great or small.

That is the message of Rabbi Meir Schuster's life: the power of one man to change the world by taking his mission seriously. He embodied what Rabbi Noach Weinberg called "the power of one." And in doing so, he delivered a message of hope for each of us in our ability to further the world toward its ultimate destiny.

Rabbi Schuster's *matzeivah*

# INDEX

Chernoff, Eddie 190, 191
Chontow, Dovid 263, 268
Chontow, Miriam 262, 263
Clyman, Ellen 287, 291
Cowan, Rabbi Yirmi 195, 196

# D

Damski, Seth 169, 184, 185
Dan-Hytman family 298
David, Rebbetzin Bruria 278
Davidson, Esther 48
Davidson, Moshe 48
Dembs, Reuven 292
Dessler, Rabbi Eliyahu Elilezer 88, 251
Drucker, Steven 198, 206, 207
Dubin, Mordechai (Mitchell) 120, 121

# E

Eade, Rabbi Moshe Chaim 128
Edelstein, Rabbi Avraham 21, 84, 85, 96,
    128, 138, 163, 168, 196, 197, 199, 200,
    206, 212, 213, 214, 216, 226, 239, 243,
    248, 252, 254, 257, 260, 267, 280, 290, 313
Edelstein, Rabbi Yosef 177
Efros, Rabbi Moshe 237
Elbaz, Rabbi Avi 214
Elfenbeim, Rabbi Gedaliah 52
Elyashiv, Rav Yosef Shalom 18, 54, 91,
    92, 93
Epstein, Josh 126, 127
Estrin, Dena 22, 94, 179, 180, 204, 208,
    224, 227, 241

# F

Feinhandler, Rabbi Aharon 98, 99, 124
Feinhandler, Sarah 98, 99, 124
Feinstein, Rabbi Moshe 189, 190
Feld, Avraham 283
Feldman, Rabbi Yitzchak 177
Feldman, Rav Aharon 18
Felsenthal, Chani 226
Felsenthal, Rabbi David 226
Fern, Gershon 161
Fierstein, Rabbi Yehuda 142, 143, 144,
    145
Finkel, Rav Nosson Tzvi 144
Frand, Rabbi Yissocher 39, 281

Freifeld, Rabbi Shlomo 318
Friedberg, Dov 174, 187, 244
Fried, Dahlia 96
Friedland, Laurie 21, 268, 282
Friedland, Sam 21, 100, 101, 260, 262,
    263, 267, 269, 282, 308
Friedland, Yonatan 269
Friedman, Binny 226
Friedman, Chani 91
Friedman, Dr. Shimon 91
Fried, Yaakov 61

# G

Gafni, Rabbi Moshe 264
Galkin, Bill 285
Galkin, Sharon 285
Garfiinkel, Shoshana 230
Garfinkel, Aaron 50
Garfinkel, Anne 47, 48
Garfinkel, Dovid 46, 47, 48, 121
Garfinkel, Esther (Schuster) 44, 45, 46,
    48, 50
Garfinkel, Herb 50, 51
Garfinkel, Rabbi Moshe 50, 51, 63, 64, 97,
    128, 229, 275
Garfinkel, Ruth (Kramer) 48, 49
Garfinkel, Shoshana 229
Gedult, Rabbi Mordechai 136
Geller, Rabbi Avi 185, 223, 224
Gershenfeld, Gila 116
Gershenfeld, Rabbi Beryl 61, 115, 116,
    125, 155, 156, 215
Gibber, Aaron 50, 92, 317
Gibber, Eli 45
Gibber, Harvey 50
Gibber, Ruth 50
Ginsburg, Beth 227, 228, 229
Ginsburg, Daniella 227
Ginsburg, Dr. Leonard 227, 228, 229, 230,
    262, 268
Glaser, Rabbi Eli 19
Glaser, Rabbi Yom Tov 125, 128, 185, 267
Glazer, Gerry 29, 30, 31, 32
Goetz, Bracha 285, 287, 304, 309
Goetz, Larry (Aryeh) 304, 309, 310
Goldberg, Rabbi Hillel 96, 184, 187, 314
Goldberg, Rabbi Shlomo (Steven) 98, 99,
    124, 300

This volume is part of
THE ARTSCROLL® SERIES
an ongoing project of
translations, commentaries and expositions on
Scripture, Mishnah, Talmud, Midrash, Halachah,
liturgy, history, the classic Rabbinic writings,
biographies and thought.

For a brochure of current publications
visit your local Hebrew bookseller
or contact the publisher:

*Mesorah Publications, ltd.*

313 Regina Avenue
Rahway, New Jersey 07065
(718) 921-9000
www.artscroll.com